To Brett.

To the most _____ _____
son a Mother could
ever have.

Love your "pain in the neck"
Mom.

George Herbert (English Vicar)

By all means use some times
to be alone
Salute thyself: see what the
soul doth wear.

Niebuhr.
The conquest of self is in a sense
the inevitable consequence of true Self
Knowledge. If the self centered self
is shattered by a genuine awareness
of its situation, there is the power of a
new life in the experience

"Lives based on having
are less free than lives
based on doing or on being"
William James.

THE
COURAGE TO
CREATE

By the same author

POWER AND INNOCENCE
LOVE AND WILL
MAN'S SEARCH FOR HIMSELF

THE
COURAGE TO
CREATE

ROLLO MAY

W · W · Norton & Company · Inc ·

NEW YORK

FIRST EDITION

"The Nature of Creativity" was first published in *Creativity and Its
Cultivation*, Harold H. Anderson, ed. (New York, 1959).

"Creativity and the Unconscious" was first published in *Voices: The
Journal of the American Academy of Psychotherapists*.

"Creativity and Encounter" was first published in *The American Journal
of Psychoanalysis* XXIV/1.

"The Delphic Oracle as Therapist" was first published in *The Reach of
Mind: Essays in Memory of Kurt Goldstein*, Marianne L. Simmel, ed. (New
York, 1968).

PRINTED IN THE UNITED STATES OF AMERICA

Library of Congress Cataloging in Publication Data
May, Rollo.
   The courage to create.
   Includes bibliographical references.
   1.   Creation (literary, artistic, etc.)
I.   Title.
BF408.M33   1975   153.3'5   75-23055

ISBN 0-393-01119-4

1 2 3 4 5 6 7 8 9

Contents

Preface

ALL MY LIFE I have been haunted by the fascinating questions of creativity. Why does an original idea in science and in art "pop up" from the unconscious at a given moment? What is the relation between talent and the creative act, and between creativity and death? Why does a mime or a dance give us such delight? How did Homer, confronting something as gross as the Trojan War, fashion it into poetry which became a guide for the ethics of the whole Greek civilization?

I have asked these questions not as one who stands on the sidelines, but as one who himself participates in art and science. I ask them out of my own excitement, for example, at watching two of my colors on a paper merge into an unpredictable third color. Is it not the distinguishing characteristic of the human being that in the hot race of evolution he pauses for a moment to paint on the cave walls at Lascaux or Altamira those brown-and-red deer and bison which still fill us with amazed admiration and awe? Suppose the apprehension of beauty is itself a way to truth? Suppose that "elegance"—as the word is used by physicists to describe their discoveries—is a key to ultimate reality? Suppose Joyce is right that the artist creates "the uncreated conscience of the race"?

These chapters are a partial record of my ponderings.

They had their birth as lectures given at colleges and universities. I had always hesitated to publish them because they seemed incomplete—the mystery of creation still remained. I then realized that this "unfinished" quality would always remain, and that it is a part of the creative process itself. This realization coincided with the fact that many people who had heard the lectures urged that they be published.

The title was suggested by Paul Tillich's *The Courage to Be*, a debt I am glad to acknowledge. But one cannot *be* in a vacuum. We express our being by creating. Creativity is a necessary sequel to being. Furthermore, the word *courage* in my title refers, beyond the first few pages of the first chapter, to that particular kind of courage essential for the creative act. This is rarely acknowledged in our discussions of creativity and even more rarely written about.

I want to express my gratitude to several friends who have read all or part of the manuscript and have discussed it with me: Ann Hyde, Magda Denes, and Elinor Roberts.

More than is usually the case, this book was a delight to compile, for it gave me cause to ponder all these questions over again. I only hope the book gives as much pleasure to the reader as it did to me in the compiling of it.

Rollo May
Holderness, New Hampshire

THE
COURAGE TO
CREATE

ONE

THE COURAGE TO CREATE

We ARE living at a time when one age is dying and the new age is not yet born. We cannot doubt this as we look about us to see the radical changes in sexual mores, in marriage styles, in family structures, in education, in religion, technology, and almost every other aspect of modern life. And behind it all is the threat of the atom bomb, which recedes into the distance but never disappears. To live with sensitivity in this age of limbo indeed requires courage.

A choice confronts us. Shall we, as we feel our foundations shaking, withdraw in anxiety and panic? Frightened by the loss of our familiar mooring places, shall we become paralyzed and cover our inaction with apathy? If we do those things, we will have surrendered our chance to participate in the forming of the future. We will have forfeited the distinctive characteristic of human beings—namely, to influence our evolution through our own awareness. We will have capitulated to the blind juggernaut of history and lost the chance to mold the future into a society more equitable and humane.

Or shall we seize the courage necessary to preserve our sensitivity, awareness, and responsibility in the face of radical change? Shall we consciously participate, on however small the scale, in the forming of the new society? I hope our choice will be the latter, for I shall speak on that basis.

We are called upon to do something new, to confront a no man's land, to push into a forest where there are no well-worn paths and from which no one has returned to guide us. This is what the existentialists call the anxiety of nothingness. To live into the future means to leap into the unknown, and this requires a degree of courage for which there is no immediate precedent and which few people realize.

1. WHAT IS COURAGE?

This courage will not be the opposite of despair. We shall often be faced with despair, as indeed every sensitive person has been during the last several decades in this country. Hence Kierkegaard and Nietszche and Camus and Sartre have proclaimed that courage is not the absence of despair; it is, rather, the capacity to move ahead *in spite of despair*.

Nor is the courage required mere stubbornness—we shall surely have to create with others. But if you do not express your own original ideas, if you do not listen to your own being, you will have betrayed yourself. Also you will have betrayed our community in failing to make your contribution to the whole.

A chief characteristic of this courage is that it requires a centeredness within our own being, without which we would feel ourselves to be a vacuum. The "emptiness" within corresponds to an apathy without; and apathy adds up, in the long run, to cowardice. That is why we must always base our commitment in the center of our own being, or else no commitment will be ultimately authentic.

Courage, furthermore, is not to be confused with rashness. What masquerades as courage may turn out to be simply a bravado used to compensate for one's unconscious fear and to prove one's machismo, like the "hot" fliers in World War II. The ultimate end of such rashness is getting one's self killed, or at least one's head battered in with a policeman's billy club—both of which are scarcely productive ways of exhibiting courage.

Courage is not a virtue or value among other personal values like love or fidelity. It is the foundation that underlies and gives reality to all other virtues and personal values. Without courage our love pales into mere dependency. Without courage our fidelity becomes conformism.

The word *courage* comes from the same stem as the French word *coeur*, meaning "heart." Thus just as one's heart, by pumping blood to one's arms, legs, and brain enables all the other physical organs to function, so courage makes possible all the psychological virtues. Without courage other values wither away into mere facsimiles of virtue.

In human beings courage is necessary to make *being* and *becoming* possible. An assertion of the self, a commitment, is essential if the self is to have any reality. This is the distinction between human beings and the rest of nature. The acorn becomes an oak by means of automatic growth; no commitment is necessary. The kitten similarly becomes a cat on the basis of instinct. *Nature* and *being* are identical in creatures like them. But a man or woman becomes fully human only by his or her choices and his or her commitment to them. People attain worth and dignity by the multitude of decisions they make from day by day. These decisions require courage. This is why Paul Tillich speaks of courage as *ontological*—it is essential to our being.

2. PHYSICAL COURAGE

This is the simplest and most obvious kind of courage. In our culture, physical courage takes its form chiefly from the myths of the frontier. Our prototypes have been the pioneer heroes who took the law into their own hands, who survived because they could draw a gun faster than their opponent, who were, above all things, self-reliant and could endure the inevitable loneliness in homesteading with the nearest neighbor twenty miles away.

But the contradictions in our heritage from this frontier are immediately clear to us. Regardless of the heroism it generated in our forebears, this kind of courage has now not only lost its usefulness, but has degenerated into brutality. When I was a child in a small Midwest town, boys were expected to fistfight. But our mothers represented a different viewpoint, so the boys often got licked at school and then whipped for fighting when they came home. This is scarcely an effective way to build character. As a psychoanalyst, I hear time and again of men who had been sensitive as boys and who could not learn to pound others into submission; consequently, they go through life with the conviction that they are cowards.

America is among the most violent of the so-called civilized nations; our homicide rate is three to ten times higher than that of the nations of Europe. An important cause of this is the influence of that frontier brutality of which we are the heirs.

We need a new kind of physical courage that will neither run rampant in violence nor require our assertion of ego-centric power *over* other people. I propose a new form of courage of the body: the use of the body not for the development of musclemen, but for the cultivation of sensitivity. This will mean the development of the capacity to listen with the body. It will be, as Nietszche remarked, a learning to think with the body. It will be a valuing of the body as the means of empathy with others, as expression of the self as a thing of beauty and as a rich source of pleasure.

Such a view of the body is already emerging in America through the influence of yoga, meditation, Zen Buddhism, and other religious psychologies from the Orient. In these traditions, the body is not condemned, but is valued as a source of justified pride. I propose this for our consideration as the kind of physical courage we will need for the new society toward which we are moving.

3. MORAL COURAGE

A second kind of courage is moral courage. The persons I have known, or have known of, who have great moral courage have generally abhorred violence. Take, for example,

Aleksander Solzhenitsyn, the Russian author who stood up alone against the might of the Soviet bureaucracy in protest against the inhuman and cruel treatment of men and women in Russian prison camps. His numerous books, written in the best prose of modern Russia, cry out against the crushing of any person, whether physically, psychologically, or spiritually. His moral courage stands out the more clearly since he is not a liberal, but a Russian nationalist. He became the symbol of a value lost sight of in a confused world—that the innate worth of a human being must be revered solely because of his or her humanity and regardless of his or her politics. A Dostoevskian character out of old Russia (as Stanley Kunitz describes him), Solzenitsyn proclaimed, "I would gladly give my life if it would advance the cause of truth."

Apprehended by the Soviet police, he was taken to prison. The story is told that he was disrobed and marched out before a firing squad. The purpose of the police was to scare him to death if they could not silence him psychologically; their bullets were blanks. Undaunted, Solzhenitsyn now lives as an exile in Switzerland, where he pursues his gadfly role and levels the same kind of criticism at other nations, like the United States, at the points where our democracy obviously stands in need of radical revision. So long as there exist persons with the moral courage of a Solzhenitsyn, we can be sure that the triumph of "man, the robot" has not yet arrived.

Solzhenitsyn's courage, like that of many persons of similar moral valor, arose not only out of his audaciousness, but also out of his compassion for the human suffering he saw about him during his own sentence in the Soviet prison camp. It is highly significant, and indeed almost a rule, that moral courage has its source in such identification through one's own sensitivity with the suffering of one's fellow human beings. I am tempted to call this "perceptual courage" because it depends on one's capacity to *perceive*, to let one's self see the suffering of other people. If we let ourselves experience the evil, we will be forced to do something about it. It is a truth, recognizable in all of us, that when we don't want to become involved, when we don't want to confront even the *issue* of whether or not we'll come to the aid of someone who is being unjustly treated, we block off our perception, we blind ourselves to the other's suffering, we cut off our empathy with the person needing help. Hence the most prevalent form of cowardice in our day hides behind the statement "I did not want to become involved."

4. SOCIAL COURAGE

The third kind of courage is the opposite to the just described apathy; I call it social courage. It is the courage to relate to other human beings, the capacity to risk one's self in the hope of achieving meaningful intimacy. It is the courage to invest one's self over a period of time in a relationship that will demand an increasing openness.

Intimacy requires courage because risk is inescapable. We cannot know at the outset how the relationship will affect us. Like a chemical mixture, if one of us is changed, both of us will be. Will we grow in self-actualization, or will it destroy us? The one thing we can be certain of is that if we let ourselves fully into the relationship for good or evil, we will not come out unaffected.

A common practice in our day is to avoid working up the courage required for authentic intimacy by shifting the issue to the body, making it a matter of simple physical courage. It is easier in our society to be naked physically than to be naked psychologically or spiritually—easier to share our body than to share our fantasies, hopes, fears, and aspirations, which are felt to be more personal and the sharing of which is experienced as making us more vulnerable. For curious reasons we are shy about sharing the things that matter most. Hence people short-circuit the more "dangerous" building of a relationship by leaping immediately into bed. After all, the body is an object and can be treated mechanically.

But intimacy that begins and remains on the physical level tends to become inauthentic, and we later find ourselves fleeing from the emptiness. Authentic social courage requires intimacy on the many levels of the personality simultaneously. Only by doing this can one overcome personal alienation. No wonder the meeting of new persons brings a throb of anxiety as well as the joy of expectation; and as we go deeper into the relationship each new depth is marked by some new joy and new anxiety. Each meeting can be a harbinger of an unknown fate in store for us but also a stimulus toward the exciting pleasure of authentically knowing another person.

Social courage requires the confronting of two different kinds of fear. These were beautifully described by one of the early psychoanalysts, Otto Rank. The first he calls the "life fear." This is the fear of living autonomously, the fear of being abandoned, the need for dependency on someone else. It shows itself in the need to throw one's self so completely into a relationship that one has no self left with which to relate. One becomes, in effect, a reflection of the

person he or she loves—which sooner or later becomes boring to the partner. This is the fear of self-actualization, as
Rank described it. Living some forty years before the days
of women's liberation, Rank averred that this kind of fear
was most typical of women.

The opposite fear Rank called the "death fear." This is
the fear of being totally absorbed by the other, the fear of
losing one's self and one's autonomy, the fear of having
one's independence taken away. This, said Rank, is the fear
most associated with men, for they seek to keep the back
door open to beat a hasty retreat in case the relationship
becomes too intimate.

Actually, if Rank had lived on into our day he would
have agreed that both kinds of fear have to be confronted,
in varying proportions to be sure, by both men and women.
All our lives we oscillate between these two fears. They
are, indeed, the forms of anxiety that lie in wait for anyone
who cares for another. But the confronting of these two
fears, and the awareness that one grows not only by being
one's self but also by participating in other selves, is necessary if we are to move toward self-realization.

Albert Camus, in *Exile and the Kingdom*, wrote a story
that illustrates these two opposite kinds of courage. "The
Artist at Work" is a tale of a poor Parisian painter who
could scarcely get enough money to buy bread for his wife
and children. When the artist is on his death bed, his best
friend finds the canvas on which the painter was working.
It is blank except for one word, unclearly written and in
very small letters, that appears in the center. The word can
either be *solitary*—being alone; keeping one's distance
from events, maintaining the peace of mind necessary for
listening to one's deeper self. Or it can be *solidary*—"living in the market place"; solidarity, involvement, or iden-

tifying with the masses, as Karl Marx put it. Opposites though they are, both solitude and solidarity are essential if the artist is to produce works that are not only significant to his or her age, but that will also speak to future generations.

5. ONE PARADOX OF COURAGE

A curious paradox characteristic of every kind of courage here confronts us. It is the seeming contradiction that *we must be fully committed, but we must also be aware at the same time that we might possibly be wrong*. This dialectic relationship between conviction and doubt is characteristic of the highest types of courage, and gives the lie to the simplistic definitions that identify courage with mere growth.

People who claim to be *absolutely* convinced that their stand is the only right one are dangerous. Such conviction is the essence not only of dogmatism, but of its more destructive cousin, fanaticism. It blocks off the user from learning new truth, and it is a dead giveaway of unconscious doubt. The person then has to double his or her protests in order to quiet not only the opposition but his or her own unconscious doubts as well.

Whenever I heard—as we all did often during the Nixon-Watergate days—the "I am absolutely convinced" tone or the "I want to make this absolutely clear" statement emanating from the White House, I braced myself, for I knew that some dishonesty was being perpetrated by the telltale sign of overemphasis. Shakespeare aptly said, "The lady [or the politician] doth protest too much, methinks." In such a time, one longs for the presence of a leader like Lincoln, who openly admitted his doubts and as openly preserved his commitment. It is infinitely safer to know that the man at the top has his doubts, as you and I have ours, yet has the courage to move ahead in spite of these doubts. In contrast to the fanatic who has stockaded himself against new truth, the person with the courage to believe and at the same time to admit his doubts is flexible and open to new learning.

Paul Cézanne strongly believed that he was discovering and painting a new form of space which would radically influence the future of art, yet he was at the same time filled with painful and ever-present doubts. The relationship between commitment and doubt is by no means an antagonistic one. Commitment is healthiest when it is not *without* doubt, but *in spite of* doubt. To believe fully and at the same moment to have doubts is not at all a contradiction: it presupposes a greater respect for truth, an awareness that truth always goes beyond anything that can be said or done at any given moment. To every thesis there is an antithesis, and to this there is a synthesis. Truth is thus a never-dying process. We then know the meaning of the statement attributed to Leibnitz: "I would walk twenty miles to listen to my worst enemy if I could learn something."

6. CREATIVE COURAGE

This bring us to the most important kind of courage of all. Whereas moral courage is the righting of wrongs, creative courage, in contrast, is the discovering of new forms, new symbols, new patterns on which a new society can be built. Every profession can and does require some creative courage. In our day, technology and engineering, diplomacy, business, and certainly teaching, all of these professions and scores of others are in the midst of radical change and require courageous persons to appreciate and direct this change. The need for creative courage is in direct proportion to the degree of change the profession is undergoing.

But those who present directly and immediately the new forms and symbols are the artists—the dramatists, the musicians, the painters, the dancers, the poets, and those poets of the religious sphere we call saints. They portray the new symbols in the form of images—poetic, aural, plastic, or dramatic, as the case may be. They live out their imaginations. The symbols only dreamt about by most human beings are expressed in graphic form by the artists. But in our appreciation of the created work—let us say a Mozart quintet—we also are performing a creative act. When we engage a painting, which we have to do especially with modern art if we are authentically to see it, we are experiencing some new moment of sensibility. Some new vision is triggered in us by our contact with the painting; something unique is born in us. This is why appreciation of the music or painting or other works of the creative person is also a creative act on our part.

If these symbols are to be understood by us, we must identify with them as we perceive them. In Beckett's play *Waiting for Godot*, there are no intellectual discussions of the failure of communication in our time; the failure is simply *presented* there on the stage. We see it most vividly, for example, when Lucky, who, at his master's order to "Think," can only sputter out a long speech that has all the pomposity of a philosophical discourse but is actually pure gibberish. As we involve ourselves more and more in the drama, we see represented on stage, larger than life, our general human failure to communicate authentically.

We see on the stage, in Beckett's play, the lone, bare tree, symbolic of the lone, bare relationship the two men have as they wait together for a Godot who never appears; and it elicits from us a similar sense of the alienation that we and multitudes of others experience. The fact that most people have no clear awareness of their alienation only makes this condition more powerful.

In Eugene O'Neill's *The Iceman Cometh*, there are no explicit discussions of the disintegration of our society; it is shown as a reality in the drama. The nobility of the human species is not talked *about*, but is presented as a vacuum on the stage. Because this nobility is such a vivid absence, an emptiness that fills the play, you leave the theater with a profound sense of the importance of being human, as you do after having seen *Macbeth* or *King Lear*. O'Neill's capacity to communicate that experience places him among the significant tragedians of history.

Artists can portray these experiences in music or words or clay or marble or on canvas because they express what Jung calls the "collective unconscious." This phrase may not be the most felicitous, but we know that each of us carries in buried dimensions of our being some basic forms, partly generic and partly experiential in origin. It is these the artist expresses.

Thus the artists—in which term I hereafter include the poets, musicians, dramatists, plastic artists, as well as saints —are a "dew" line, to use McLuhan's phrase; they give us a "distant early warning" of what is happening to our culture. In the art of our day we see symbols galore of alienation and anxiety. But at the same time there is form amid discord, beauty amid ugliness, some human love in the midst of hatred—a love that temporarily triumphs over death but always loses out in the long run. The artists thus express the spiritual meaning of their culture. Our problem is: Can we read their meaning aright?

Take Giotto in what is called the "little Renaissance", which burgeoned in the fourteenth century. In contrast to the two-dimensional medieval mosaics, Giotto presents a new way of seeing life and nature: he gives his paintings three dimensions, and we now see human beings and animals expressing and calling forth from us such specific human emotions as care, or pity, or grief, or joy. In the previous, two-dimensional mosaics in the churches of the Middle Ages, we feel no human being is necessary to see them—they have their own relationship to God. But in Giotto, a human being *viewing* the picture is required; and this human being must take his stance as an *individual* in relation to the picture. Thus the new humanism and the new relation to nature that were to become central in the Renaissance are here born, a hundred years *before* the Renaissance proper.

In our endeavor to grasp these symbols of art, we find ourselves in a realm that beggars our usual conscious thinking. Our task is quite beyond the reach of logic. It brings us to an area in which there are many paradoxes. Take the idea expressed in Shakespeare's four lines at the end of Sonnet 64:

> Ruin hath taught me thus to ruminate,
> That time will come and take my love away.
> This thought is as a death, which cannot choose
> But weep to have that which it fears to lose.

If you have been trained to accept the logic of our society, you will ask: "Why does he have to 'weep to have' his love? Why can he not enjoy his love?" Thus our logic pushes us always toward adjustment—an adjustment to a crazy world and to a crazy life. And worse yet, we cut ourselves off from understanding the profound depths of experience that Shakespeare is here expressing.

We have all had such experiences, but we tend to cover them over. We may look at an autumn tree so beautiful in its brilliant colors that we feel like weeping; or we may hear music so lovely that we are overcome with sadness. The craven thought then creeps into our consciousness that maybe it would have been better not to have seen the tree at all or not to have heard the music. Then we wouldn't be faced with this uncomfortable paradox— knowing that "time will come and take my love away," that everything we love will die. But the essence of being human is that, in the brief moment we exist on this spinning planet, we can love some persons and some things, in spite of the fact that time and death will ultimately claim us all. That we yearn to stretch the brief moment, to postpone our death a year or so is surely understandable. But such postponement is bound to be a frustrating and ultimately a losing battle.

By the creative act, however, we *are* able to reach beyond our own death. This is why creativity is so important and why we need to confront the problem of the relationship between creativity and death.

7

Consider James Joyce, who is often cited as the greatest of modern novelists. At the very end of *A Portrait of the Artist as a Young Man*, he has his young hero write in his diary:

Welcome, O life! I go to encounter for the millionth time the reality of experience and to forge in the smithy of my soul the uncreated conscience of my race.

What a rich and profound statement that is!—"I go to en- counter for the millionth time." In other words, every cre- ative encounter is a *new* event; every time requires another assertion of courage. What Kierkegaard said about love is also true of creativity: every-person must start at the be- ginning. And to encounter "the reality of experience" is surely the basis for all creativity. The task will be "to forge in the smithy of my soul," as arduous as the blacksmith's task of bending red-hot iron in his smithy to make some- thing of value for human life.

But note especially the last words, to forge "the uncre- ated conscience of my race." Joyce is here saying that con- science is not something handed down ready-made from Mount Sinai, despite reports to the contrary. It is created, first of all, out of the inspiration derived from the artist's symbols and forms. Every authentic artist is engaged in this creating of the conscience of the race, even though he or she may be unaware of the fact. The artist is not a mor- alist by conscious intention, but is concerned only with hearing and expressing the vision within his or her own being. But out of the symbols the artist sees and creates— as Giotto created the forms for the Renaissance—there is later hewn the ethical structure of the society.

Why is creativity so difficult? And why does it require so much courage? Is it not simply a matter of clearing away the dead forms, the defunct symbols and the myths that have become lifeless? No. Joyce's metaphor is much more accurate: it is as difficult as forging in the smithy of one's soul. We are faced with a puzzling riddle indeed.

Some help comes from George Bernard Shaw. Having attended a concert given by the violinist Heifitz, he wrote the following letter when he got home:

My dear Mr. Heifitz,

My wife and I were overwhelmed by your concert. If you continue to play with such beauty, you will certainly die young. No one can play with such perfection without provoking the jealousy of the gods. I earnestly implore you to play something badly every night before going to bed. . . .

Beneath Shaw's humorous words there is, as there often was with him, a profound truth—creativity provokes the jealousy of the gods. This is why authentic creativity takes so much courage: *an active battle with the gods is occurring.*

I cannot give you any complete explanation of why this is so; I can only share my reflections. Down through the ages, authentically creative figures have consistently found themselves in such a struggle. Degas once wrote, "A painter paints a picture with the same feeling as that with which a criminal commits a crime." In Judaism and Christianity the second of the Ten Commandments adjures us, "You shall not make yourself a graven image, or any likeness of anything that is in the heavens above or that is in the earth beneath, or that is in the water under the earth." I am aware that the ostensible purpose of this commandment was to protect the Jewish people from idol worship in those idol-strewn times.

But the commandment also expresses the timeless fear that every society harbors of its artists, poets, and saints. For they are the ones who threaten the status quo, which each society is devoted to protecting. It is clearest in the struggles occurring in Russia to control the utterances of the poets and the styles of the artists; but it is true also in our own country, if not so blatant. Yet in spite of this divine prohibition, and despite the courage necessary to flout it, countless Jews and Christians through the ages have devoted themselves to painting and sculpting and have continued to make graven images and produce symbols in one form or another. Many of them have had the same experience of a battle with the gods.

A host of other riddles, which I can only cite without comment, are bound up with this major one. One is that genius and psychosis are so close to each other. Another is that creativity carries such an inexplicable guilt feeling. A third is that so many artists and poets commit suicide, and often at the very height of their achievement.

As I tried to puzzle out the riddle of the battle with the gods, I went back to the prototypes in human cultural history, to those myths that illuminate how people have understood the creative act. I do not use this term *myth* in the common present-day deteriorated meaning of "falsehood." This is an error that could be committed only by a society that has become so inebriated with adding up empirical facts that it seals off the deeper wisdom of human history. I use *myth* as meaning, rather, a dramatic presentation of the moral wisdom of the race. The myth uses the totality of the senses rather than just the intellect.

In ancient Greek civilization, there is the myth of Prometheus, a Titan living on Mount Olympus, who saw that human beings were without fire. His stealing fire from the gods and giving it to humankind is taken henceforth by the Greeks as the beginning of civilization, not only in cooking and in the weaving of textiles, but in philosophy, science, drama, and in culture itself.

But the important point is that *Zeus was outraged.* He

decreed that Prometheus be punished by being bound to Mount Caucasus, where a vulture was to come each morning and eat away his liver which would grow again at night. This element in the myth, incidentally, is a vivid symbol of the creative process. All artists have at some time had the experience at the end of the day of feeling tired, spent, and so certain they can never express their vision that they vow to forget it and start all over again on something else the next morning. But during the night their "liver grows back again." They arise full of energy and go back with renewed hope to their task, again to strive in the smithy of their soul.

Least anyone think the myth of Prometheus can be brushed aside as merely an idiosyncractic tale concoted by playful Greeks, let me remind you that in the Judeo-Christian tradition almost exactly the same truth is presented. I refer to the myth of Adam and Eve. This is the drama of the emerging of moral consciousness. As Kierkegaard said in relation to this myth (and to all myths), the truth that happens internally is presented as though it were external. The myth of Adam is re-enacted in every infant, beginning a few months after birth and developing into recognizable form at the age of two or three, though ideally it should continue enlarging all the rest of one's life. The eating of the apple of the tree of the knowledge of good and evil symbolizes the dawn of human consciousness, moral conscience and consciousness being at this point synonymous. The innocence of the Garden of Eden—the womb and the "dreaming consciousness" (the phrase is Kierkegaard's) of gestation and the first month of life—are destroyed forever.

The function of psychoanalysis is to increase this consciousness, indeed to *help* people eat of the tree of the knowledge of good and evil. It should not surprise us if this experience is as terrifying for many people as it was for Oedipus. Any theory of "resistance" that omits the terror of human consciousness is incomplete and probably wrong.

In place of innocent bliss, the infant now experiences anxiety and guilt feelings. Also, as part of the child's legacy is the sense of individual responsibility, and, most important of all, developing only later, the capacity to love. The "shadow" side of this process is the emergence of repressions and, concomitantly, neurosis. A fateful event indeed! If you call this the "fall of man," you should join Hegel and other penetrating analysts of history who have proclaimed that it was a "fall upward"; for without this experience there would be neither creativity nor consciousness as we know them.

But, again, Yahweh was angry. Adam and Eve were driven out of the garden by an angel with a flaming sword. The troublesome paradox confronts us in that both the Greek and the Judeo-Christian myths present creativity and consciousness as being born in rebellion against an omnipotent force. Are we to conclude that these chief gods, Zeus and Yahweh, did not wish humankind to have moral consciousness and the arts of civilization? It is a mystery indeed.

The most obvious explanation is that the creative artist and poet and saint must fight the *actual* (as contrasted to the ideal) gods of our society—the god of conformism as well as the gods of apathy, material success, and exploitative power. These are the "idols" of our society that are worshiped by multitudes of people. But this point does not go deeply enough to give us an answer to the riddle.

In my search for some illumination, I went back again to the myths to read them more carefully. I discovered that at the end of the myth of Prometheus there is the curious addendum: Prometheus could be freed from his chains and his torture only when an immortal would renounce his immortality as expiation for Prometheus. This was done by Chiron (who is, incidentally, another fascinating symbol—half horse and half man, renowned for his wisdom and skill in medicine and healing, he brought up Asclepius, the god of medicine). This conclusion to the myth tells us that the riddle is connected with the problem of death.

The same with Adam and Eve. Enraged at their eating of the tree of the knowledge of good and evil, Yahweh cries out that He is afraid they will eat of the tree of eternal life and become like "one of us." So! Again the riddle has to do with the problem of death, of which eternal life is one aspect.

The battle with the gods thus hinges on our own mortality! Creativity is a yearning for immortality. We human beings know that we must die. We have, strangely enough, a word for death. We know that each of us must develop the courage to confront death. Yet we also must rebel and struggle against it. Creativity comes from this struggle— out of the rebellion the creative act is born. Creativity is not merely the innocent spontaneity of our youth and childhood; it must also be married to the passion of the adult human being, which is a passion to live beyond one's death. Michelangelo's writhing, unfinished statues of slaves, struggling in their prisons of stone, are the most fitting symbol for our human condition.

8

When I use the word *rebel* for the artist, I do not refer to revolutionary or to such things as taking over the dean's office; that is a different matter. Artists are generally soft-spoken persons who are concerned with their inner visions and images. But that is precisely what makes them feared by any coercive society. For they are the bearers of the human being's age-old capacity to be insurgent. They love to emerse themselves in chaos in order to put it into form, just as God created form out of chaos in Genesis. Forever unsatisfied with the mundane, the apathetic, the conventional, they always push on to newer worlds. Thus are they the creators of the "uncreated conscience of the race."

This requires an intensity of emotion, a heightened vitality—for is not the vital forever in opposition to death? We could call this intensity by many different names: I choose to call it rage. Stanley Kunitz, contemporary poet, state that "the poet writes his poems out of his rage." This rage is necessary to ignite the poet's passion, to call forth his abilities, to bring together in ecstasy his flamelike insights, that he may surpass himself in his poems. The rage is against injustice, of which there is certainly plenty in our society. But ultimately it is rage against the prototype of all injustice—death.

We recall the first lines of a poem by another contemporary poet, Dylan Thomas, on the death of his father:

> Do not go gentle into that good night,
> Old age should burn and rave at close of day;
> Rage, rage against the dying of the light.

And the poem ends:

> And you, my father, there on the sad height,
> Curse, bless, me now with your fierce tears, I pray.
> Do not go gentle into that good night.
> Rage, rage against the dying of the light.

Note that he does not ask merely to be blessed. "Curse
. . . me . . . with your *fierce* tears." Note also that it is
Dylan Thomas, and not his father, who writes the poem.
The father had to confront death and in some way accept
it. But the son expresses the eternally insurgent spirit—and
as a result we have the piercing elegance of this poem.

This rage has nothing at all to do with rational concepts
of death, in which we stand outside the experience of death
and make objective, statistical comments about it. That
always has to do with someone else's death, not our own.
We all know that each generation, whether of leaves or
grass or human beings or any living things, must die in
order for a new generation be born. I am speaking of death
in a different sense. A child has a dog, and the dog dies.
The child's grief is mixed with deep anger. If someone tries
to explain death in the objective, evolutionary way to him
—everything dies, and dogs die sooner than human beings
—he may well strike out against the explainer. The child
probably knows all that anyway. His real sense of loss and
betrayal comes from the fact that his love for his dog and
the dog's devotion to him are now gone. It is the personal,
subjective experience of death of which I am speaking.

As we grow older we learn how to understand each other
better. Hopefully, we learn also to love more authentically.
Understanding and love require a wisdom that comes only
with age. But at the highest point in the development of

that wisdom, we will be blotted out. No longer will we see
the trees turning scarlet in the autumn. No longer will we
see the grass pushing up so tenderly in the spring. Each of
us will become only a memory that will grow fainter every
year.

This most difficult of truths is put by another modern
poet, Marianne Moore, into these words:

> What is our innocence,
> what is our guilt? All are
>   naked, none is safe. And whence
> is courage . . .

And then, after considering death and how we can confront
it, she ends her poem:

> So he who strongly feels,
> behaves. The very bird,
>   grown taller as he sings, steels
> his form straight up. Though he is captive,
> his mighty singing
> says, satisfaction is a lowly
> thing, how pure a thing is joy.
>   This is mortality,
>   this is eternity.

Thus mortality is at last brought into antiphony with its
opposite, eternity.

9

For many·people the relating of rebellion to religion will
be a hard truth. It brings with it the final paradox. In religion, it is not the sycophants or those who cling most
faithfully to the status quo who are ultimately praised. It
is the insurgents. Recall how often in human history the

saint and the rebel have been the same person. Socrates was a rebel, and he was sentenced to drink hemlock. Jesus was a rebel, and he was crucified for it. Joan of Arc was a rebel, and she was burned at the stake.

Yet each of these figures and hundreds like them, though ostricized by their contemporaries, were recognized and worshiped by the following ages as having made the most significant creative contributions in ethics and religion to civilization.

Those we call saints rebelled against an outmoded and inadequate form of God on the basis of their new insights into divinity. The teachings that led to their deaths raised the ethical and spiritual levels of their societies. They were aware that Zeus, the jealous god of Mount Olympus, would no longer do. Hence Prometheus stands for a religion of compassion. They rebelled against Yahweh, the primitive tribal god of the Hebrews who gloried in the deaths of thousands of Philistines. In place of him came the new visions of Amos and Isaiah and Jeremiah of the god of love and justice. Their rebellion was motivated by new insights into the meaning of godliness. They rebelled, as Paul Tillich has so beautifully stated, against God in the name of the God beyond God. The continuous emergence of the God beyond God is the mark of creative courage in the religious sphere.

Whatever sphere we may be in, there is a profound joy in the realization that we are helping to form the structure of the new world. This is creative courage, however minor or fortuitous our creations may be. We can then say, with Joyce, Welcome, O life! We go for the millionth time to forge in the smithy of our souls the uncreated conscience of the race.

TWO

THE NATURE OF
CREATIVITY

W HEN WE examine the psychological studies and
writings on creativity over the past fifty years, the
first thing that strikes us is the general paucity of material
and the inadequacy of the work. In academic psychology
after the time of William James and during the first half
of this century, the subject was generally avoided as unscientific, mysterious, disturbing, and too corruptive of the
scientific training of graduate students. And when some
studies of creativity actually were made, they dealt with
areas so peripheral that creative people themselves felt they
had next to nothing to do with real creativity. Essentially
we have come up with truisms or irrelevancies at which
the artists and poets smile and about which they say, "Interesting, yes. But that's not what goes on within me in the
creative act." Fortunately during the last twenty years a

change has been occurring, but it is still true that creativity is a stepchild of psychology.

And in psychoanalysis and depth psychology the situation has been little better. I well recall an incident of some twenty years ago that brought vividly home to me the oversimplification and inadequacy of the depth-psychology theories of creativity. One summer I was traveling with a group of seventeen artists through central Europe, studying and painting peasant art. While we were in Vienna, Alfred Adler, whom I had known and whose summer school I had attended, invited us all to his home for a private lecture. In the course of his lecture, in his parlor, Adler touched upon his *compensatory theory of creativity* —that human beings produce art, science, and other aspects of culture to compensate for their own inadequacies. The oyster producing the pearl to cover up the grain of sand intruding into its shell is often cited as a simple illustration. Beethoven's deafness was one of the many famous examples Adler cited, showing how highly creative individuals compensate for some defect or organ inferiority by their creative acts. Adler also believed that civilization was created by human beings to compensate for their relatively weak position on this unfriendly crust of earth as well as for their inadequacy of tooth and claw in the animal world. Then Adler, having entirely forgotten he was addressing a group of artists, looked around the room and remarked, "Since I see that very few of you are wearing glasses, I assume that you are not interested in art." The oversimplification this theory of compensation is subject to was thus dramatically exposed.

The theory does have some merit and is one of the important hypotheses that must be considered by students in the field. But its error is that it does not deal with *the crea-tive process as such*. Compensatory trends in an individual will influence the forms his or her creating will take, but they do not explain the process of creativity itself. Compensa-tory needs influence the particular *bent* or direction in cul-ture or science, but they do not explain the *creation* of the culture or science.

Because of this I learned very early in my psychological career to regard with a good deal of skepticism current the-ories explaining creativity. And I learned always to ask the question: Does the theory deal with creativity itself, or does it deal only with some artifact, some partial, periph-eral aspect, of the creative act?

The other widely current psychoanalytic theories about creativity have two characteristics. First, they are *reductive* —that is, they reduce creativity to some other process. Sec-ond, they generally make it specifically an expression of *neurotic* patterns. The usual definition of creativity in psy-choanalytic circles is "regression in the service of the ego." Immediately the term *regression* indicates the reductive approach. I emphatically disagree with the implication that creativity is to be understood by reducing it to some other process, or that it is essentially an expression of neurosis.

Creativity is certainly associated with serious psycho-logical problems in our particular culture—Van Gogh went psychotic, Gauguin seems to have been schizoid, Poe was alcoholic, and Virginia Woolf was seriously depressed. Ob-viously creativity and originality are associated with per-sons who do not fit into their culture. But this does not necessarily mean that the creativity is the *product* of the neurosis.

The association of creativity with neurosis presents us

with a dilemma—namely, if by psychoanalysis we cured the artists of their neuroses would they no longer create? This dichotomy, as well as many others, arises from the reductive theories. Furthermore, if we create out of some *transfer* of affect or drive, as implied in sublimation, or if our creativity is merely the by-product of an endeavor to accomplish something else, as in compensation, does not our very creative act then have only a pseudo value? We must indeed take a strong stand against the implications, however they may creep in, that talent is a disease and creativity is a neurosis.

1. WHAT IS CREATIVITY?

When we define creativity, we must make the distinction between its pseudo forms, on the one hand—that is, creativity as a superficial aestheticism. And, on the other, its authentic form—that is, the process of *bringing something new into being*. The crucial distinction is between art as artificiality (as in "artifice" or "artful") and genuine art.

This is a distinction that artists and philosophers have struggled all through the centuries to make clear. Plato, for example, demoted his poets and his artists down to the sixth circle of reality because, he said, they deal only with appearances and not with reality itself. He was referring to art as decoration, a way of making life prettier, a dealing with semblances. But in his later, beautiful dialogue, the *Symposium*, he described what he called the *true artists*— namely, those who give birth to some new reality. These poets and other creative persons are the ones who express being itself, he held. As I would put it, these are the ones who enlarge human consciousness. Their creativity is the most basic manifestation of a man or woman fulfilling his or her own being in the world.

Now we must make the above distinction clear if our inquiries into creativity are to get below the surface. We are thus not dealing with hobbies, do-it-yourself movements, Sunday painting, or other forms of filling up leisure time. Nowhere has the meaning of creativity been more disastrously lost than in the idea that it is something you do only on week ends!

The creative process must be explored not as the product of sickness, but as representing the highest degree of emotional health, as the expression of the normal people in the act of actualizing themselves. Creativity must be seen in the work of the scientist as well as in that of the artist, in the thinker as well as in the aesthetician; and one must not rule out the extent to which it is present in captains of modern technology as well as in a mother's normal relationship with her child. Creativity, as *Webster's* rightly indicates, is basically the process of *making*, of *bringing into being*.

2. THE CREATIVE PROCESS

Let us now inquire into the nature of the creative process, and seek our answers by trying to describe as accurately as possible what actually happens in individuals at the moment of the creative act. I shall speak mostly about artists because I know them, have worked with them, and, to some extent, am one myself. This does not mean that I underestimate creativity in other activities. I assume that the following analysis of the nature of creativity will apply to all men and women during their creative moments.

The first thing we notice in a creative act is that it is an *encounter*. Artists encounter the landscape they propose to paint—they look at it, observe it from this angle and that. They are, as we say, absorbed in it. Or, in the case of abstract painters, the encounter may be with an idea, an inner vision, that in turn may be led off by the brilliant colors on the palette or the inviting rough whiteness of the canvas. The paint, the canvas, and the other materials then become a secondary part of this encounter; they are the language of it, the *media*, as we rightly put it. Or scientists confront their experiment, their laboratory task, in a similar situation of encounter.

The encounter may or may not involve voluntary effort —that is, "will power." A healthy child's play, for example, also has the essential features of encounter, and we know it is one of the important prototypes of adult creativity. The essential point is not the presence or absence of voluntary effort, but the degree of absorption, the degree of intensity (which we shall deal with in detail later); there must be a specific quality of *engagement*.

Now we come upon one important distinction between pseudo, escapist creativity on the one hand and that which is genuine on the other. *Escapist creativity is that which lacks encounter.* This was illustrated vividly to me when I worked with a young man in psychoanalysis. A talented professional, this man had rich and varied creative potentialities, but he always stopped just short of actualizing them. He would suddenly get the idea for an excellent story, would work it out in his mind to a full outline which could have then been written up without much further ado, and would relish and enjoy the ecstasy of the experience. Then he would stop there, writing down nothing at all. It was as though the experience of *seeing himself as one who was able to write, as being just about to write,* had within it what he was really seeking and brought its own reward. Hence he never actually created.

This was a fairly baffling problem to him and to me. We had analyzed many aspects of it: his father had been a somewhat gifted writer but a failure; his mother had made much of his father's writings, but had shown only contempt for him in other realms. The young man, an only child, had been pampered and overprotected by his mother and often had been shown preference over his father—for instance, by being served special food at meals. The patient was clearly competing with his father, and faced a dire threat if he should succeed. All this and more we had analyzed in some detail. A vital link of experience, however, was missing.

One day the patient came in to announce that he had made an exciting discovery. The evening before, while reading, he had gotten his customary sudden creative flow of ideas for a story and had taken his usual pleasure in the fact. At the same time he had had a peculiar sexual feeling. He had then recalled for the first time that he had always had this sexual feeling at precisely such an abortively creative moment.

I shall not go into the complex analysis of the associations, which demonstrated that this sexual feeling was both a desire for comfort and sensual gratification of a passive sort and a desire for the unconditional admiration of any woman. I only wish to indicate that the upshot was clearly that his creative "bursts" of ideas were ways of getting admiration, gratification from his mother; that he needed to show mother and other women what a fine, gifted person he was. And once he had done that by getting the beautiful, lofty visions, he had achieved what he wanted. He was not really interested in this context in creating, but in being about to create; creativity was in the service of something quite else.

Now no matter how you may interpret the causes of this pattern, one central feature is clear—*the encounter was lacking.* Is not this the essence of escapist art? Everything is there but the encounter. And is not this the central feature of many kinds of artistic exhibitionism—what Rank calls the *artiste manqué?* We cannot make a valid distinction by saying one kind of art is neurotic and the other healthy. Who is to judge that? We can only say that in exhibitionistic, escapist forms of creativity there is no real encounter, no engagement with reality. That isn't what the young man is after; he wants to be passively accepted and admired by mother. In cases of this kind it is accurate to speak of *regression* in the negative sense. But the crucial point is that we are dealing with something quite different from creativity.

The concept of encounter also enables us to make clearer the important distinction between *talent* and *creativity.* Talent may well have its neurological correlates and can be studied as "given" to a person. A man or woman may have talent whether he or she uses it or not; talent can probably be measured in the person as such. But creativity can be seen only in the act. If we were purists, we would not speak of a "creative person," but only of *a creative act.* Sometimes, as in the case of Picasso, we have great talent and at the same time great encounter and, as a result, great creativity. Sometimes we have great talent and truncated creativity, as many people felt in the case of Scott Fitzgerald. Sometimes we have a highly creative person who seems not to have much talent. It was said of the novelist Thomas Wolfe, who was one of the highly creative figures of the American scene, that he was a "genius without talent." But he was so creative because he threw himself so completely into his material and the challenge of saying it—he was great because of the intensity of his encounter.

3. INTENSITY OF THE ENCOUNTER

This leads us to the second element in the creative act— namely, the *intensity* of the encounter. *Absorption, being caught up in, wholly involved,* and so on, are used commonly to describe the state of the artist or scientist when creating or even the child at play. By whatever name one calls it, genuine creativity is characterized by an intensity of awareness, a heightened consciousness.

Artists, as well as you and I in moments of intensive encounter, experience quite clear neurological changes. These include quickened heart beat; higher blood pressure; increased intensity and constriction of vision, with eyelids narrowed so that we can see more vividly the scene we are painting; we become oblivious to things around us (as well as to the passage of time). We experience a lessening of appetite—persons engaged in a creative act lose interest in eating at the moment, and may work right through mealtime without noticing it. Now all of these correspond to an inhibiting of the functioning of the parasympathetic division of the autonomic nervous system (which has to do with ease, comfort, nourishment) and an activation of the sympathetic nervous division. And, lo and behold, we have the same picture that Walter B. Cannon described as the "flight-fight" mechanism, the energizing of the organism for fighting or fleeing. This is the neurological correlate of what we find, in broad terms, in anxiety and fear.

But what the artist or creative scientist feels is *not* anxiety or fear; it is *joy*. I use the word in contrast to happiness or pleasure. The artist, at the moment of creating, does not experience gratification or satisfaction (though this may be the case later, after he or she has a highball or a pipe in the evening. Rather, it is *joy*, joy defined as the emotion that goes with heightened consciousness, the mood that accompanies the experience of actualizing one's own potentialities.

Now this intensity of awareness is not necessarily connected with conscious purpose or willing. It may occur in reverie or in dreams, or from so-called unconscious levels. An eminent New York professor related an illustrative story. He had been searching for a particular chemical formula for some time, but without success. One night, while he was sleeping, he had a dream in which the formula was worked out and displayed before him. He woke up, and in the darkness he excitedly wrote it down on a piece of tissue, the only thing he could find. But the next morning he could not read his own scribbling. Every night thereafter, upon going to bed, he would concentrate his hopes on dreaming the dream again. Fortunately, after some nights he did, and he then wrote the formula down for good. It was the formula he had sought and for which he received the Nobel prize.

Though not rewarded so dramatically, we have all had similar experiences. Processes of forming, making, building go on even if we are not consciously aware of them at the time. William James once said that we learn to swim in the winter and to skate in the summer. Whether you wish to interpret these phenomena in terms of some formulation of the unconscious, or prefer to follow William James in connecting them with some neurological processes that continue even when we are not working on them, or prefer some other approach, as I do, it is still clear that creativity goes on in varying degrees of intensity on levels not directly under the control of conscious willing. Hence the heightened awareness we are speaking of does not at all mean increased self-consciousness. It is rather correlated with abandon and absorption, and it involves a heightening of awareness in the whole personality.

But let it be said immediately that unconscious insights or answers to problems that come in reverie do not come hit or miss. They may indeed occur at times of relaxation, or in fantasy, or at other times when we alternate play with work. But what is entirely clear is that they pertain to those areas in which the person consciously has worked laboriously and with dedication. *Purpose* in the human being is a much more complex phenomenon than what used to be called will power. Purpose involves all levels of experience. We cannot *will* to have insights. We cannot *will* creativity. But we can *will* to give ourselves to the encounter with intensity of dedication and commitment. The deeper aspects of awareness are activated to the extent that the person is committed to the encounter.

We must also point out that this "intensity of encounter" is not to be identified with what is called the *Dionysian* aspect of creativity. You will find this word *Dionysian* used often in books on creative works. Taken from the name of the Greek god of intoxication and other forms of ecstasy, the term refers to the upsurge of vitality, the abandon, which characterized the ancient orgiastic revels of Dionysus. Nietzsche, in his important book *The Birth of Tragedy*, cites the Dionysian principle of surging vitality and the Apollonian principle of form and rational order as the two dialectical principles that operate in creativity. This dichotomy is assumed by many students and writers.

The Dionysian aspect of intensity can be studied psychoanalytically easily enough. Probably almost every artist has tried at some time or other to paint while under the influence of alcohol. What happens generally is what one would expect, and it happens in proportion to how much alcohol is consumed—namely, that the artist *thinks* he or she is doing wonderful stuff, indeed much better than usual, but in actual fact, as is noted the next morning while looking at the picture, has really performed less well than usual. Certainly Dionysian periods of abandon are valuable, particularly in our mechanized civilization where creativity and the arts are all but starved to death by the routine of punching clocks and attending endless committee meetings, and by the pressures to produce ever greater quantities of papers and books, pressures that have infested the academic world more lethally than the industrial world. I long for the health-giving effects of the periods of "carnival," such as they still have in the Mediterranean countries.

But the intensity of the creative act should be *related to the encounter objectively,* and not released merely by something the artist "takes." Alcohol is a depressant, and possibly necessary in an industrial civilization; but when one needs it regularly to feel free of inhibitions, he or she is misnaming the problem. The issue really is why the inhibitions are there in the first place. The psychological studies of the upsurge of vitality and other effects that occur when such drugs are taken are exceedingly interesting; but one must sharply distinguish this from the intensity that accompanies the encounter itself. The encounter is not something that occurs merely because we ourselves have subjectively changed; it represents, rather, a real relationship with the objective world.

The important and profound aspect of the Dionysian principle is that of *ecstasy.* It was in connection with Dionysian revels that Greek drama was developed, a magnificent summit of creativity which achieved a union of *form and passion* with *order and vitality. Ecstasy* is the technical term for the process in which this union occurs.

The topic of ecstasy is one to which we should give more active attention in psychology. I use the word, of course, not in its popular and cheapened sense of "hysteria," but in its historical, etymological sense of "ex-stasis"—that is, literally to "stand out from," to be freed from the usual split between subject and object which is a perpetual dichotomy in most human activity. *Ecstasy* is the accurate term for the intensity of consciousness that occurs in the creative act. But it is not to be thought of merely as a Bacchic "letting go"; it involves the total person, with the subconscious and unconscious acting in unity with the conscious. It is not, thus, *irrational*; it is, rather, suprarational. It brings intellectual, volitional, and emotional functions into play all together.

What I am saying may sound strange in the light of our traditional academic psychology. It *should* sound strange. Our traditional psychology has been founded on the dichotomy between subject and object which has been the central characteristic of Western thought for the past four centuries. Ludwig Binswanger calls this dichotomy "the cancer of all psychology and psychiatry up to now." [1] It is not avoided by behaviorism or operationalism, which would define experience only in objective terms. Nor is it avoided by isolating the creative experience as a purely subjective phenomenon.

Most psychological and other modern schools of thought still assume this split without being aware of it. We have tended to set reason over against emotions, and have assumed, as an outgrowth of this dichotomy, that we could observe something most accurately if our emotions were not involved—that is to say, we would be least biased if we had no emotional stake at all in the matter at hand. I think this is an egregious error. There are now data in Rorschach responses, for example, that indicate that people can more accurately observe precisely when they are emotionally involved—that is, reason works better when emotions are present; the person sees sharper and more accurately when his emotions are engaged. Indeed, we cannot really see an object unless we have some emotional involvement with it. It may well be that reason works best in the state of ecstasy.

The Dionysian and the Apollonian must be related to

each other. Dionysian vitality rests on this question: What manner of encounter releases the vitality? What particular relation to landscape or inner vision or idea heightens the consciousness, brings forth the intensity?

4. ENCOUNTER AS INTERRELATING WITH THE WORLD

We arrive finally in analyzing the creative act in terms of the question What is this intense encounter *with?* An encounter is always a meeting between two poles. The subjective pole is the conscious person in the creative act itself. But what is the objective pole of this dialectical relationship? I shall use a term that will sound too simple: it is the artist's or scientist's encounter with his *world.* I do not mean world as environment or as the "sum total" of things; nor do I refer at all to objects about a subject.

World is the pattern of meaningful relations in which a person exists and in the design of which he or she participates. It has objective reality, to be sure, but it is not simply that. World is interrelated with the person at every moment. A continual dialectical process goes on between world and self and self and world; one implies the other, and neither can be understood if we omit the other. This is why one can never localize creativity as a *subjective* phenomenon; one can never study it simply in terms of what goes on within the person. The pole of world is an inseparable part of the creativity of an individual. What occurs is always a *process,* a *doing*—specifically a process interrelating the person and his or her world.

How artists encounter their world is illustrated in the

work of every genuinely creative painter. Out of the many possible examples of this, I shall choose the superb exhibition of the paintings of Mondrian shown at the Guggenheim Museum in New York in 1957–58. From his first realistic works in 1904 and 1905, all the way to his later geometrical rectangles and squares in the 1930s, one can see him struggling to find the underlying forms of the objects, particularly trees, that he was painting. He seems to have loved trees. The paintings around 1910, beginning somewhat like Cézanne, move further and further into the underlying meaning of tree—the trunk rises organically from the ground into which the roots have penetrated; the branches curve and bend into the trees and hills of the background in cubistic form, beautifully illustrative of what the underlying essence of tree is to most of us. Then we see Mondrian struggling more and more deeply to find the "ground forms" of nature; now it is less tree and more the eternal geometric forms underlying all reality. Finally we see him pushing inexorably toward the squares and rectangles that are the ultimate form of purely abstract art. Impersonal? To be sure. The individual self is lost. But is this not precisely a reflection of Mondrian's world—the world of the decades of the twenties and thirties, the world in the period of emerging fascism, communism, conformism, military power, in which the individual not only feels lost, but *is* lost, alienated from nature and others as well as himself? Mondrian's paintings express creative strength *in* such a world, an affirmation in spite of the "lostness" of the individual. In this sense his work is a search for the foundation of individuality that can withstand these antihuman political developments.

It is absurd to think of artists simply as "painting nature," as though they were only anachronistic photographers of trees and lakes and mountains. For them, nature is a medium, a language by which they reveal their world. What genuine painters do is to reveal the underlying psychological and spiritual conditions of their relationship to their world; thus in the works of a great painter we have a reflection of the emotional and spiritual condition of human beings in that period of history. If you wish to understand the psychological and spiritual temper of any historical period, you can do no better than to look long and searchingly at its art. For in the art the underlying spiritual meaning of the period is expressed directly in symbols. This is not because artists are didactic or set out to teach or to make propaganda; to the extent that they do, their power of expression is broken; their direct relation to the inarticulate, or, if you will, "unconscious" levels of the culture is destroyed. They have the power to reveal the underlying meaning of any period precisely because the essence of art is the powerful and alive encounter between the artist and his or her world.

Nowhere was this encounter demonstrated more vividly than in the famous seventy-fifth anniversary exhibit of Picasso's works, presented in New York in 1957. Broader in temperament than Mondrian, Picasso is a spokesman for his time *par excellence*. Even in his early works around 1900, his vast talent was already visible. And in the stark, realistic paintings of peasants and poor people in the first decade of this century, his passionate relationship to human suffering was shown. You can then see the spiritual temper of each succeeding decade in his work.

In the early 1920s, for example, we find Picasso painting classical Greek figures, particularly bathers by the sea. An aura of escapism hovers about these pictures in the exhibit. Was not the 1920s, the decade after the first World War, in reality a period of escapism in the Western world? Toward the end of the twenties and in the early thirties, these bathers by the sea become pieces of metal, mechanical, gray-blue curving steel. Beautiful indeed, but impersonal, unhuman. And here one was gripped in the exhibit with an ominous foreboding—the prediction of the beginning of the time when people were to become impersonal, objectivized, numbers. It was the ominous prediction of the beginnings of "man, the robot."

Then in 1937 comes the great painting *Guernica*, with figures torn apart, split from each other, all in stark white, gray, and black. It was Picasso's pained outrage against the inhumanity of the bombing of the helpless Spanish town of Guernica by fascist planes in the Spanish revolution; but it is much more than that. It is the most vivid portrayal imaginable of the atomistic, split-up, fragmentized state of contemporary human beings, and implies the conformism, emptiness, and despair that were to go along with this. Then in the late thirties and forties, Picasso's portraits become more and more machinelike—people turned literally into metal. Faces become distorted. It is as though persons, individuals, do not exist any more; their places are taken by hideous witches. Pictures now are not *named*, but *numbered*. The bright colors the artist used in his earlier periods and which were so delightful are now largely gone. In these rooms at the exhibit one feels as though darkness has settled upon the earth at noon. As in the novels of Kafka, one gets a stark and gripping feeling of the modern individual's loss of humanity. The first time I saw this exhibit, I was so overcome with the foreboding picture of human beings losing their faces, their individuality, their humanity, and the prediction of the robot to come, that I could look no longer and had to hurry out of the room and onto the street again.

To be sure, all the way through Picasso preserves his own sanity by "playing" with paintings and sculptures of animals and his own children. But it is clear that the main stream is a portrayal of our modern condition, which has been psychologically portrayed by Riesman, Mumford, Tillich, and others. The whole is an unforgettable portrait of modern man and woman in the process of losing their person and their humanity.

In this sense genuine artists are so bound up with their age that they cannot communicate separated from it. In this sense, too, the historical situation conditions the creativity. For the consciousness which obtains in creativity is not the superficial level of objectified intellectualization, but is an encounter with the world on a level that undercuts the subject-object split. "Creativity," to rephrase our definition, "is the encounter of the intensively conscious human being with his or her world."

THREE

CREATIVITY AND
THE UNCONSCIOUS

Everyone uses from time to time such expressions as, "a thought pops up," an idea comes "from the blue" or "dawns" or "comes as though out of a dream," or "it suddenly hit me." These are various ways of describing a common experience: the breakthrough of ideas from some depth below the level of awareness. I shall call this realm "the unconscious" as a catchall for the subconscious, preconscious, and other dimensions below awareness.

When I use the phrase "the unconscious," I, of course, mean it as a shorthand. There is no such thing as *"the* unconscious"; it is, rather, unconscious dimensions (or aspects or sources) of experience. I define this unconscious as *the potentialities for awareness or action which the individual cannot or will not actualize.* These potentialities are the source of what can be called "free creativity."

The exploration of unconscious phenomena has a fascinating relationship to creativity. What are the nature and characteristics of the creativity that has its source in these unconscious depths of personality?

1

I wish to begin our exploration of this topic by relating an incident from my own experience. When I was a graduate student doing research on *The Meaning of Anxiety*, I studied anxiety in a group of unmarried mothers—i.e., pregnant young women in their late teens and early twenties in a shelter home in New York City.[1] I had a good, sound hypothesis on anxiety, approved by my professors and approved by me—that the predisposition toward anxiety in individuals would be proportionate to the degree to which they had been rejected by their mothers. In psychoanalysis and psychology this had been a generally accepted hypothesis. I assumed the anxiety of people like these young women would be cued off by the anxiety-creating situation of being unwed and pregnant, and I could then study more openly the original source of their anxiety—namely the maternal rejection.

Now I discovered that half the young women fitted my hypothesis beautifully. But the other half did not fit it at all. This latter group included young women from Harlem and the Lower East Side who had been radically rejected by their mothers. One of them, whom I shall call Helen, was from a family of twelve children whose mother drove them out of the house on the first day of summer to stay with their father, the caretaker of a barge that went up and down the Hudson River. Helen was pregnant by her father. At the time she was in the shelter, he was in Sing Sing on a charge of rape by Helen's older sister. Like the other young women of this group, Helen would say to me, "We have troubles, but we don't worry."

This was a very curious thing to me and I had a hard time believing the data. But the facts seemed clear. As far as I could tell by the Rorschach, TAT, and other tests I used, these radically rejected young women did not carry any unusual degree of anxiety. Forced out of the house by their mothers, they simply made their friends among other youngsters on the street. Hence, there was not the predisposition to anxiety we would have expected according to what we know in psychology.

How could this be? Had the rejected young women who had not experienced anxiety become hardened, apathetic, so that they did not feel the rejection? The answer to that seemed clearly no. Were they psychopathic or sociopathic types, who also don't experience anxiety? Again, no. I felt myself caught by an insoluble problem.

Late one day, putting aside my books and papers in the little office I used in that shelter house, I walked down the street toward the subway. I was tired. I tried to put the whole troublesome business out of my mind. About fifty feet away from the entrance to the Eighth Street station, it suddenly struck me "out of the blue," as the not-unfitting expression goes, that those young women who didn't fit my hypothesis *were all from the proletarian class*. And as quickly as that idea struck me, other ideas poured out. I think I had not taken another step on the sidewalk when a whole new hypothesis broke loose in my mind. I realized my entire theory would have to be changed. I saw at that instant that it is not rejection by the mother that is the original trauma which is the source of anxiety; it is rather *rejection that is lied about.*

The proletarian mothers rejected their children, but they never made any bones about it. The children knew they were rejected; they went out on the streets and found other companions. There was never any subterfuge about their situation. They knew their world—bad or good—and they could orient themselves to it. But the middle-class young women were always lied to in their families. They were rejected by mothers who pretended they loved them. This was really the source of their anxiety, not the sheer rejection. I saw, in that instantaneous way that characterizes insights from these deeper sources, that anxiety comes from *not being able to know the world you're in, not being able to orient yourself in your own existence.* I was convinced there, on the street—and later thought and experience only convinced me the more—that this is a better, more accurate, and more elegant theory, than my first.

2

What was going on at the moment when this breakthrough occurred? Taking this experience of mine as a start, we notice, first of all, that the insight broke into my conscious mind *against* what I had been trying to think rationally. I had a good, sound thesis and I had been working very hard trying to prove it. The unconscious, so to speak, *broke through in opposition to the conscious belief to which I was clinging.*

Carl Jung often made the point that there is a polarity,

a kind of opposition, between unconscious experience and consciousness. He believed the relationship was compensatory: consciousness controls the wild, illogical vagaries of the unconscious, while the unconscious keeps consciousness from drying up in banal, empty, arid rationality. The compensation also works on specific problems: if I consciously bend too far one way on some issue, my unconscious will lean the other way. This is, of course, the reason why the more we are unconsciously smitten with doubts about an idea, the more dogmatically we fight for it in our conscious arguments. This is also why persons as different as Saint Paul on the Damascus road and the alcoholic in the Bowery go through such radical conversions—the repressed unconscious side of the dialectic erupts and takes over the personality. The unconscious seems to take delight (if I may so express it) in breaking through—and breaking up—exactly what we cling to most rigidly in our conscious thinking.

What occurs in this breakthrough is not simply growth; it is much more dynamic. It is not a mere expansion of awareness; it is rather a kind of battle. A dynamic struggle goes on within a person between what he or she consciously thinks on the one hand and, on the other, some insight, some perspective that is struggling to be born. The insight is then born with anxiety, guilt, and the joy and gratification that is inseparable from the actualizing of a new idea or vision.

The guilt that is present when this breakthrough occurs has its source in the fact that the insight must destroy something. My insight destroyed my other hypothesis and would destroy what a number of my professors believed, a fact that caused me some concern. Whenever there is a breakthrough of a significant idea in science or a significant new form in art, the new idea will destroy what a lot of people believe is essential to the survival of their intellectual and spiritual world. This is the source of guilt in genuine creative work. As Picasso remarked, "Every act of creation is first of all an act of destruction."

The breakthrough carries with it also an element of anxiety. For it not only broke down my previous hypothesis, it shook my self-world relationship. At such a time I find myself having to seek a new foundation, the existence of which I as yet don't know. This is the source of the anxious feeling that comes at the moment of the breakthrough; it is not possible that there be a genuinely new idea without this shake up occurring to some degree.

But beyond guilt and anxiety, as I said above, the main feeling that comes with the breakthrough is one of gratification. We have seen something new. We have the joy of participating in what the physicists and other natural scientists call an experience of "elegance."

3

A second thing that occurred in the breakthrough of this insight is that *everything around me became suddenly vivid*. I can remember that on the particular street down which I walked the houses were painted an ugly shade of green that I normally would prefer to forget immediately. But by virtue of the vividness of this experience, the colors all around were sharpened and were imbedded in my experience, and that ugly green still exists in my memory. The moment the insight broke through, there was a special translucence that enveloped the world, and my vision was given a special clarity. I am convinced that this is the usual accompaniment of the breakthrough of unconscious experience into consciousness. Here is again part of the reason the experience scares us so much: the world, both inwardly and outwardly, takes on an intensity that may be momentarily overwhelming. This is one aspect of what is called ecstasy—the uniting of unconscious experience with consciousness, a union that is not *in abstracto,* but a dynamic, immediate fusion.

I want to emphasize that I did not get my insight as though I were dreaming, with the world and myself opaque and cloudy. It is a popular misconception that perception is dull when one is experiencing this state of insight. I believe that perception is actually sharper. True, one aspect of it resembles a dream in that self and world may become kaleidoscopic; but another aspect of the experience is a sharpened perception, a vividness, a translucence of relationship to the things around us. The world becomes vivid and unforgettable. Thus the breakthrough of material from unconscious dimensions involves a heightening of sensory experience.

We could, indeed, define the whole experience that we are talking about as *a state of heightened consciousness.* Unconsciousness is the depth dimension of consciousness, and when it surges up into consciousness in this kind of polar struggle the result is an intensification of consciousness. It heightens not only the capacity to think, but also the sensory processes; and it certainly intensifies memory.

There is a third thing we observe when such insights occur—that is, *the insight never comes hit or miss, but in accordance with a pattern of which one essential element is our own commitment*. The breakthrough does not come by just "taking it easy," by "letting the unconscious do it." The insight, rather, is born from unconscious levels exactly in the areas in which we are most intensively consciously committed. The insight came to me on that problem to which, up till the moment I put my books and papers away in the little office that I occupied, I had devoted my best and most energetic conscious thought. The idea, the new form which suddenly becomes present, *came in order to complete an incomplete Gestalt with which I was struggling in conscious awareness*. One can quite accurately speak of this incomplete Gestalt, this unfinished pattern, this unformed form, as constituting the "call" that was answered by the unconscious.

The fourth characteristic of this experience is that *the insight comes at a moment of transition between work and relaxation*. It comes at a break in periods of voluntary effort. My breakthrough came when I had put away my books and was walking toward the subway, my mind far away from that problem. It is as though intense application to the problem—thinking about it, struggling with it —starts and keeps the work process going; but some part of the pattern that is different from what I am trying to work out is struggling to be born. Hence the tension that is involved in creative activity. If we are too rigid, dogmatic, or bound to previous conclusions, we will, of course, never let this new element come into our consciousness; we will never let ourselves be aware of the knowledge that exists on another level within us. But the insight often cannot be born until the conscious tension, the conscious application, is relaxed. Hence the well-known phenomenon that the unconscious breakthrough requires the alternation of intense, conscious work and relaxation, with the unconscious insight often occurring, as in my case, at the moment of the shift.

Albert Einstein once asked a friend of mine in Princeton, "Why is it I get my best ideas in the morning while I'm shaving?" My friend answered, as I have been trying to say here, that often the mind needs the relaxation of inner controls—needs to be freed in reverie or day dreaming—for the unaccustomed ideas to emerge.

4

Let us now consider the experience, more complex and richer than mine, of one of the great mathematicians of the late nineteenth and early twentieth centuries, Jules Henri Poincaré. In his autobiography, Poincaré tells us with admirable clarity how his new insights and new theories came to him, and he describes vividly the circumstances surrounding the occurrence of one "breakthrough."

> For fifteen days I strove to prove that there could not be any functions like those I have since called Fuchsian functions. I was then very ignorant; every day I seated myself at my work table, stayed an hour or two, tried a great number of combinations and reached no results. One evening, contrary to my custom, I drank black coffee and could not sleep. Ideas rose in crowds; I felt them collide until pairs interlocked, so to speak, making a stable combination. By the next morning I had established the existence of a class of Fuchsian functions, those which come from the hypergeometric series; I had only to write out the results, which took but a few hours.[2]

Still a young man, he was then called into the military service, and for some months nothing happened in his thinking. One day in a town in southern France he was getting on a bus and talking with another soldier. As he was about to put his foot on the step—he pinpoints the moment that exactly—there broke into his mind the answer to how these new mathematical functions that he had discovered were related to the conventional mathematics he had been working on before. When I read Poincaré's experience—which was after the above incident in my own life—I was struck by how similar it was in this special precision and vividness. He got up on the step, entered the bus, continued without pause his conversation with his friend, but was completely and instaneously convinced of the way these functions were related to general mathematics.

To continue with a later portion of his autobiography, when he returned from army service:

Then I turned my attention to the study of some arithmetical questions apparently without much success and without a suspicion of any connection with my preceding researches. Disgusted with my failure, I went to spend a few days at the seaside, and thought of something else. One morning, walking on the bluff, the idea came to me, with just the same characteristics of brevity, suddenness and immediate certainty, that the arithmetic transformations of indeterminate ternary quadratic forms were identical with those of non-Euclidean geometry.[3]

Poincaré, turning psychologist for the moment, asks himself the question we posed above: What is going on in the mind that these ideas should break through at this moment? This is what he proposes in answer to his question:

Most striking at first is this appearance of sudden illumination, a manifest sign of long, unconscious prior work. The role of this unconscious work in mathematical invention appears to me incontestable, and traces of it would be found in other cases where it is less evident. Often when one works at a hard question, nothing good is accomplished at the first attack. Then one takes a rest, longer or shorter, and sits down anew to the work. During the first half-hour, as before, nothing is found, and then all of a sudden the decisive idea presents itself to the mind. It might be said that the conscious work has been more fruitful because it has been interrupted and the rest has given back to the mind its force and freshness.[4]

Is the appearance of the illumination due to the relief from fatigue—i.e., simply taking a rest? No, he answers:

It is more probable that this rest has been filled out with unconscious work and that the result of this work has afterward revealed itself to the geometer just as in the cases I have cited; only the revelation, instead of coming during a walk or a journey, has happened during a period of conscious work, but independently of this work which plays at most a role of excitant, as if it were the goad stimulating the results already reached during rest, but remaining unconscious, to assume the conscious form.[5]

He then continues with another penetrating comment on the practical aspects of the breakthrough:

There is another remark to be made about the conditions of this unconscious work: it is possible, and of a certainty it is only fruitful, if it is on the one hand preceded and on the other hand followed by a period of conscious work. These sudden inspirations (and the examples already cited sufficiently prove this) never happen except after some days of voluntary effort which has appeared absolutely fruitless and whence nothing good seems to have come, where the way taken seems totally astray. These efforts then have not been as sterile as one thinks; they have set agoing the unconscious machine and without them it would not have moved and would have produced nothing.[6]

Let us summarize some of the most significant points so far in Poincaré's testimony. He sees the characteristics of the experience as follows: (1) the *suddenness* of the illumination; (2) that the insight may occur, and to some extent *must* occur, *against* what one has clung to consciously in one's theories; (3) the *vividness* of the incident and the whole scene that surrounds it; (4) the *brevity* and *consciseness* of the insight, along with the experience of *immediate certainty*. Continuing with the practical conditions which he cites as necessary for this experience are (5) hard work on the topic *prior to the breakthrough*; (6) a *rest*, in which the "unconscious work" has been given a chance to proceed on its own and after which the breakthrough may occur (which is a special case of the more general point); (7) the necessity of *alternating work and relaxation*, with the insight often coming at the moment of the break between the two, or at least within the break.

This last point is particularly interesting. It is probably something everyone has learned: professors will lecture with more inspiration if they occasionally alternate the classroom with the beach; authors will write better when, as Macaulay used to do, they write for two hours, then pitch quoits, and then go back to their writing. But certainly more than the mere mechanical alternation is involved.

I propose that in our day this alternation of the market place and mountain requires the capacity for the *constructive use of solitude*. It requires that we be able to retire from a world that is "too much with us," that we be able to be quiet, that we let the solitude work for us and in us. It is a characteristic of our time that many people are afraid of solitude: to be alone is a sign one is a social failure, for no one would be alone if he or she could help it. It often occurs to me that people living in our modern, hectic civilization, amid the constant din of radio and TV, subjecting themselves to every kind of stimulation whether of the passive sort of TV or the more active sort of conversation, work, and activity, that people with such constant preoccupations find it exceedingly difficult to let insights from unconscious depths break through. Of course, when an individual is afraid of the irrational—that is, of the unconscious dimensions of experience—he tries to keep busiest, tries to keep most "noise" going on about him. The avoidance of the anxiety of solitude by constant agitated diversion is what Kierkegaard, in a nice simile, likened to the settlers in the early days of America who used to beat on pots and pans at night to make enough din to keep the wolves away. Obviously if we are to experience insights from our unconscious, we need to be able to give ourselves to solitude.

Poincaré finally asks: What determines *why* a given idea comes through from the unconscious? Why this particular insight and not one of a dozen others? Is it because a particular insight is the answer which is empirically most accurate? No, he answers. Is it because it is the insight which will pragmatically work best? Again, no. What Poincaré proposes as the selective factor resulting in this given insight seems to me to be in some ways the most important and gripping point in his whole analysis:

The useful combinations [that come through from the unconscious] are precisely the most beautiful, I mean those best able to charm this special sensibility that all mathematicians know, but of which the profane are so ignorant as often to be tempted to smile at it.

. . . Among the great numbers of combinations blindly formed by the subliminal self, almost all are without interest and without utility; but just for that reason they are also without effect upon the esthetic sensibility. Consciousness will never know them; only certain ones are harmonious, and, consequently, at once useful and beautiful. They will be capable of touching this special sensibility of the geometer of which I have just spoken, and which, once aroused, will call our attention to them, and thus give them occasion to become conscious.[7]

This is why the mathematicians and physicists talk about the "elegance" of a theory. The utility is subsumed as part of the character of being beautiful. The harmony of an internal form, the inner consistency of a theory, the character of beauty that touches one's sensibilities—these are significant factors determining why a given idea emerges. As a psychoanalyst, I can only add that my experience in helping people achieve insights reveals the same phenomenon—that insights emerge not chiefly because they are "rationally true" or even helpful, but because they have a certain form, the form that is beautiful because it completes an incomplete Gestalt.

When this breakthrough of a creative insight into consciousness occurs, we have the subjective conviction that the form should be this way and no other way. It is characteristic of the creative experience that it strikes us as true —with the "immediate certainty" of Poincaré. And we think, nothing else could have been true in that situation, and we wonder why we were so stupid as not to have seen it earlier. The reason, of course, is that we were not psychologically ready to see it. We could not yet *intend* the new truth or creative form in art or scientific theory. We were not yet open on the level of intentionality. But the "truth" itself is simply there. This reminds us of what the Zen Buddhists keep saying—that at these moments is reflected and revealed a reality of the universe that does not depend merely on our own subjectivity, but is as though we only had our eyes closed and suddenly we open them and there it is, as simple as can be. The new reality has a kind of immutable, eternal quality. The experience that "this is the way reality is and isn't it strange we didn't see it sooner" may have a religious quality with artists. This is why many artists feel that something holy is going on when they paint, that there is something in the act of creating which is like a religious revelation.

5

We now consider some dilemmas which arise from the relation of the unconscious to techniques and machines. No discussion of creativity and the unconscious in our society can possibly avoid these difficult and important problems.

We live in a world that has become mechanized to an amazingly high degree. Irrational unconscious phenomena are always a threat to this mechanization. Poets may be delightful creatures in the meadow or the garret, but they are menaces on the assembly line. Mechanization requires uniformity, predictability, and orderliness; and the very fact that unconscious phenomena are original and irrational is already an inevitable threat to bourgeois order and uniformity.

This is one reason people in our modern Western civilization have been afraid of unconscious and irrational experience. For the potentialities that surge up in them from deeper mental wells simply don't fit the technology which has become so essential for our world. What people today do out of fear of irrational elements in themselves as well as in other people is *to put tools and mechanics between themselves and the unconscious world.* This protects them from being grasped by the frightening and threatening aspects of irrational experience. I am saying nothing whatever, I am sure it will be understood, against technology or techniques or mechanics in themselves. What I am saying is that the danger always exists that our technology will serve as a buffer between us and nature, a block between us and the deeper dimensions of our own experience. Tools and techniques ought to be an *extension* of consciousness, but they can just as easily be a *protection* from consciousness. Then tools become defense mechanisms—specifically against the wider and more complex dimensions of consciousness that we call the unconscious. Our mechanisms and technology then make us "uncertain in the impulses of the spirit," as the physicist Heisenberg puts it.[8]

Western civilization since the Renaissance has centrally emphasized techniques and mechanics. Thus it is understandable that the creative impulses of ourselves and our forefathers, again since the Renaissance, should have been channeled into the making of technical things—creativity directed toward the advance and application of science. Such channeling of creativity into technical pursuits is appropriate on one level but serves as a psychological defense on a deeper level. This means that technology will be clung to, believed in, and depended on far beyond its legitimate sphere, since it also serves as a defense against our fears of irrational phenomena. Thus the very success of technological creativity—and that its success is magnificent does not need to be heralded by me—is a threat to its own existence. For if we are not open to the unconscious, irrational, and transrational aspects of creativity, then our science and technology have helped to block us off from what I shall call "creativity of the spirit." By this I mean creativity that has nothing to do with technical use; I mean creativity in art, poetry, music, and other areas that exist for our delight and the deepening and enlarging of meaning in our lives rather than for making money or for increasing technical power.

To the extent that we lose this free, original creativity of the spirit as it is exemplified in poetry and music and art, we shall also lose our scientific creativity. Scientists themselves, particularly the physicists, have told us that the creativity of science is bound up with the freedom of human beings to create in the free, pure sense. In modern physics it is very clear that the discoveries that later become utilized for our technological gains are generally made in the first place because a physicist lets his imagination go and discovers something simply for the joy of discovery. But this always runs the risk of radically upsetting our previously nicely worked-out theories, as it did when Einstein introduced his theory of relativity, and Heisenberg introduced his principle of indeterminacy. My point here is more than the conventional distinction between "pure" and "applied" science. The creativity of the spirit *does* and *must* threaten the structure and presuppositions of our rational, orderly society and way of life. Unconscious, irrational urges are bound by their very nature to be a threat to our rationality, and the anxiety we experience thereupon is inescapable.

I am proposing that the creativity coming from the preconscious and unconscious is not only important for art and poetry and music; but is essential in the long run also for our science. To shrink from the anxiety this entails, and block off the threatening new insights and forms this engenders, is not only to render our society banal and progressively more empty, but also to cut off as well the headwaters in the rough and rocky mountains of the stream that later becomes the river of creativity in our science. The new physicists and mathematicians, for fairly obvious reasons, have been furthest ahead in realizing this interrelation between unconscious, irrational illumination and scientific discovery.

Let me now give an illustration of the problem we face. In the several times I have been on television, I have been struck by two different feelings. One was wonder at the fact that my words, spoken in the studio, could be delivered instantaneously into the living rooms of half a million people. The other was that whenever I got an original idea, whenever in these programs I began to struggle with some unformed, new concept, whenever I had an original thought that might cross some frontier of the discussion, at that point I was cut off. I have no resentment against emcees who do this; they know their business, and they realize that if what goes on in the program does not fit in the world of listeners all the way from Georgia to Wyoming, the viewers will get up, go to the kitchen, get a beer, come back, and switch on a Western.

When you have the potentialities for tremendous mass communication, you inevitably tend to communicate on the level of the half-million people who are listening. What you say must have some place in their world, must at least be partly known to them. Inevitably, then, originality, the breaking of frontiers, the radical newness of ideas and images are at best dubious and at worst totally unacceptable. Mass communication—wonder as it may be technologically and something to be appreciated and valued—presents us with a serious danger, the danger of conformism, due to the fact that we all view the same things at the same time in all the cities of the country. This very fact throws considerable weight on the side of regularity and uniformity and against originality and freer creativity.

6

Just as the poet is a menace to conformity, he is also a constant threat to political dictators. He is always on the verge of blowing up the assembly line of political power.

We have had powerful and poignant demonstrations of this in Soviet Russia. It appeared chiefly in the prosecution and purge of artists and writers under Stalin, who was pathologically anxious when faced with the threat that the creative unconscious posed to his political system. Indeed, some students believe that the present situation in Russia shows an ongoing struggle between rationality and what we have been calling "free creativity." George Reavey, in his introduction to the work of the Russian poet Yevgeny Yevtushenko writes:

There is something about the poet and his poetic utterance that has a terrifying effect on some Russians, and especially on the Authorities, be they Tzarist or Soviet. It is as though *poetry were an irrational force which must be bridled and subjugated and even destroyed.*[9]

Reavey cites the tragic fate that has befallen so many Russian poets, and suggests that "it is as though Russia were frightened by the expanding image of its culture and, feeling threatened by the possible loss of its own simple theoretical identity, must needs shatter anything more

The Courage to Create

complex as something alien to itself." He feels that this "may be due to an inherent strain of puritanism. Or to the reaction of an archaic form of despotic paternalism." Or to the present painful effects of a too sudden transition from serfdom to industrialization. I would also raise the question as to whether there is among Russians less cultural and psychological defense against irrational elements in themselves and their society than among people of other nations. Don't Russians, in fact, live closer to irrational elements than the older European countries, and, therefore, being more threatened by untamed irrationality, have to make a greater effort to control it by regulation?

Could not the same question be fruitfully raised about the United States—that is, are not our emphasis on pragmatic rationalism, our practical controls, and our behavioristic ways of thinking defenses against the irrational elements that were present on the frontiers of our society only a hundred years ago? These irrational elements are always bursting out—often to our considerable embarrassment—in the prairie fires of revival movements of the nineteenth century, in the Ku Klux Klan, and in McCarthyism, to name mainly negative examples.

But there is a special point I'd like to make here about preoccupation in the United States with "behavior." The sciences of man in America are called *"behavioral* sciences," the American Psychological Association's national television program was called "Accent on *Behavior,*" and our chief original and only extensive contribution to psychological schools is *behaviorism*, in contrast to the many European schools—psychoanalysis, Gestalt structuralism, existential psychology, etc. Practically all of us as children have heard: "Behave yourself! Behave! Behave!" The relation between moralistic puritanism and this preoccupation with behavior is by no means entirely fictitious or accidental. Is not our emphasis on behavior a carry-over of *our* "inherent strain of puritanism," as Reavey suggests may be the case in Russia? I am, of course, entirely aware of the argument that we have to study behavior because that's the only thing that can be studied with any kind of objectivity. But this could well be—and I propose it is— a parochial prejudice raised to the level of a scientific principle. If we accept it as a presupposition, does it not lead to the greatest mistake of all, from the point of view of this chapter—namely, a denial by fiat of the significance of irrational, subjective activity by subsuming it under the guise of its external results?

In any case, Reavey states that even though Stalin is dead, the situation of the poet in Russia is still precarious because the younger poets and some of the hitherto muzzled older poets have become more determined to express their real feelings and to interpret the truth as they see it. These poets have not only been condemning the corrupt substitution of falsehood for truth in Russia, but are trying to rejuvenate the language of Russian poetry by clearing it of political clichés and "father images." During Stalinism this was condemned as "ideological co-existence" with the "bourgeois world," and the poet was cut down for anything that "seemed to endanger the closed, exclusive system of Soviet Realism." The only trouble is, any kind of "closed, exclusive system" destroys poetry as it does all art. Reavey continues:

In a speech pronounced in 1921, Alexander Blok, the great Russian poet, had argued that "tranquility and freedom" were "essential to the poet in order to set harmony free." But he went on to say, "the Soviet authorities also take away our tranquility and freedom. *Not outward but creative tranquility.* Not the childish do-as-you-will, not the freedom to play the liberal, but *the creative will*—the secret freedom. And the poet is dying, because there is no longer anything to breathe; life has lost its meaning from him." [10]

This is a powerful statement of my thesis—namely, that a *sine qua non* of creativity is the freedom of artists to give all the elements within themselves free play in order to open up the possibility of what Blok excellently calls "the creative will," [11] The negative part of Blok's statement is true of poetry in Stalin's regime, and was in this country during the McCarthy period. This "creative tranquility" and this "secret freedom" are precisely what the dogmatists cannot tolerate. Stanley Kunitz believes the poet is inevitably the adversary of the state. The poet, he says, is a witness to the possibility of revelation. This the politically rigid cannot stand.

Dogmatists of all kinds—scientific, economic, moral, as well as political—are threatened by the creative freedom of the artist. This is necessarily and inevitably so. We cannot escape our anxiety over the fact that the artists together with creative persons of all sorts, are the possible destroyers of our nicely ordered systems. For the creative impulse is the speaking of the voice and the expressing of the forms of the preconscious and unconscious; and this is, by its very nature, a threat to rationality and external control. The dogmatists then try to take over the artist. The church, in certain periods, harnessed him to prescribed subjects and methods. Capitalism tries to take over the artist by buying him. And Soviet realism tried to do so by social proscription. The result, by the very nature of the creative impulse, is fatal to art. If it were possible to control the artist—and I do not believe it is—it would mean the death of art.

FOUR

CREATIVITY AND ENCOUNTER

I WISH TO PROPOSE a theory and to make some remarks about it, arising largely out of my contacts and discussions with artists and poets. The theory is: *Creativity occurs in an act of encounter and is to be understood with this encounter as its center.*

Cézanne sees a tree. He sees it in a way no one else has ever seen it. He experiences, as he no doubt would have said, "being grasped by the tree." The arching grandeur of the tree, the mothering spread, the delicate balance as the tree grips the earth—all these and many more characteristics of the tree are absorbed into his perception and are felt throughout his nervous structure. These are part of the vision he experiences. This vision involves an omission of some aspects of the scene and a greater emphasis on other aspects and the ensuing rearrangement of the whole; but it is more than the sum of all these. Primarily it is a vision that is now not tree, but Tree; the concrete tree Cézanne looked at is formed into the essence of tree. However original and unrepeatable his vision is, it is still a vision of all trees triggered by his encounter with this particular one.

The painting that issues out of this encounter between a human being, Cézanne, and an objective reality, the tree, is literally new, unique and original. Something is born, comes into being, something that did not exist before—which is as good a definition of creativity as we can get. Thereafter everyone who looks at the painting with intensity of awareness and lets it speak to him or her will see the tree with the unique powerful movement, the intimacy between the tree and the landscape, and the architectural beauty which literally did not exist in our relation with trees until Cézanne experienced and painted them. I can say without exaggeration that I never really *saw* a tree until I had seen and absorbed Cézanne's paintings of them.

1

The very fact that the creative act is such an encounter between two poles is what makes it so hard to study. It is easy enough to find the subjective pole, the person, but it is much harder to define the objective pole, the "world" or "reality." Since my emphasis here is on the encounter itself, I shall not worry too much at the moment about such definitions. In his book *Poetry and Experience*, Archibald MacLeish uses the most universal terms possible for the two poles of the encounter: "Being and Non-being."

He quotes a Chinese poet: "We poets struggle with Non-being to force it to yield Being. We knock upon silence for an answering music." [1]

"Consider what this means," MacLeish ruminates. "The 'Being' which the poem is to contain derives from 'Non-being,' not from the poet. And the 'music' which the poem is to own comes not from us who make the poem but from the silence; comes in *answer* to our knock. The verbs are eloquent: 'struggle,' 'force,' 'knock.' The poet's labor is to struggle with the meaninglessness and silence of the world until he can force it to mean; until he can make the silence answer and the Non-being be. It is a labor which undertakes to 'know' the world not by exegesis or demonstration or proofs but directly, as a man knows apple in the mouth." [2] This is a beautifully expressed antidote to our common assumption that the subjective projection is *all* that occurs in the creative act, and a reminder of the inescapable mystery that surrounds the creative process.

The vision of the artist or the poet is the intermediate determinant between the subject (the person) and the objective pole (the world-waiting-to-be). It will be non-being until the poet's struggle brings forth an answering meaning. The greatness of a poem or a painting is not that it portrays the *thing* observed or experienced, but that it portrays the artist's or the poet's vision cued off by his encounter with the reality. Hence the poem or the painting is unique, original, never to be duplicated. No matter how many times Monet returned to paint the cathedral at Rouen, each canvas was a new painting expressing a new vision.

Here we must guard against one of the most serious errors in the psychoanalytic interpretation of creativity.

This is the attempt to find something within the individual which is then projected onto the work of art, or some early experience which is transferred to the canvas or written into the poem. Obviously, early experiences play exceedingly important roles in determining how artists will encounter their world. But these subjective data can never explain the encounter itself.

Even in the cases of abstract artists, where the process of painting seems most subjective, the relationship between being and non-being is certainly present and may be sparked by the artist's encountering the brilliant colors on the palette or the inviting rough whiteness of the canvas. Painters have described the excitement of this moment: it seems like a re-enactment of the creation story, with being suddenly becoming alive and possessing a vitality of its own. Mark Tobey fills his canvases with elliptical, calligraphic lines, beautiful whirls that seem at first glance to be completely abstract and to come from nowhere at all except his own subjective musing. But I shall never forget how struck I was, on visiting Tobey's studio one day, to see strewn around books on astronomy and photographs of the Milky Way. I knew then that Tobey experiences the movement of the stars and solar constellations as the external pole of his encounter.

The receptivity of the artist must never be confused with passivity. Receptivity is the artist's holding him- or herself alive and open to hear what being may speak. Such receptivity requires a nimbleness, a fine-honed sensitivity in order to let one's self be the vehicle of whatever vision may emerge. It is the opposite of the authoritarian demands impelled by "will power." I am quite aware of all the jokes that appear in *The New Yorker* and elsewhere showing the artist sitting disconsolately in front of the easel, brush in passive hand, waiting for the inspiration to come. But an artist's "waiting," funny as it may look in cartoons, is not to be confused with laziness or passivity. It requires a high degree of attention, as when a diver is poised on the end of the springboard, not jumping but holding his or her muscles in sensitive balance for the right second. It is an active listening, keyed to hear the answer, alert to see whatever can be glimpsed when the vision or the words do come. It is a waiting for the birthing process to begin to move in its own organic time. It is necessary that the artist have this sense of timing, that he or she respect these periods of receptivity as part of the mystery of creativity and creation.

2

A remarkable example of the creative encounter is given in the small book written by James Lord in recounting his experience of posing for Alberto Giacometti. Having been friends for some time, these two men could be entirely open with each other. Lord often made notes directly after the posing session of what Giacometti had said and done, and out of them he has put together this valuable monograph about the experience of encounter that occurs in creativity.

He reveals, first, the great degree of anxiety and agony that the encounter generated in Giacometti. When Lord would arrive at the studio for his sitting, Giacometti would often disconsolately occupy himself half an hour or more doing odds and ends with his sculpture, literally afraid to start on the painting. When he did bring himself to get into the painting, the anxiety became overt. At one point, writes Lord, Giacometti started gasping and stamping his foot:

> "Your head is going away!" he exclaimed. "It's going away completely!"
> "It will come back again," I said.
> He shook his head. "Not necessarily. Maybe the canvas will become completely empty. And then what will become of me? I'll die of it!" . . .
> He reached into his pocket, pulled out his handkerchief, stared at it for a moment, as though he didn't know what it was, then with a moan threw it onto the floor. Suddenly he shouted very loudly, "I shriek! I scream!" [3]

Lord goes on at another point:

> To talk to his model while he is working distracts him, I think, from the constant anxiety which is a result of his conviction that he cannot hope to represent on the canvas what he sees before him. This anxiety often bursts forth in the form of melan choly gasps, furious expletives, and occasional loud cries of rage and/or distress. He suffers. There is no doubt about it. . . .
> Giacometti is committed to his work in a particularly intense and total way. The creative compulsion is never wholly absent from him, never leaves him a moment of complete peace.[4]

So intense is the encounter that he often identifies the painting on the easel with the actual flesh-and-blood person posing. One day his foot accidentally struck the catch that holds the easel shelf at the proper level, which caused the canvas to fall abruptly for a foot or two.

> "Oh, excuse me!" he said. I laughed and observed that he'd excused himself as though he'd caused me to fall instead of the painting. "That's exactly what I did feel," he answered.[5]

In Giacometti this anxiety was associated, as it was in his revered Cézanne, with a great deal of self-doubt.

In order to go on, to hope, to believe that there is some chance of his actually creating what he ideally visualizes, he is obliged to feel that it is necessary to start his entire career over again every day, as it were, from scratch. . . . he often feels that the particular sculpture or painting on which he happens to be working at the moment is that one which will for the very first time express what he subjectively experiences in response to an objective reality.[6]

Lord correctly assumes that the anxiety is related to the gap between the ideal vision that the artist is trying to paint and the objective results. Here he discusses the contradiction that every artist experiences:

This fundamental contradiction, arising from the hopeless discrepancy between conception and realization, is at the root of all artistic creation, and it helps explain the anguish which seems to be an unavoidable component of that experience. Even as "happy" an artist as Renoir was not immune to it.[7]

What meant something, what alone existed with a life of its own was his [Giacometti's] indefatigable, interminable struggle via the act of painting to express in visual terms a perception of reality that had happened to coincide momentarily with my head [which Giacometti was then trying to paint]. To achieve this was of course impossible, because what is essentially abstract can never be made concrete without altering its essence. But he was committed, he was, in fact *condemned* to the attempt, which at times seemed rather like the task of Sisyphus.[8]

One day Lord happened to see Giacometti in a café.

And, indeed, miserable was what he did seem to be. This, I thought, was the true Giacometti, sitting alone at the back of a café, oblivious to the admiration and recognition of the world, staring into a void from which no solace could come, tormented by the hopeless dichotomy of his ideal yet *condemned by that helplessness to struggle as long as he lived to try to overcome it.* What consolation was it that the newspapers of many countries spoke of him, that museums everywhere exhibited his works, that people he would never know knew and admired him. None. None at all.[9]

When we see the intimate feelings and inner experiences of an eminent artist like Giacometti, we smile at the absurd talk in some psychotherapeutic circles of "adjusting" people, making people "happy," or training out of them by simple behavior modification techniques all pain and grief and conflict and anxiety. How hard for humankind to absorb the deeper meaning of the myth of Sisyphus!—to see that "success" and "applause" are the bitch goddesses we always secretly knew they were. To see that the purpose of human existence in a man like Giacometti has nothing whatever to do with reassurance or conflict-free adjustment.

Giacometti was rather devoted—"condemned," to use Lord's fitting term—to the struggle to perceive and reproduce the world around him through his own vision of being human. He knew there was no other alternative for him. This challenge gave his life meaning. He and his kind seek to bring their own visions of what it means to be human, and to see through that vision to a world of reality, however ephemeral, however consistently that reality vanishes each time you concentrate on it. How absurd are the rationalistic assumptions that all one has to do is to remove from the world its curtains of superstition and ignorance and there suddenly will be reality, pristine and pure!

Giacometti sought to see reality through his ideal vision.

He sought to find the *ground forms,* the basic structure of reality, below the strewn surface of the arena where bitch goddesses cavort. He could not escape devoting himself unstintingly to the question: *Is there some place where reality speaks our language, where it answers us if we but understand the hieroglyphics?* He knew the rest of us would be no more successful than he was in finding the answer; but we have his contribution to work with, and thus we are helped.

3

Out of the encounter is born the work of art. This is true not only of painting, but of poetry and other forms of creativity. W. H. Auden once remarked to me in private conversation: "The poet marries the language, and out of this marriage the poem is born." How *active* this makes language in the creation of a poem! It is not that language is merely a tool of communication, or that we only use language to express our ideas; it is just as true that language uses *us.* Language is the symbolic repository of the meaningful experience of ourselves and our fellow human beings down through history, and, as such, it reaches out to grasp us in the creating of a poem. We must not forget that the original Greek and Hebrew words meaning "to know" meant also "to have sexual relations." One reads in the Bible "Abraham *knew* his wife and she conceived." The etymology of the term demonstrates the prototypical fact that knowledge itself—as well as poetry, art, and other creative products—arises out of the dynamic encounter between subjective and objective poles.

The sexual metaphor indeed expresses the importance of encounter. In sexual intercourse the two persons encounter each other; they withdraw partially to unite with each other again, experiencing every nuance of knowing, not knowing, in order to know each other again. The man becomes united with the woman and the woman with the man, and the partial withdrawal can be seen as the expedient by which both have the ectastatic experience of being filled again. Each is active and passive in his and her way. It is a demonstration that the *process* of knowing is what is important; if the male simply rests within the woman, nothing will happen beyond the prolonging of the wonder of the intimacy. It is the continuous experiencing of encounter and re-encounter that is the significant happening from the viewpoint of ultimate creativity. Sexual intercourse is the ultimate intimacy of two beings in the fullest and richest encounter possible. It is highly significant that this is the experience that is also the highest form of creativity in the respect that it can produce a new being.

The particular forms the offspring take in poems, drama, and the plastic arts are *symbols* and *myths*. Symbols (like Cézanne's tree) or myths (like that of Oedipus) express the relationship between conscious and unconscious experience, between one's individual present existence and human history. Symbol and myth are the living, immediate forms that emerge from encounter, and they consist of the dialectic interrelationship—the living, active, continuous mutual influence in which any change in one is bound to bring a change in the other—of subjective and objective poles. They are born out of the heightened consciousness of the encounter we are describing; and they have their power to grasp us because they require from us and give us an experience of heightened consciousness.

Thus in the history of culture artistic discovery precedes other forms. As Sir Herbert Read puts it, "On the basis of this [artistic] activity, a 'symbolic discourse' becomes possible, and religion, philosophy and science follow as consequent modes of thought." This is not to say that reason is the more civilized form and art the more *primitive* one, in a pejorative sense—an egregious error unfortunately often found in our rationalistic Western culture. This is, rather, to say that the creative encounter in the art form is "total"—it expresses a wholeness of experience; and science and philosophy abstract partial aspects for their subsequent study.

4

One distinguishing characteristic of the encounter is the degree of *intensity*, or what I would call *passion*. I am not referring here to the *quantity* of emotion. I mean a *quality* of commitment, which may be present in little experiences—such as a brief glance out the window at a tree—that do not necessarily involve any great quantity of emotion. But these temporally brief experiences may have a considerable significance for the sensitive person, here viewed as the person with a capacity for passion. Hans Hofmann, venerable dean of abstract painters in this country and one of our most expert and experienced teachers, remarked that art students these days have a great deal of talent but that they lack passion or commitment. Hofmann went on to say, interestingly enough, that his men students get married early for reasons of security and become dependent on their wives, and that often it is only through their wives that he, as their teacher, can draw out their talent. The fact that talent is plentiful but passion is lacking seems to me to be a fundamental facet of the problem of creativity in many fields today, and our ways of approaching creativity by evading the encounter have played directly into this trend. We worship technique—talent—as a way of evading the anxiety of the direct encounter.

Kierkegaard understood this so well! "The present writer . . ." he wrote about himself, "can easily foresee his fate in an age when passion has been obliterated in favor of learning, in an age when an author who wants to have readers must take care to write in such a way that the book can easily be perused during the afternoon nap."

5

At this point we see the inadequacy of the concept commonly used in psychoanalytic circles to explain creativity —"regression in the service of the ego." In my own endeavors to understand creative people in psychoanalysis and to understand the creative act in general, I find this theory unsatisfactory. This is not only because of its negative character, but chiefly because it proposes a partial solution that diverts us from the center of the creative act and therefore away from any full understanding of creativity.

In supporting the theory of "regression in the service of

the ego," Ernest Kris cites the work of the minor poet A. E. Housman, who, in his autobiography, describes his way of writing poetry as follows. After a full morning of teaching classes in Latin at Oxford, Housman would have lunch, with which he would drink a pint of beer, and would then take a walk. And in this somnambulistic mood, his poems would come to him. Kris, in line with this theory, correlates *passiveness and receptivity* with creativity. It is true that most of us find an appeal in such lines of Housman:

> Be still, my soul, be still;
> the arms you bear are brittle . . .

And the appeal does call forth a nostalgic, regressive mood in us as readers as well as, ostensibly, in Housman himself.

I grant, thus, that creativity often *seems* to be a regressive phenomenon, and does bring out archaic, infantile, unconscious psychic contents in the artist. But is this not parallel to what Poincaré points out (see Chapter Three, pp. 64–65) when he discusses how his insights come in periods of rest after his great labors? He specifically cautions us *not* to assume that it is the rest that produces the creativity. The rest—or regression—only serves to release the person from his or her intense efforts and the accompanying inhibitions, so that the creative impulse can have free rein to express itself. When the archaic elements in a poem or a picture have genuine power to move others, and when they have a universality of meaning—that is, when they are genuine symbols—it is because some encounter is occurring on a more basic, comprehensive level.

If, however, we take as a contrast some lines from one

of the major poets of our day, William Butler Yeats, we find a quite different mood. In "The Second Coming," Yeats describes modern man's condition:

> Things fall apart; the center cannot hold;
> Mere anarchy is loosed upon the world . . .

He then tells us what he sees:

> The Second Coming! Hardly are those words out
> When a vast image . . .
> Troubles my sight; somewhere in sands of the desert
> A shape with lion body and the head of a man,
> A gaze blank and pitiless as the sun,
> Is moving its slow thighs . . .
> And what rough beast, its hour come round at last,
> Slouches towards Bethlehem to be born?

What tremendous power in this last symbol! It is a new revelation, with beauty but with terrible meaning in relation to the situation in which we modern human beings find ourselves. The reason Yeats has such power is that he writes out of an intensity of consciousness that includes archaic elements because they are part of him, as they are of every person, and will emerge in any intensely aware moment. But the symbol has its power precisely from the fact that it is an encounter that also includes the most dedicated and passionate intellectual effort. In writing this poem Yeats was *receptive*, but by no stretch of the imagination passive. "The poet's labor," MacLeish tells us, is "not to wait until the cry gathers of itself in his own throat." [10]

Obviously, poetic and creative insights of all sorts come to us in moments of relaxation. They come not haphazardly, however, but come only in those areas in which we are intensively committed and on which we concentrate in our waking, conscious experience. It may be, as we have said, that the insights can break through only in moments of relaxation; but to say this is to describe *how* they come rather than to explain their genesis. My poet friends tell me that if you want to write poetry, or even read it, the hour after a full lunch and a pint of beer is just the time *not* to pick. Choose rather the moments in which you are capable of your highest, most intense consciousness. If you write poetry during your afternoon nap, it will be perused that way.

The issue here is not simply which poets you happen to like. It is much more basic—namely, the nature of the symbols and myths that are born in the creative act. Symbol and myth do bring into awareness infantile, archaic dreads, unconscious longings, and similar primitive psychic content. This is their *regressive* aspect. But they also bring out new meaning, new forms, and disclose a reality that was literally not present before, a reality that is not merely subjective but has a second pole which is outside ourselves. This is the *progressive* side of symbol and myth. This aspect points ahead. It is integrative. It is a progressive revealing of structure in our relation to nature and our own existence, as the French philosopher Paul Ricoeur so well states. It is a road to universals beyond discrete personal experience. It is this *progressive* aspect of symbols and myths that is almost completely omitted in the traditional Freudian psychoanalytic approach.

This heightened consciousness, which we have identified as characteristic of the encounter, the state in which the dichotomy between subjective experience and objective reality is overcome and symbols which reveal new meaning are born, is historically termed *ecstasy*. Like passion, ecstasy is a quality of emotion (or, more accurately, a quality of relationship one side of which is emotional) rather than a quantity. Ecstasy is a temporary transcending of the subject-object dichotomy. It is interesting that in psychology we dodge that problem, Maslow's work on the peak experience being a notable exception. Or, when we do speak of ecstasy we are implicitly pejorative or assume that it is neurotic.

The experience of encounter also brings with it *anxiety*. I need not remind you, after our discussion of Giacometti's experience, of the "fear and trembling" of artists and creative people in their moments of creative encounter. The myth of Prometheus is the classical expression of this anxiety. W. H. Auden once remarked that he always experiences anxiety when he writes poetry except when he is "playing." *Playing* may be defined as encounter in which anxiety is temporarily bracketed. But in mature creativity, anxiety must be confronted if the artist (and the rest of us who benefit from his work later on) is to experience the joy in the creative work.

I am impressed by Frank Barron's studies of creative persons in art and science,[11] for he shows them dirctly confronting their anxiety. Barron designated his "creative persons" as those who were recognized by their peers as having made distinguished contributions to their field. He showed them as well as a control group of "normal" people a series of Rorschachlike cards, some of which had orderly, systematic designs on them and others disorderly, unsymmetrical, and chaotic designs. The "normal" people selected the orderly, symmetrical cards as the designs they liked the most—they liked their universe to be "in shape." But the creative persons selected the chaotic, disorderly cards—they found these more challenging and interesting. They could be like God in the Book of Genesis, creating order out of chaos. They chose the "broken" universe; they got joy out of encountering it and forming it into order. They could accept the anxiety and use it in molding their disorderly universe "closer to the heart's desire."

According to the theory proposed here, anxiety is understandably a concomitant of the shaking of the self-world relationship that occurs in the encounter. Our sense of identity is threatened; the world is not as we experienced it before, and since self and world are always correlated, *we* no longer are what we were before. Past, present, and future form a new Gestalt. Obviously this is only rarely true in a complete sense (Gauguin going to the South Sea Islands, or Van Gogh becoming psychotic), but it is true that the creative encounter does change to some degree the self-world relationship. The anxiety we feel is temporary rootlessness, disorientation; it is the anxiety of nothingness.

Creative people, as I see them, are distinguished by the fact that they can live with anxiety, even though a high price may be paid in terms of insecurity, sensitivity, and defenselessness for the gift of the "divine madness," to borrow the term used by the classical Greeks. They do not run away from non-being, but by encountering and wrestling with it, force it to produce being. They knock on silence for an answering music; they pursue meaninglessness until they can force it to mean.*

* Since I have come out in support of meditation earlier (Chapter One), I feel it necessary to state my disagreement with a claim of one kind of relaxation, namely transcendental meditation, that it is the "science of creative intelligence" and stimulates creative think-

ing. True, it does further one aspect of creativity—namely spontaneity, intuitively "feeling one's self into the universe," and similar things associated with the "comfort" Maharishi talks about so often. These are the aspects of creativity associated with children's play. But TM completely omits the element of encounter which is essential for mature creativity. The aspects of struggle, of tension, of constructive stress—the emotions that Giacometti was experiencing in Lord's account—are forgotten in TM.

I have discussed this matter with Frank Barron, psychologist at the University of California at Santa Cruz and, in my judgment, the foremost authority on the psychology of creativity in this country. Barron, like myself, has addressed regional conferences of TM. The card test mentioned above has been given to some groups of transcendental meditators. The results (not yet published) were negative —that is, the meditators tended to choose the cards with orderly and symmetrical forms. This is the opposite to Barron's results with especially creative persons. Also Gary Swartz studied teachers of transcendental meditation and found that on tests of creativity they scored worse or only as well as control groups. (See *Psychology Today*, July, 1975, p. 50).

When I am engaged in writing something important to me, I find that if I engage in the customary twenty-minute meditation period before writing, my universe has become too straightened out, too orderly. Then I have nothing to write about. My encounter has vanished into thin air. My "problems" are all solved. I feel bliss, to be sure; but I cannot write.

I prefer, therefore, to endure the chaos, to face "complexity and perplexity," as Barron puts it. Then I am impelled by this chaos to seek order, to struggle with it until I can find a deeper, underlying form. I believe I am then engaged in what MacLeish describes as struggling with the meaninglessness and silence of the world until I can force it to mean, until I can make the silence answer and the non-being be. After the morning's period of writing, I can then use meditation for its authentic purpose—namely a deep relaxation of mind and body.

It is unfortunate for the movement—in that it presages a strong reaction against the movement sometime in the future—that its leaders are not more open to the limitations of TM and of Maharishi. All descriptions I have seen of TM blandly assume that Maharishi's gospel has no limitations at all. To those who wish a more complete picture, I recommend the article by Constance Holden, "Maharishi International University: 'Science of Creative Intelligence,' " *Science*, Vol. 187 (March 28, 1975), 1176.

FIVE

THE DELPHIC ORACLE AS THERAPIST

I<small>N THE MOUNTAINS</small> at Delphi stands a shrine that for many centuries was of great importance to ancient Greece. The Greeks had a genius for locating their shrines in lovely places, but Delphi is especially magnificent with a long valley stretching between massive ranges on one side and on the other the deep blue-green of the Bay of Cornith. It is a place where one immediately feels the awe and the sense of grandeur which befits the nature of the shrine. Here the Greeks found help in meeting their anxiety. In this temple, from the chaotic archaic age down through classical times, Apollo gave counsel through his priestesses. Socrates was even to find there inscribed on the wall of the entrance hall to the temple his famous dictum "Know thyself," which has become the central touchstone for psychotherapy ever since.

The sensitive Greek, anxious about himself, his family, and his future in those upset times, could find guidance here, for Apollo knew the meaning of "the complicated games the gods play with humanity," writes Prof. E. R. Dodds. In his excellent study of the irrational in ancient Greek culture, he continues:

Without Delphi, Greek society could scarcely have endured the tensions to which it was subjected in the Archaic Age. The crushing sense of human ignorance and human insecurity, the dread of divine *phthonos*, the dread of *miasma*—the accumulated burden of these things would have been unendurable without the assurance which such an omniscient divine counsellor could give, the assurance that behind the seeming chaos there was knowledge and purpose.[1]

The anxiety that Apollo helped people meet was the apprehension that accompanies a formative, fermenting, creative, powerfully expanding period. It is important to see that it was not neurotic anxiety, characterized by withdrawal, inhibition, and the blocking off of vitality. The archaic period in ancient Greece was the time of emergence and vital growth fraught with distress that resulted from the chaos of expanding outer and inner limits. The Greeks were experiencing the anxiety of new possibilities —psychologically, politically, aesthetically, and spiritually. These new possibilities, and the anxiety that always accompanies such challenges, were forced upon them whether they wished it or not.

The shrine at Delphi rose to prominence at a time when the old stability and order of the family were crumbling and the individual soon would have to be responsible for himself. In Homeric Greece, Odysseus' wife Penelope and son Telemachus could oversee the estate whether Odysseus was there or at the wars in Troy or tossed for ten years on the "wine-dark sea." But now, in the archaic period, families must be welded into cities. Each young Telemachus felt himself standing on the brink of the time when he would have to choose his own future and find his own place as part of a new city. How fertile the myth of the young Telemachus has been for modern writers who are searching for their own identity. James Joyce presents one aspect of it in *Ulysses*. Thomas Wolfe refers often to Telemachus as the myth of the search for the father, which was Wolfe's search as truly as it was the ancient Greek's. Wolfe, like any modern Telemachus, found that the hard, cold truth was "you can't go home again."

The city-states were struggling in anarchy, tyrant following tyrant (a term that in Greek does not have the usual destructive connotation it carries in English).[2] The upsurging leaders tried to weld the new power into some order. New forms of governing the city-states, new laws, and new interpretations of the gods were emerging, all of which gave the individual new psychological powers. In such a period of change and growth, *emergence* is often experienced by the individual as *emergency* with all its attendant stress.

Into this ferment came the symbol of Apollo and his shrine at Delphi and the rich myths on which they were based.

1

It is important to remember that Apollo is the god of *form*, the god of reason and logic. Thus it is no accident that his shrine became the important one in this chaotic time and that through this god of proportion and balance the citizens sought assurance that there was meaning and purpose behind the seeming chaos. Form and proportion and the golden mean were essential if these men and women were to control their deep passions, not in order to tame these passions but to turn to constructive use the daimonic powers that the Greeks knew so well in nature and in themselves. Apollo is also the god of art since form—elegance—is an essential characteristic of beauty. Indeed, Parnassus, the mountain at Delphi on whose flank Apollo's shrine stood, has become a symbol in all Western languages for devotion to the virtues of the mind.

We appreciate more of the rich meaning of such a myth when we note that Apollo is the god of light—not only the light of the sun, but the light of the mind, the light of reason, the light of insight. He is often called Helios, the word in Greek for "sun," and Phoebus Apollo, the god of brightness and radiance. Finally, we note the most cogent point of all: Apollo is the god of healing and well-being, and his son Asclepius is the god of medicine.

All of these attributes of Apollo, created as they were by collective unconscious processes in the mythology of the dark pre-Homeric centuries, are interwoven with fantastic literal as well as figurative significance. How consistent and meaningful it is that this is the god of good counsel, of psychological and spiritual insight, who will give guidance to a highly vital, formative age! An Athenian setting out on the trip to Delphi to consult Apollo would be turning over in his imagination at almost every moment in the journey this figure of the god of light and healing. Spinoza adjured us to fix our attention on a desired virtue, and we would thus tend to acquire it. Our Greek would be doing this on his trip, and the psychological processes of anticipation, hope, and faith would already be at work. Thus he would be proleptically participating in his own "cure." His conscious intentions and his deeper intentionality would be already committed to the event about to take place. For the one who participates in them, symbols and myths carry their own healing power.

This chapter is thus an essay on the *creating of one's self*. The self is made up, on its growing edge, of the models, forms, metaphors, myths, and all other kinds of psychic content which give it direction in its self-creation. This is a process that goes on continuously. As Kierkegaard well said, the self is only that which it is in the process of becoming. Despite the obvious determinism in human life —especially in the physical aspect of one's self in such simple things as color of eyes, height, relative length of life, and so on—there is also, clearly, this element of self-directing, self-forming. Thinking and self-creating are inseparable. When we become aware of all the fantasies in which we see ourselves in the future, pilot ourselves this way or that, this becomes obvious.

This continuous influencing of the direction of a person's development goes on in the ancient Greek or the modern American, deny it as we wish. Spinoza's counsel, mentioned above, is one way this piloting function can be actualized. The mass of myths dealing with the reincarnation of an individual into one or another life form, its status dependent on how this person has lived his or her life, attests to the awareness in the experience of the race that the individual does have some responsibility for how he or she lives. Sartre's argument that we invent ourselves by virtue of the multitude of our choices may be overstated, but its partial truth must nevertheless be admitted.

Human freedom involves our capacity to pause between stimulus and response and, in that pause, to choose the one response toward which we wish to throw our weight. The capacity to create ourselves, based upon this freedom, is inseparable from consciousness or self-awareness.

We are concerned here with how the oracle at Delphi furthers this process of self-creation. Clearly self-creating is actualized by our hopes, our ideals, our images, and all sorts of imagined constructs that we may hold from time to time in the forefront of our attention. These "models" function consciously as well as unconsciously; they are shown in fantasy as well as in overt behavior. The summary terms for this process are *symbols* and *myths*. And the shrine of Apollo at Delphi was a concrete expression of these symbols and myths, and it was where they were embodied in ritual.

2

We can see in the superb statues of Apollo carved at this time—the archaic figure with his strong, straight form, his calm beauty of head, his ordered features which are eloquent with controlled passion, even down to the slight "knowing" smile on the almost straight mouth—how this god could be the symbol in which the Greek artists as well as other citizens of that period perceived their longed-for order. There is a curious feature in these statues that I have seen: the eyes are *dilated,* made more open than is normal in the head of a living man or in classical Greek statues. If you walk through the archaic Greek room of the National Museum in Athens, you will be struck by the fact that the dilated eyes of the marble figures of Apollo give an expression of great alertness. What a contrast to the relaxed, almost sleepy eyes of the familiar fourth-century head of Hermes by Praxiteles.

These dilated eyes of the archaic Apollo are characteristic of apprehension. They express the anxiety—the excessive awareness, the "looking about" on all sides lest something unknown might happen—that goes with living in a fomenting age. There is a remarkable parallel between these eyes and the eyes in the figures Michelangelo painted in another formative period, the Renaissance. Almost all of Michelangelo's human beings, powerful and triumphant as they appear at first glance, have, on closer inspection, the dilated eyes which are a telltale sign of anxiety. And as if to demonstrate that he is expressing the inner tensions not only of his age but of himself as a member of his age, Michelangelo in his self-portraits paints eyes that are again markedly distended in the way that is typical of apprehension.

The poet Rilke also was struck by Apollo's prominent eyes with their quality of seeing deeply. In his "Archaic Torso of Apollo," he speaks of ". . . his legendary head in which the eyeballs ripened," and then continues,

> . . . But
> his torso still glows like a candelabrum
> in which his gaze, only turned low,
>
> holds and gleams. Else could not the curve
> of the breast blind you, nor in the slight turn

of the loins could a smile be running
to that middle, which carried procreation.

Else would this stone be standing maimed and short
under the shoulders' translucent plunge
nor flimmering like the fell of beasts of prey

nor breaking out of all its contours
like a star: for there is no place
that does not see you. You must change your life.[3]

In this vivid picture we note how well Rilke catches the
essence of *controlled passion*—not inhibited or repressed
passion, as was to be the goal during the later Hellenistic
age of the Greek teachers who had become afraid of vital
drives. What a far cry is Rilke's interpretation from Vic-
torian inhibition and repression of drives. These early
Greeks, who wept and made love and killed with zest,
gloried in passion and Eros and the daimonic. (Persons in
therapy nowadays, considering the strange spectacle in
ancient Greece, remark on the fact that it is the *strong*
person like Odysseus or Achilles who weeps.) But the
Greeks knew also that these drives had to be directed and
controlled. It was the essence, they believed, of a man of
virtue (*arete*) that he choose his passions rather than be
chosen by them. In this lies the explanation of why they
did not need to go through the self-castrating practice of
denying Eros and the daimonic, as modern Western man
does.

The sense of the archaic period is shown even in Rilke's
curious last sentence, which seems at first (but only at
first) to be a *non sequitur:* "You must change your life."
This is the call of passionate beauty, the demand that
beauty makes on us by its very presence that we also par-

ticipate in the new form. Not at all moralistic (the call has nothing whatever to do with right or wrong), it is nevertheless an imperious demand which grasps us with the insistence that we take into our own lives this new harmonious form.

3

How the oracle of Apollo functioned and where the advice it gave came from are, of course, fascinating questions. But unfortunately little seems to be known on this subject. The shrine was veiled in secrecy; those who directed it could not only give counsel to others but could also keep their own. Plato tells us that a "prophetic madness" overcame the Pythia, the priestess who served in the temple as mouthpiece for Apollo. From this "madness" there emerged some "creative insight," so Plato believed, which represented deeper-than-normal levels of consciousness. "It is to their madness," he writes in his *Phaedrus*, "that we owe the many benefits that the Pythia of Delphi and the priestesses of Dodona were able to bestow upon Greece both privately and in public life, for when they were in their right minds their achievements amounted to little or nothing." [4] This is a clear statement of one side of a controversy that has raged through human history about the source of inspiration—to what extent does creativity come from madness?

Apollo spoke in the first person through the Pythia. Her voice changed and became husky, throaty, and quavering like that of a modern medium. The god was said to enter her at the very moment of her seizure, or *enthusiasm*, as the root of that term, *en-theo* ("in god"), literally suggests.

Before the "seance" the priestess went through several ritualistic acts, such as special bathing and perhaps drinking from a sacred spring, presumedly with the customary autosuggestive effects. But the oft-repeated statement that she breathed vapors issuing from a fissure in the rocks of the shrine which induced a hypnotic effect is disposed of summarily by Professor Dodds:

As for the famous "vapours" to which the Pythia's inspiration was once confidently ascribed, they are a Hellenistic invention. . . . Plutarch, who knew the facts, saw the difficulties of the vapour theory, and seems finally to have rejected it altogether; but like the Stoic philosophers, nineteenth-century scholars seized with relief on a nice solid materialist explanation.[5]

Dodds goes on to remark pithily that "less has been heard of this theory since the French excavations showed that there are to-day no vapours, and no 'chasm' from which vapours could once have come." [6] Obviously such explanations are needless in view of the present-day evidence of anthropology and abnormal psychology.

The Pythian priestesses themselves seemed to be simple, uneducated women (Plutarch tells of one who was the daughter of a peasant). But modern scholars have a high respect for the intelligence system of the oracle. The decisions of Delphi showed sufficient signs of a consistent policy to convince scholars that human intelligence, intuition, and insight did play a decisive role in the process. Although Apollo committed some notorious blunders in his predictions and advice, especially during the Persian wars, the Greeks, with an attitude like many people in psychotherapy have toward their therapist today, forgave him evidently because of the useful advice and help he had given at other times.

The point that interests us most is the function of the shrine as a communal symbol that had the power to draw out the preconscious and unconscious collective insights of the Greeks. Delphi's communal, collective aspect had a sound foundation: the shrine was originally devoted to the earth goddesses before being dedicated to Apollo. Also it is collective in the sense that Dionysus, Apollo's opposite, was also a strong influence at Delphi. Greek vases show Apollo, presumably at Delphi, grasping Dionysus' hand. Plutarch does not exaggerate much when he writes, "as regards the Delphic oracle the part played by Dionysus was no less than Apollo's." [7]

Any genuine symbol, with its accompanying ceremonial rite, becomes the mirror that reflects insights, new possibilities, new wisdom, and other psychological and spiritual phenomena that we do not dare experience on our own. We cannot for two reasons. The first is our own anxiety: the new insights often—and, we could even say, typically—would frighten us too much were we to take full and lonely responsibility for them. In an age of ferment such insights may come frequently, and they require more psychological and spiritual responsibility than most individuals are prepared to bear. In dreams people can let themselves do things—such as killing their parent or their child, or thinking "my mother hated me," for instance— that would normally be too horrible to think or say in ordinary speech. We hesitate to think these and similar things even in daydreams since such fantasies are felt to carry more individual responsibility than night dreams. But if we can have a dream say it, or have Apollo through his oracle say it, we can be much more frank about our new truth.

The second reason is we escape hubris. Socrates could

assert that Apollo at Delphi had pronounced him the wisest man then living, a claim—whether it be Socratic wit or not—he could never have made on his own.

How did one interpret the counsel of the priestesses? This is the same as asking: How does one interpret a symbol? The divinations of the priestess were generally couched in poetry and often were uttered "in wild, ono- matopoeic cries as well as articulate speech, and this 'raw material' certainly had to be interpreted and worked over." [8] Like mediumistic statements of all ages, these were sufficiently cryptic not only to leave the way open for interpretation, but to *require* it. And often they were susceptible to two or many different interpretations.

The process was like the interpretation of a dream. Harry Stack Sullivan used to teach young analysts-in-train- ing not to enterpret a dream as if it were the law of the Medes and the Persians, but to suggest two different mean- ings to the person being analyzed, thus requiring him or her to choose between them. The value of dreams, like these divinations, is not that they give a specific answer, but that they open up new areas of psychic reality, shake us out of our customary ruts, and throw light on a new segment of our lives. Thus the sayings of the shrine, like dreams, were not to be received passively; *the recipients had to "live" themselves into the message.*

During the Persian wars, for example, when the anx- ious Athenians had petitioned Apollo to give them guid- ance, word came from the oracle adjuring them to trust in "the wooden wall." The meaning of this enigma was hotly debated. As Herodotus tells the story, "Certain of the old men were of opinion that the god meant to tell them the acropolis would escape, for this was anciently defended by a wooden palisade. Others maintained that the god referred to wooden ships, which had best be at once got ready." Thereupon another part of the oracle caused debate, for some thought they should sail away without a fight and establish themselves in a new land. But Themistocles convinced the people that they were intended to engage in a sea fight near Salamis, which they did, destroying Xerxes' fleet in one of the decisive battles of history.[9]

Whatever the intention of the Delphic priests, the effect of ambiguous prophecies was to force the suppliants to think out their situation anew, to reconsider their plans, and to conceive of new possibilities.

Apollo, indeed, was nicknamed the "ambiguous one." Lest some budding therapists take this as an excuse for their own ambiguity, let us here note a difference between modern therapy and the divinations of the oracle. The utterances of the priestess are on a level closer to the recipients' unconscious, closer to *actual* dreams, in contrast to the interpretation of dreams in a therapeutic hour. Apollo speaks from deeper dimensions of consciousness in the citizen and the collective group (i.e., the city). Thus there can be a creative ambiguity, which occurs both in the original saying (or dream) and in the citizen's (or patient's) interpretation of it. The oracle hence has an advantage over the contemporary therapist. In any case, I believe a therapist ought to be as succinct as possible, and leave the inescapable ambiguity to the patient!

The counsels of Delphi were not advice in the strict sense, but rather were stimulants to the individual and to the group to look inward, to consult their own intuition and wisdom. The oracles put the problem in a new context so that it could be seen in a different way, a way in which new and as yet unimagined possibilities would become evident. It is a common misconception that such shrines, as well as modern therapy, tend to make the individual more passive. This would be bad therapy and a misinterpretation of the oracles. Both should do exactly the opposite; they should require individuals to recognize their own possibilities, enlightening new aspects of themselves and their interpersonal relationships. This process taps the source of creativity in people. It turns them inward toward their own creative springs.

In the *Apologia*, Socrates tells us how he tried to puzzle out what the god meant by telling his friend Chaerephon that no one in the world was wiser than he (Socrates). The philosopher came to the conclusion that it meant he was wisest because he admitted his own ignorance. The god also counseled Socrates to "know thyself." Ever since that time, thoughtful men like Nietzsche and Kierkegaard have been trying to fathom the meaning of the god's advice, and we are still stimulated to find new meanings in it. Nietzsche even interprets it as meaning just opposite to what one would conclude at first glance: "What did the god mean who proclaimed 'Know thyself' to Socrates? Did he perchance mean, 'Cease to be concerned about thyself,' 'Be objective'?" Like the true symbols and/or myths they are, these utterances of the god yield unending richness as new and interesting meanings are unfolded.

4

There is another reason why an oracle can be significant as the embodiment of the unconscious collective insights of the group. A symbol or myth acts like a projective screen in drawing out the insight. Like Rorschach cards or Murray's Thematic Apperception Test, the oracle and its ceremonies are a screen that stimulates wonder and calls imagination into action.

But I must hasten to insert a caution. The process going on at such a place and time may be called "projection," but we must insist that it is not "projection" in any pejorative sense of the word, either in the psychoanalytical one in which an individual "projects" what is "sick" and therefore what he or she cannot face, nor in the empirical psychological sense in which it is implied that the process is simply subjective and that the cards or TAT pictures have nothing to do with the result. In my judgment, both of these pejorative uses of *projection* result from the common failure of Western man to understand the nature of symbol and myth.

The "screen" is not merely a blank mirror. It is, rather, *the objective pole necessary for calling forth the subjective processes of consciousness.* The Rorschach cards *are* definite and real forms of black and color, even though no one ever before has "seen" in them the things you or I may see in them. Such "projection" is in no sense a "regression" by definition or something less respectable than being able to say what you want to say in rational sentences without the cards. It is rather a legitimate and healthy exercise of imagination.

This process goes on all the time in art. Paint and canvas are objective things that have powerful and existential influences on the artist in bringing out his or her ideas and visions. Indeed, the artist is in a dialectical relation not only with paint and canvas, but with the shapes he or she sees in nature. The poet and the musician are in a similar relationship with their inherited language and musical notes. The artist, the poet, and the musician dare to bring forth new forms, new kinds of vitality and meaning. They are, at least partially, protected from "going crazy" in this process of radical emergence by the form given by the media—namely the paints, the marble, the words, the musical notes.

The shrine of Apollo at Delphi thus can most felicitously be seen as a communal symbol. We can postulate, then, that its insights come by a communal symbolic process involving both subjective and objective factors in a dialectical relation with each other. For anyone who authentically uses the oracle, new forms, new ideal possibilities, new ethical and religious structures may be born from levels of experience that underlie and transcend the individual's customary waking consciousness. We have noted that Plato calls this process the ecstasy of "prophetic madness." Ecstasy is a time-honored method of transcending our ordinary consciousness and a way of helping us arrive at insights we could not attain otherwise. An element of ecstasy, however slight, is part and parcel of every genuine symbol and myth; for if we genuinely participate in the symbol or myth, we are for that moment taken "out of" and "beyond" ourselves.

The psychological approach to symbol and myth is only one of several possible avenues. In taking this approach I do not wish to "psychologize away" the myth's religious meaning. From this religious aspect of myth we get the insight (revelation) that comes from the dialectical interplay of the subjective elements in the individual and the objective fact of the oracle. To the genuine believer, the myth is never purely psychological. It always includes an element of revelation, whether from the Greek Apollo, or the Hebrew Elohim, or the Oriental "Being." If we completely psychologized away this religious element, we would be unable to appreciate the power with which Aeschylus and Sophocles wrote their dramas and even unable to understand what they are talking about. Aeschylus and Sophocles and the other dramatists could write great tragedies because of the religious dimensions of the myths, which gave a structural undergirding to their belief in the dignity of the race and the meaning of its destiny.

SIX

⟨⟩

ON THE LIMITS
OF CREATIVITY

O N A SATURDAY evening at an Esalen week end in New York recently, a panel discussion on the human prospect was held. The panel consisted of such insightful and stimulating persons as Joyce Carol Oates, Gregory Bateson, and William Irwin Thompson. The audience was made up of seven or eight hundred eager individuals, expectantly set for an interesting discussion at the very least. In his opening remarks, the chairman emphasized the theme that "the possibilities of the human being are unlimited."

But strange to say, there seemed, as the meeting went on, to be no problems to discuss. The vast vacuum filling the room was felt by both the panel and the audience alike. All the exciting issues that the participants on the panel had approached so eagerly had mysteriously vanished. As the discussion limped along to the end of an almost fruitless evening, the common question seemed to be: What had gone wrong?

I propose that the statement, "human possibilities are unlimited" is de-energizing. If you take it at face value, there is no real problem anymore. You can only stand up and sing hallelujah and then go home. Every problem will sooner or later be overcome by these unlimited possibilities; there remain only temporary difficulties that will go away of their own accord when the time comes. Contrary to the chairman's intention, statements like his actually terrorize the listener: it is like putting someone into a canoe and pushing him out into the Atlantic toward England with the cheery comment, "The sky's the limit." The canoer is only too aware of the fact that an inescapably real limit is also the bottom of the ocean.

In these notes I shall explore the hypothesis that limits are not only unavoidable in human life, they are also valuable. I shall also discuss the phenomenon that *creativity itself requires limits*, for the creative act arises out of the struggle of human beings with and against that which limits them.

To begin with, there is the inescapable physical limitation of death. We can postpone our death slightly, but nevertheless each of us will die and at some future time unknown to and unpredictable by us. Sickness is another limit. When we overwork we get ill in one form or another. There are obvious neurological limits. If the blood stops flowing to the brain for as little as a couple of minutes, a stroke or some other kind of serious damage occurs. Despite the fact that we can improve our intelligence to some degree, it remains radically limited by our physical and emotional environment.

There are also metaphysical limitations which are even more interesting. Each of us was born into a certain family in a certain country at a certain historical moment, all with no choice on our part. If we try to deny these facts—like Jay Gatsby in Fitzgerald's *The Great Gatsby*—we blind ourselves to reality and come to grief. True, we can surpass to some extent the limitations of our family backgrounds or our historical situation, but such transcendence can occur only to those who accept the fact of their limitation to begin with.

1. THE VALUE OF LIMITS

Consciousness itself is born out of the awareness of these limits. Human consciousness is the distinguishing feature of our existence; without limitations we would never have developed it. Consciousness is the awareness that emerges out of the dialectical tension between possibilities and limitations. Infants begin to be aware of limits when they experience the ball as different from themselves; mother is a limiting factor for them in that she does not feed them every time they cry for food. Through a multitude of such limiting experiences they learn to develop the capacity to differentiate themselves from others and from objects and to delay gratification. If there had been no limits, there would be no consciousness.

Our discussion so far may seem, at first glance, to be discouraging, but not when we probe more deeply. It is not by accident that the Hebrew myth that marks the beginning of human consciousness, Adam and Eve in the Garden of Eden, is portrayed in the context of a rebellion.

Consciousness is born in the struggle against a limit, called there a prohibition. Going beyond the limit set by Yahweh is then punished by the acquiring of other limits which operate inwardly in the human being—anxiety, the feeling of alienation and guilt. But valuable qualities also come out of this experience of rebellion—the sense of personal responsibility and ultimately the possibility, born out of loneliness, of human love. Confronting limits for the human personality actually turns out to be *expansive. Limiting and expanding* thus go together.

Alfred Adler proposed that civilization arose out of our physical limitations, or what Adler called inferiority. Tooth for tooth and claw for claw, men and women were inferior to the wild animals. In the struggle against these limitations for their survival, human beings evolved their intelligence.

Heraclitus said, "Conflict is both king of all and father of all." [1] He was referring to the theme I am here stating: conflict presupposes limits, and the struggle with limits is actually the source of creative productions. The limits are as necessary as those provided by the banks of a river, without which the water would be dispersed on the earth and there would be no river—that is, the river is constituted by the tension between the flowing water and the banks. Art in the same way requires limits as a necessary factor in its birth.

Creativity arises out of the tension between spontaneity and limitations, the latter (like the river banks) forcing the spontaneity into the various forms which are essential to the work of art or poem. Again listen to Heraclitus: unwise people "do not understand how that which differs with itself is in agreement: harmony consists of opposing tension, like that of the bow and the lyre." [2] In a discussion of how he composed his music, Duke Ellington explained that since his trumpet player could reach certain notes beautifully but not other notes, and the same with his trombonist, he had to write his music within those limits. "It's good to have limits," he remarked.

True, in our age there is occurring a new valuation of spontaneity and a strong reaction against rigidity. This goes along with a rediscovery of the values of the childlike capacity to play. In modern art, as we all know, there has evolved a new interest in children's painting as well as in peasant and primitive art, and these kinds of spontaneity often are used as models for adult art work. This is especially true in psychotherapy. The great majority of patients experience themselves as stifled and inhibited by the excessive and rigid limits insisted on by their parents. One of their reasons for coming for therapy in the first place is this conviction that all of this needs to be thrown overboard. Even if it is simplistic, this urge toward spontaneity obviously should be valued by the therapist. People must recover the "lost" aspects of their personalities, lost under a pile of inhibitions, if they are to become integrated in any effective sense.

But we must not forget that these stages in therapy, like children's art, are interim stages. Children's art is characterized by an unfinished quality. Despite the apparent similarity with nonobjective art, it still lacks the tension necessary for authentic mature art. It is a promise but not yet an achievement. Sooner or later the growing person's art must relate itself to the dialectic tension that comes out of confronting limits and is present in all forms of mature art. Michelangelo's writhing slaves; Van Gogh's fiercely twisting cypress trees; Cézanne's lovely yellow-green landscapes of southern France, reminding us of the freshness of eternal spring—these works have that spontaneity, but they also have the mature quality that comes from the absorption of tension. This makes them much more than "interesting"; it makes them great. The controlled and transcended tension present in the work of art is the result of the artists' successful struggle with and against limits.

2. FORM AS A LIMITATION IN CREATIVITY

The significance of limits in art is seen most clearly when we consider the question of form. Form provides the essential boundaries and structure for the creative act. It is no accident that the art critic Clive Bell, in his books about Cézanne, cites "significant form" as the key to understanding the great painter's work.

Let us say I draw a rabbit on a blackboard. You say, "There's a rabbit." In reality there is nothing at all on the blackboard except the simple line I have made: no protrusion, nothing three dimensional, no indentation. It is the same blackboard as it was, and there can be no rabbit "on" it. You see only my chalk line, which may be infinitesimally narrow. This line limits the content. It says what space is *within* the picture and what is *outside*—it is a pure limiting to that particular form. The rabbit appears because you have accepted my communication that this space within the line is that which I wish to demarcate.

There is in this limiting a nonmaterial character, a spiritual character if you will, that is necessary in all creativity. Hence, *form* and, similarly, *design*, *plan*, and *pattern* all refer to a nonmaterial meaning present in the limits.

Our discussion of form demonstrates something else— that the object you see is a product both of your subjectivity *and* external reality. The form is born out of a dialectical relation between my brain (which is subjective, *in* me) and the object that I see external to me (which is objective). As Immanuel Kant insisted, we not only know the world, but the world at the same time conforms to our ways of knowing. Incidentally, note the word *conform*— the world forms itself "with," it takes on our forms.

The trouble begins whenever anyone dogmatically sets himself or herself up to defend either extreme. On the one hand, when an individual insists on his or her own subjectivity and follows exclusively his or her own imagination, we have a person whose flights of fancy may be interesting but who never really relates to the objective world. When, on the other hand, an individual insists that there is nothing "there" except empirical reality, we have a technologically minded person who would impoverish and oversimplify his or her and our lives. Our perception is determined by our imagination as well as by the empirical facts of the outside world.

Speaking of poetry, Coleridge distinguished between two kinds of form. One is external to the poet—the mechanical form, let us say, of the sonnet. This consists of an arbitrary agreement that the sonnet will consist of fourteen lines in a certain pattern. The other kind of form is organic. This is inner form. It comes from the poet, and consists of the passion he or she puts into the poem. The organic aspect of form causes it to grow on its own; it speaks to us down through the ages revealing new meaning to each generation. Centuries later we may find meaning in it that even the author did not know was there.

When you write a poem, you discover that the very necessity of fitting your meaning into such and such a form requires you to search in your imagination for new meanings. You reject certain ways of saying it; you select others, always trying to form the poem again. In your forming, you arrive at new and more profound meanings than you had even dreamed of. Form is not a mere lopping off of meaning that you don't have room to put into your poem; it is an aid to finding new meaning, a stimulus to condensing your meaning, to simplifying and purifying it, and to discovering on a more universal dimension the essence you wish to express. How much meaning Shakespeare could put into his plays *because* they were written in blank verse rather than prose, or his sonnets *because* they were fourteen lines!

In our day the concept of form is often attacked because of its relation to "formality" and "formalism," both of which—so we are told—are to be avoided like the plague. I agree that in transitional times like our own, when honesty of style is difficult to come by, formalism and formality should be required to demonstrate their authenticity. But in the attack on these often bastardized kinds of formalism, it is not form itself that is being accused, but special kinds of form—generally the conformist, dead kinds, which actually do lack an inner, organic vitality.

We should remember, moreover, that all spontaneity carries with it its own form. Anything expressed in language, for example, carries the forms given to it by that language. How different a poem originally written in English sounds when translated into the exquisite music of the French language or into the profound and powerful sentiments of the German language! Another example is the rebellion in the name of spontaneity against picture frames, as shown in those paintings that reach out over their frames, dramatically breaking the latter's too limiting boundaries. This act borrows its spontaneous power from the assumption of a frame to start with.

The juxtaposition of spontaneity and form are, of course, present all through human history. It is the ancient but ever-modern struggle of the Dionysian versus the Apollonian. In transitional periods this dichotomy comes completely out in the open since old forms do have to be transcended. I can, therefore, understand the rebellion in our day against form and limits as expressed in the cry "We have unlimited potentialities." But when these movements try to throw form or limits out entirely, they become self-destructive and noncreative. Never is form itself superseded so long as creativity endures. If form were to vanish, spontaneity would vanish with it.

3. IMAGINATION AND FORM

Imagination is the outreaching of mind. It is the individual's capacity to accept the bombardment of the conscious mind with ideas, impulses, images, and every other sort of psychic phenomena welling up from the preconscious. It is the capacity to "dream dreams and see visions," to consider diverse possibilities, and to endure the tension involved in holding these possibilities before one's attention. Imagination is casting off mooring ropes, taking one's chances that there will be new mooring posts in the vastness ahead.

In creative endeavors the imagination operates in jux-

taposition with form. When these endeavors are successful, it is because imagination infuses form with its own
vitality. The question is: How far can we let our imagination loose? Can we give it rein? Dare to think the un-
thinkable? Dare to conceive of, and move among, new
visions?

At such times we face the danger of losing our orienta-
tion, the danger of complete isolation. Will we lose our
accepted language, which makes communication possible
in a shared world? Will we lose the boundaries that en-
able us to orient ourselves to what we call reality? This,
again, is the problem of form or, stated differently, the
awareness of limits.

Psychologically speaking, this is experienced by many
people as psychosis. Hence some psychotics walk close to
the wall in hospitals. They keep oriented to the edges, always preserving their localization in the external environment. Having no localization inwardly, they find it
especially important to retain whatever outward localization is available.

As director of a large mental hospital in Germany which
received many brain-injured soldiers during the war, Dr.
Kurt Goldstein found that these patients suffered radical
limitation of their capacities for imagination. He observed
that they had to keep their closets in rigid array, shoes always placed in just this position, shirts hung in just that
place. Whenever a closet was upset, the patient became
panicky. He could not orient himself to the new arrange-
ment, could not imagine a new "form" that would bring
order out of the chaos. The patient was then thrown into
what Goldstein called the "catastrophic situation." Or
when asked to write his name on a sheet of paper, the
brain-injured person would write the name in some corner

close to the boundaries. He could not tolerate the possibility of becoming lost in the open spaces. His capacities for abstract thought, for transcending the immediate facts in terms of the possible—what I call, in this context, imagination—were severely curtailed. He felt powerless to change the environment to make it adequate to his needs.

Such behavior is indicative of what life is when imaginative powers are cut off. The limits have always to be kept clear and visible. Lacking the ability to shift forms, these patients found their world radically truncated. Any "limitless" existence was experienced by them as being highly dangerous.

Not brain-injured, you and I nevertheless can experience a similar anxiety in the reverse situation—that is, in the creative act. The boundaries of our world shift under our feet and we tremble while waiting to see whether any new form will take the place of the lost boundary or whether we can create out of this chaos some new order.

As imagination gives vitality to form, form keeps imagination from driving us into psychosis. This is the ultimate necessity of limits. Artists are the ones who have the capacity to see original visions. They typically have powerful imaginations and, at the same time, a sufficiently developed sense of form to avoid being led into the catastrophic situation. They are the frontier scouts who go out ahead of the rest of us to explore the future. We can surely tolerate their special dependencies and harmless idiosyncrasies. For we will be better prepared for the future if we can listen seriously to them.

There is a curiously sharp sense of joy—or perhaps better expressed, a sense of mild ecstasy—that comes when you find the particular form required by your creation. Let us say you have been puzzling about it for days when suddenly you get the insight that unlocks the door—you see how to write that line, what combination of colors is needed in your picture, how to form that theme you may be writing for a class, or you hit upon the theory to fit your new facts. I have often wondered about this special sense of joy; it so often seems out of proportion to what actually has happened.

I may have worked at my desk morning after morning trying to find a way to express some important idea. When my "insight" suddenly breaks through—which may happen when I am chopping wood in the afternoon—I experience a strange lightness in my step as though a great load were taken off my shoulders, a sense of joy on a deeper level that continues without any relation whatever to the mundane tasks that I may be performing at the time. It cannot be just that the problem at hand has been answered—that generally brings only a sense of relief. What is the source of this curious pleasure?

I propose that it is the experience of this-is-the-way-things-are-meant-to-be. If only for that moment, we participate in the myth of creation. Order comes out of disorder, form out of chaos, as it did in the creation of the universe. The sense of joy comes from our participation, no matter how slight, in being as such. The paradox is that at that moment we also experience more vividly our own limitations. We discover the *amor fati* that Nietzsche writes about—the love of one's fate. No wonder it gives a sense of ecstasy!

SEVEN

PASSION FOR FORM

For many years I have been convinced that something occurs in the creative working of the imagination that is more fundamental—but more puzzling—than we have assumed in contemporary psychology. In our day of dedication to facts and hard-headed objectivity, we have disparaged imagination: it gets us away from "reality"; it taints our work with "subjectivity"; and, worst of all, it is said to be unscientific. As a result, art and imagination are often taken as the "frosting" to life rather than as the solid food. No wonder people think of "art" in terms of its cognate, "artificial," or even consider it a luxury that slyly fools us, "artifice." Throughout Western history our dilemma has been whether imagination shall turn out to be artifice or the source of being.

What if imagination and art are not frosting at all, but the fountainhead of human experience? What if our logic and science derive from art forms and are fundamentally dependent on them rather than art being merely a decoration for our work when science and logic have produced it? These are the hypotheses I propose here.

This same problem is related to psychotherapy in ways that are much more profound than merely the play on words. In other words, is psychotherapy an artifice, a process that is characterized by artificiality, or is it a process that can give birth to new being?

1

Pondering these hypotheses, I brought data to my aid from the dreams of persons in therapy. By dreaming, persons in analysis, I saw, are doing something on a level quite below that of psychodynamics. They are struggling with their world—to make sense out of nonsense, meaning out of chaos, coherence out of conflict. They are doing it by imagination, by constructing new forms and relationships in their world, and by achieving through proportion and perspective a world in which they can survive and live with some meaning.

Here is a simple dream. It was related by an intelligent man who seems younger than his thirty years, coming from a culture where fathers have considerable authority.

I was in the sea playing with some large porpoises. I like porpoises and wanted these to be like pets. Then I began to get afraid, thinking that the big porpoises would hurt me. I went out of the water, on the shore, and now I seem to be a cat hanging by its tail from a tree. The cat is curled up in a tear-drop form, but its eyes are big and seductive, one of them winking. A porpoise comes up, and, like a father cajoling a youngster out of bed with "get up and get going," it hits the cat lightly. The cat then becomes afraid with a real panic and bounds off in a straight line into the higher rocks, away from the sea.

Let us put aside such obvious symbols as the big porpoises being father and so on—symbols that are almost always confused with symptoms. I ask you to take the dream as an abstract painting, to look at it as pure form and motion.

We see first a smallish form, namely the boy, playing with the larger forms, the porpoises. Imagine the former as a small circle, and the latter as large circles. The playing movement conveys a kind of love in the dream, which we could express by lines toward each other converging in the play. In the second scene we see the smaller form (the boy in his fright) moving in a line out of the sea and away from the larger forms. The third scene shows the smaller form as a cat, now in an elliptical, tearlike, form, the coyness of the cat's eyes being seductive. The big form now coming toward the cat moves into the cajoling act and the lines here, it seems to me, would be confused. This is a typical neurotic phase consisting of the dreamer trying to resolve his relationship with his father and the world. And, of course, it does not work. The fourth and last scene is the panic in which the smaller form, the cat, moves rapidly out of the scene. It dashes toward the higher rocks. The motion is in a straight line off the canvas. The whole dream can be seen as an endeavor through form and motion to resolve this young man's relationship, in its love and its fear, to his father and father figures.

The resolution is a vivid failure. But the "painting" or play, Ionescolike though it be, shows like many a contemporary drama the vital tension in the irresolution of conflict. Therapeutically speaking, the patient is certainly

facing his conflicts, albeit he can at the moment do nothing but flee.

We also can see in these scenes a progression of planes:
first, the plane of the sea; second, the higher plane of the
land with the tree; and third, the highest plane of all,
namely the rocks on the mountain to which the cat leaps.
These may be conceived as higher levels of consciousness
to which the dreamer climbs. This expansion of consciousness may represent an important gain for the patient
even though in the dream the actual resolution of the
problem is a failure.

When we turn such a dream into an abstract painting,
we are on a deeper level than psychodynamics. I do not
mean we should leave out the contents of the dreams of
our patients. I mean we should go beyond contents to
the ground forms. We shall then be dealing with basic
forms that only later, and derivatively, become *formula-
tions.*

From the most obvious viewpoint, the son is trying to
work out a better relationship with his father, to be accepted as a comrade, let us say. But on a deeper level he
is trying to construct a world that makes sense, that has
space and motion and keeps these in some proportion, a
world that he can live in. *You can live without a father
who accepts you, but you cannot live without a world that
makes some sense to you.* Symbol in this sense no longer
means symptom. As I have pointed out elsewhere, [1] *symbol* returns to its original and root meaning of "drawing
together" (*sym-ballein*). The problem—the neurosis and
its elements—is described by the antonym of *symbolic,*
namely *diabolic* (*dia-ballein*), "pulling apart."

Dreams are *par excellence* the realm of symbols and

myths. I use the term *myth* not in the pejorative sense of "falsehood," but in the sense of *a form of universal truth* revealed in some partial way to the dreamer. These are ways human consciousness makes sense of the world. Persons in therapy, like all of us, are trying to make sense out of nonsense, trying to put the world into some perspective, trying to form out of the chaos they are suffering some order and harmony.

After having studied a series of dreams of persons in therapy, I am convinced that there is one quality that is always present, a quality I call *passion for form*. The patient constructs in his "unconscious" a drama; it has a beginning, something happens and is "flashed on the stage," and then it comes to some kind of denouement. I have noted the forms in the dreams being repeated, revised, remolded, and then, like a motif in a symphony, returning triumphantly to be drawn together to make a meaningful whole of the series.

2

I found that one fruitful approach is *to take the dream as a series of spatial forms*. I refer now to a thirty-year-old woman in therapy. In one stage in her dreams, a female character, for example, would move onto the stage of the dream; then another female would enter; a male would appear; the females would exit together. This kind of movement in space occurred in the Lesbian period of this particular person's analysis. In later dreams she, the patient, would enter; then the female, who was present, would exit; a man would enter and he would sit beside her.

I began to see a curious geometric communication, a progression of spatial forms. Perhaps the meaning of her dreams, and the progress of her analysis, could be better understood by how she constructed these forms moving in space—of which she was quite unaware—than in what she verbalized about her dreams.

Then I began to notice the presence of triangles in this person's dreams. First, in her dreams referring to her infantile period, it was the triangle of father, mother, and baby. In what I took to be her adolescent phase, the triangle was composed of two women and a man, and she, as one of the women, moved in space toward the man. Then after some months of analysis, in a Lesbian phase, the triangle consisted of two women and a man with the two women standing together. In a still later period the triangles turned into rectangles: two men were in the dream with two women, assumedly her boy friend, herself, her mother, and her father. Her development then became a process of working through rectangles to form eventually a new triangle, her man, herself, and a child. These dreams occurred in the middle and later parts of the analysis.

That the symbol of the triangle is fundamental can be seen by the fact that it refers to a number of different levels simultaneously. A triangle has three lines; it has the lowest possible number of straight lines required to make a geometric form that has content. This is the mathematical, "pure form" level. The triangle is fundamental in early, neolithic art—*vide* designs on the vases of this period. This is the aesthetic level. It is present in science—triangulation is the way the Egyptians figured their relation to the stars. The triangle is the basic symbol in medieval philosophy and theology—*vide* the Trinity. It is fundamental in Gothic art, a graphic example of which is Mont-Saint-Michel, the triangle of rock rising from the sea capped by the Gothic triangle of man-built architecture which, in turn, ends in a pinnacle pointing toward heaven —a magnificent art form in which we have the triangle of nature, man, and God. And finally, psychologically speaking, we have the basic human triangle—man, woman, and child.

The importance of forms is revealed in the inescapable unity of the body with the world. The body is always a part of the world. I sit on this chair; the chair is on a floor in this building; and the building, in turn, rests on the mountain of stone that is Manhattan Island. Whenever I walk, my body is interrelated with the world in which and on which I take my steps. This presupposes some harmony between body and world. We know from physics that the earth rises infinitesimally to meet my step, as any two bodies attract each other. The *balance* essential in walking is one that is not solely in my body; it can be understood only as a relationship of my body to the ground on which it stands and walks. The earth is there to meet each foot as it falls, and the rhythm of my walking depends on my faith that the earth will be there.

Our active need for form is shown in the fact that we automatically construct it in an infinite number of ways. The mime Marcel Marceau stands upon the stage impersonating a man taking his dog out for a walk. Marceau's arm is outstretched as though holding the dog's leash. As his arm jerks back and forth, everyone in the audience "sees" the dog straining at the leash to sniff this or that in the bushes. Indeed, the dog and the leash are the most "real" parts of the scene even though there is no dog and no leash on the stage at all. Only part of the Gestalt is there—the man Marceau and his arm. The rest is entirely supplied by our imagination as viewers. The incomplete Gestalt is completed in our fantasy. Another mime, Jean-Louis Barrault, who plays a deaf-mute in the film *Les Enfants du Paradis,* goes through the whole account of the man who has had his pocket picked in the crowd—he makes one movement for the fat stomach of the victim, another movement for the dour expression of the companion, and so on until we have a vivid picture of the entire event of the pickpocketing. But not a word has been spoken. There is only a mime making a few artful motions. All of the gaps are automatically filled by our imagination.

The human imagination leaps to form the whole, to complete the scene in order to make sense of it. The instantaneous way this is done shows how we are driven to construct the remainder of the scene. To fill the gaps is essential if the scene is to have meaning. That we may do this in misleading ways—at times in neurotic or paranoid ways—does not gainsay the central point. Our passion for form expresses our yearning to make the world adequate to our needs and desires, and, more important, to experience ourselves as having significance.

The phrase "passion for form," may be interesting, but it is also problematical. If we used just the word *form,* it would sound too abstract; but when it is combined with passion, we see that what is meant is not form in any intellectual sense, but rather in a wholistic scene. What is occurring in the person, hidden as it may be by passivity or other neurotic symptoms, is a conflict-filled passion to make sense out of a crisis-ridden life.

Plato told us long ago how passion, or, as he put it, Eros, moves toward the creation of form. Eros moves toward the making of meaning and the revealing of Being. Originally a daimon called love, Eros is the lover of wisdom, and the force in us that brings to birth both wisdom and beauty. Plato says through Socrates that "human nature will not easily find a helper better than love [Eros]." [2] "All creation or passage of non-being into being is poetry or making," Plato writes, "and the processes of all art are creative; and the masters of arts are all poets or makers." [3] Through Eros or the passion of love, which is daimonic and constructive at the same time, Plato looks forward to "at last the vision . . . of a single science, which is the science of beauty everywhere." [4]

Thus the mathematicians and physicists talk about the "elegance" of a theory. Utility is subsumed as part of the character of being beautiful. The harmony of an internal form, the inner consistency of a theory, the character of beauty that touches your sensibilities—these are significant factors that determine why one given insight comes into consciousness rather than another. As a psychoanalyst, I can only add that my experience in helping people achieve insights from unconscious dimensions within themselves reveals the same phenomenon—insights emerge not chiefly because they are "intellectually true" or even because they are helpful, but because they have a certain *form*, the form that is beautiful because it completes what is incomplete in us.

This idea, this new form that suddenly presents itself, comes in order to complete a hitherto incomplete Gestalt with which we are struggling in conscious awareness. One can quite accurately speak of this unfinished pattern, this unformed form, as constituting the "call" to which our preconscious, out of its maelstrom, gives an answer.

4

By passion for form I mean a principle of human experience that is analogous to several of the most important ideas in Western history. Kant proposed that our understanding is not simply a reflection of the objective world around us, but it also *constitutes* this world. It is not that objects simply speak to *us*; they also conform to our ways of knowing. The mind thus is an active process of forming and re-forming the world.

Interpreting dreams as dramas of the patient's relationship to his or her world, I asked myself whether there is not on a deeper and more inclusive level in human experience something parallel to what Kant was talking about. That is, is it not only our *intellectual* understanding that plays a role in our forming and re-forming the world in the process of knowing it, but do not *imagination* and *emotions* also play a critical role? It must be the *totality* of ourselves that understands, not simply reason. And it is the totality of ourselves that fashions the images to which the world conforms.

Not only does reason form and re-form the world, but the "preconscious," with its impulses and needs, does so also and does so on the basis of wish and intentionality. Human beings not only think but feel and will as they make form in their world. This is why I use the word *pas-*

sion, the sum of erotic and dynamic tendencies, in the phrase "passion for form." Persons in therapy—or anybody for that matter—are not simply engaged in knowing their world: what they are engaged in is a passionate re-forming of their world by virtue of their interrelationship with it.

This passion for form is a way of trying to find and constitute meaning in life. And this is what genuine creativity is. Imagination, broadly defined, seems to me to be a principle in human life underlying even reason, for the rational functions, according to our definitions, can lead to understanding—can participate in the constituting of reality—only as they are creative. Creativity is thus involved in our every experience as we try to make meaning in our self-world relationship.

Philosopher Alfred North Whitehead also speaks in effect of this passion for form. Whitehead has constructed a philosophy based not on reason alone, but one that includes what he calls "feeling." By feeling he does not mean simply affect. As I understand it he means the total capacity of the human organism to experience his or her world. Whitehead reformulates Descartes' original principle as follows:

Descartes was wrong when he said "Cogito, ergo sum"—I think, therefore I am. It is never bare thought or bare existence that we are aware of. I find myself rather as essentially a unity of emotions, of enjoyment, of hopes, of fears, of regrets, valuations of alternatives, decisions—all of these are subjective reactions to my environment as I am active in my nature. My unity which is Descartes' "I am" is my *process of shaping this welter of material into a consistent pattern of feelings.*[5]

What I am calling passion for form is, if I understand Whitehead aright, a central aspect of what he is describing as the experience of identity.* I am able to shape feelings, sensibilities, enjoyments, hopes into a pattern that makes me aware of myself as man or woman. But I cannot shape them into a pattern as a purely subjective act. I can do it only as I am related to the immediate objective world in which I live.

Passion can destroy the self. But this is not passion for form; it is passion gone beserk. Passion obviously can be diabolic as well as symbolic—it can deform as well as form; it can destroy meaning and produce chaos again. When sexual powers emerge in puberty, passion often does destroy form temporarily. But sex also has great creative potentialities precisely because it is passion. Unless one's development is radically pathological, there will also occur in the adolescent a growth toward a new form, in manhood or womanhood, in contrast to his or her previous state as girl or boy.

5

The urgent need in everyone to give form to his or her life can be illustrated by the case of a young man who consulted with me when I was writing this chapter. He was the only son in a professional family where his mother and father had quarreled and had fought almost continuously,

---

* A friend of mine, on reading this chapter in manuscript, sent me the following original poem, which I quote with permission:

I am, therefore I love
the total sensibility
that looked at me
out of your undefended face
immediately.
I love, therefore I am.

according to his memory, since he was born. He had never been able to concentrate or apply himself to his studies in school. As a boy when he was supposed to be studying in his room, he would hear his father coming up the stairs and immediately open a schoolbook to cover over the magazine on mechanics he had been looking at. He recalled that his father, a successful but apparently very cold man, had often promised to take him on various trips as a reward if he successfully got through his schoolwork. But none of those trips ever materialized.

His mother had made him her confidante, covertly supporting him in his conflicts with his father. He and his mother used to sit out in the backyard summer evenings talking until late at night—they were "partners," they "grooved together," as he put it. His father exercised pull to get him accepted into college in another part of the country; but the young man spent three months there never going out of his room until his father came to fetch him home.

Living at home he worked as a carpenter, and later as a construction worker in the Peace Corps. He then came to New York where he supported himself as a plumber, doing sculpture on the side, until by a kind of lucky accident he got a job as instructor in crafts at a university an hour outside the city. But in his job he was unable to assert himself or to talk clearly and directly to either students or faculty. He was overawed by the young Ivy League graduates on the faculty who monopolized faculty meetings with their chatter which he felt was pompous and artificial. In this dazed and ineffectual state, he first began work with me. I found him an unusually sensitive person, generous, talented (he gave me a wire sculptured figure he

had made in my waiting room which I found delightful).
He was seriously withdrawn and apparently accomplish-
ing practically nothing in his job or life.

We worked together a couple of times a week for most
of a year, in which time he made unusually commendable
progress in his interpersonal relationships. He now worked
effectually and had entirely overcome his neurotic awe of
fellow faculty members. He and I agreed that since he was
now functioning actively and well we would stop our work
for the time being. We were both aware, however, that we
had never been able to explore adequately his relationship
with his mother.

He came back a year later. He had married in the meantime, but this did not seem to present any special problems. What cued off the present impasse was a visit he
and his wife had made the previous month to his mother,
who by that time was in a mental hospital. They found her
sitting by the nurses' desk in the corridor "waiting for her
cigarette." She went into her room to talk with them, but
soon came out again to continue waiting out the hour until the time for her rationed cigarette.

Coming back on the train, the young man was very depressed. He had known theoretically about his mother's
increasingly senile condition, but was unable to make
emotional sense of it. His withdrawn, apathetic state was
similar to but also different from his condition the first time
he had come. He was now able to communicate with me
directly and openly. His problem was localized, specific,
in contrast to the generalized daze he had been suffering
from the first time he came. His relationship to his mother
was in chaos. In that segment of his life he felt no form
at all, only a gnawing confusion.

After our first session the daze he was under lifted, but the problem remained. This is often the function of *communication* in the therapeutic hour: it enables the person to overcome his or her sense of alienation from the human kind. But it does not suffice in itself for a genuine experience of new form. It assuages, but it doesn't produce the new form. An overcoming of the chaos on a deeper level is required, and this can only be done with some kind of insight.

In this second hour we reviewed at length his mother's attachment to him and the understandable upset he would feel at her present condition, even though he had known it had been coming on for years. She had privately made him the "crown prince." I pointed out that she had been a powerful woman in these fights with his father, that she had wooed him away from his father and had exploited him in her endeavors to defeat his father. In contrast to his illusion that they had been partners or that they had "grooved," he actually had been a hostage, a little person used in much bigger battles. When he mentioned his surprise at seeing these things, he brought to my mind a story, which I told him. A man was selling hamburgers allegedly made of rabbit meat at an amazingly low price. When people asked him how he did it, he admitted that he was using some horse meat. But when this did not suffice as an explanation, he confessed it was 50 per cent horse meat and 50 per cent rabbit meat. When they continued to ask him what he meant, he stated, "One rabbit to one horse."

The graphic image of the rabbit and horse gave him a powerful "aha" experience, much greater than any he would have gotten from an intellectual explanation. He continued to marvel at his being the rabbit not in any derogatory sense, but with the felt realization of how helpless he must have been in his childhood. A heavy load of guilt and previously unexpressible hostility was lifted off his back. The image gave him a way of getting at long last to his negative feelings toward his mother. Many details of his background now fell into place, and he seemed to be able to cut the psychological umbilical cord which he previously did not know existed.

Curiously, persons in such situations give the impression of having had all along the necessary strength at hand to make these changes; it was just a matter of waiting for the "sun of order" to melt away "the fog of confusion" (to change the metaphor into Delphic-oracle terms). The "passion" in his example is shown by the alacrity with which he grasped this insight and by the immediacy with which he re-formed his psychological world. He gave the impression—which again is typical for the experience—of having stored up the strength at previous stages until it was finally possible, on getting the right piece of the jigsaw puzzle, to suddenly seize that strength and exercise it.

In our third and last session he told me of his newly-made decision to resign his post at the university, and to find a studio in which he could devote himself entirely to his sculpture.

The communication with me in the first session may be seen as the preliminary step in this creative process. Then came the "aha" experience as the needed insight, preferably as an image, is born in the individual's consciousness. The third step is the making of the decisions, which the young man did between the second and third sessions, as *a result* of the newly achieved form. The therapist cannot predict the exact nature of such decisions; they are *a living out of the new form.*

The creative process is the expression of this passion for

form. It is the struggle against disintegration, the struggle to bring into existence new kinds of being that give harmony and integration.

Plato has for our summation some charming advice:

For he who would proceed aright in this manner should begin in youth to visit beautiful forms; and first, if he be guided by his instructor aright, to love one such form only—out of that he should create fair thoughts; and soon he will of himself perceive that the beauty of one form is akin to the beauty of another, and that beauty in every form is one and the same.[6]

Notes

TWO The Nature of Creativity, pp. 36–54

1. Ludwig Binswanger, in *Existence: A New Dimension in Psychology and Psychiatry*, eds. Rollo May, Ernest Angel, and Henri F. Ellenberger (New York, 1958), p. 11.

THREE Creativity and the Unconscious, pp. 55–76

1. This was in the mid-1940s, when being pregnant and unwed was considerably more traumatic than now.
2. Henri Poincaré, "Mathematical Creation," from *The Foundation of Science*, trans. George Bruce Halsted, in *The Creative Process*, ed. Brewster Ghiselin (New York, 1952), p. 36.
3. *Ibid.*, p. 37.
4. *Ibid.*, p. 38.
5. *Ibid.*
6. *Ibid.*
7. *Ibid.*, p. 40.
8. Werner Heisenberg, "The Representation of Nature in Contemporary Physics," in *Symbolism in Religion and Literature*, ed. Rollo May (New York, 1960), p. 225.
9. Yevgeny Yevtushenko, *The Poetry of Yevgeny Yevtushenko, 1953–1965*, trans. George Reavey (New York, 1965), pp. x–xi. Emphasis mine.
10. *Ibid.*, p. vii.
11. *Ibid.*, p. viii–ix.

FOUR   Creativity and Encounter, pp. 77–94

1. Archibald MacLeish, *Poetry and Experience* (Boston, 1961),
pp. 8–9.
2. *Ibid.*
3. James Lord, *A Giacometti Portrait* (New York, 1964), p. 26.
4. *Ibid.*, p. 22.
5. *Ibid.*, p. 23.
6. *Ibid.*, p. 18.
7. *Ibid.*, p. 24.
8. *Ibid.*, p. 41 (italics mine).
9. *Ibid.*, p. 38 (italics mine).
10. MacLeish, pp. 8–9.
11. Frank Barron, "Creation and Encounter," *Scientific American* (September, 1958), 1–9.

FIVE   The Delphic Oracle as Therapist, pp. 95–111

1. E. R. Dodds, *The Greeks and the Irrational* (Berkeley, 1964),
p. 75.
2. The word *tyrannos* refers simply to an absolute ruler, of the
type normally spawned in eras of political ferment and change. Some
of these "tyrants," like Pisistratus, the "tyrant of Athens" of the
late sixth century, are regarded as benefactors by historians as well
as by modern Greeks. I well recall my surprise when I first heard
the boys of the school in Greece in which I taught speak of Pisistratus with the same quality of admiration, if not the same quantity,
as people in this country speak of George Washington.
3. *Translations from the Poetry of Rainer Maria Rilke*, trans.
M. D. Herter Norton (New York, 1938), p. 181.
4. Robert Flacelière, *Greek Oracles*, trans. Douglas Garman
(New York, 1965), p. 49.
5. Dodds, p. 73.
6. *Ibid.*
7. Flacelière, p. 37.
8. Flacelière, p. 52.
9. Herodotus, *The Histories*, Book VII, 140–144.

SIX   On the Limits of Creativity, pp. 112–123

1. Heraclitus, p. 28, Ancilla to the Pre-Socratic Philosophers, A complete translation of the Fragments in Diels, by Kathleen Freeman, Harvard U. Press, Cambridge, Mass., 1970.
2. *Ibid.*, p. 28.

SEVEN   Passion for Form, pp. 124–140

1. Rollo May, "The Meaning of Symbols," in *Symbolism in Religion and Literature,* ed. Rollo May (New York, 1960), pp. 11–50.
2. Plato, *Symposium,* trans. Benjamin Jowett, in *The Portable Greek Reader,* ed. W. H. Auden (New York, 1948), p. 499.
3. *Ibid.*, p. 497.
4. Elsewhere in this book I have noted that the mathematician Poincaré echoes a similar emphasis on Eros as bringing forth both beauty and truth at once. (See pp. 67–68.)|
5. *Alfred North Whitehead: His Reflections on Man and Nature,* selected by Ruth Nanda Anshen (New York, 1961), p. 28. Emphasis mine.
6. Plato, p. 496.

William Stafford
    To tell & tell from the
roof of the house over the flat
world to anyone listening

Stories that could be true
                    Harper + Row

Hume
Kant
Leibniz
Plato.

From Our Many Selves by Elizabeth
i Coron

I have too many Selves to know
the one,
In too complex a schooling I was bred.
Child of too many cities, who
have gone
Down all the bright cross-roads of the
World's desires,
And at too many altars bowed my head
To light too many fires.

Eunice Tietjens.

He who, in the vale of
obscurity; can brave adversity
can behave with tranquillity
and indifference is truly
great.

Olive Goldsmith.

William Murray put it beautifully.

Until one is committed, there is hesitancy the chance to draw back, always ineffectiveness. Concerning all acts of creation there is one elementary truth, the ignorance of which kills countless ideas and splendid plans. That the moment one definitely commits oneself, the Providence moves, too. All sorts of things occur to help one that would never otherwise have occurred. A whole stream of events issues from the decision raising in one's favour all manner of unforseen incidents & meetings & material assistance which no man could have dreamed would have come his way"

Goethe said: —

Whatever you can do, or dream you can, begin it.

Boldness has genius, power & magic in it.

of us have come to appreciate from her creative content online. *Unfollow Me* is a continuation of Busby's work and it is for this moment as well as the next. It demands a follow, a like, a heart emoji, and a reader who is not afraid to be floored by Busby's incisive take on so many old inequities that ghost us still."

—Darnell L. Moore, author of *No Ashes in the Fire: Coming of Age Black and Free in America*

"Frank, incisive, brutally funny, and moving, Busby has a gift for vivifying the keenest cultural observations with cutting, unflinching prose. I devoured this book."

—Amanda Montell, author of *Wordslut* and *Cultish*

"*Unfollow Me* is an emotionally risky, trope-turning manifesto of a book. Whether she's writing a letter to white hippiecrites, describing the disassociation that comes with online personas, or exploring the hell that can be microfame, her excavation is distinctive and nuanced. Jill Louise Busby for President."

—Chloe Caldwell, author of *I'll Tell You in Person and Women*

"*Unfollow Me* challenges how we think about each other and ourselves in a way that is nuanced, funny, and vulnerable. Reading this book is like listening to your smartest friend."

—Mia Mercado, author of *Weird But Normal*

Praise for *Unfollow Me*

"Jill lets us know out the gate that she ain't come to play. This book is real, raw, and unrelenting. Dark, satirical, full of brilliance and badassness. Now is definitely not the time to be unfollowing Jill."   —Killer Mike

"For anyone who has ever heard they were too much, not enough, and right on time all in the same day, this book will assure you that you're not crazy. A pleasure, even in all its painful, powerful truths."   —Meshell Ndegeocello

"*Unfollow Me* reminds me of just how much courage I lack. It forced me to challenge who I've presented myself as, and to confront the invisible but thick tether between irreverence and conformity, especially as it pertains to conversations and stances around identity and technology. Her voice is sharp, but what's sharper is the feeling that Busby is asking us to complicate our arguments and muster up the moxie to sort and see our many selves in a more honest light. And for that, I am grateful."
          —Jason Reynolds, #1 *New York Times*
          bestselling author of *Miles Morales: Spider-Man*,
          the *Track* series, *Long Way Down*, and *Stamped*,
          a collaboration with Ibram X. Kendi

"Jill Louise Busby has gifted us words that sing on the page with the insightful, poetic and witty euphony that many

UNFOLLOW ME

UNFOLLOW ME

ESSAYS ON COMPLICITY

JILL LOUISE BUSBY

BLOOMSBURY PUBLISHING

NEW YORK · LONDON · OXFORD · NEW DELHI · SYDNEY

BLOOMSBURY PUBLISHING
Bloomsbury Publishing Inc.
1385 Broadway, New York, NY 10018, USA

BLOOMSBURY, BLOOMSBURY PUBLISHING, and the
Diana logo are trademarks of Bloomsbury Publishing Plc

First published in the United States 2021

The definitions for the terms *mutualism*, *parasitism*, and *commensalism* on
page 110 were adapted from the Biology Online dictionary, Wikipedia,
and *Encyclopaedia Britannica Kids Online*; *aggressive mimicry* and *Batesian
mimicry* on pages 112 and 115 from *Encyclopaedia Britannica Online*;
and *matter* on pages 156, 161, and 171 from the
Oxford English Dictionary Online.

ISBN: HB: 978-1-63557-711-2; EBOOK: 978-1-63557-712-9

LIBRARY OF CONGRESS CATALOGING-IN-PUBLICATION DATA IS AVAILABLE

2 4 6 8 10 9 7 5 3 1

Typeset by Westchester Publishing Services
Printed and bound in the USA

This book is dedicated to my mother,
my brother, and you. Yes, you.

Truth fights for itself. If you are open to it,
it will use you as a weapon.

—JILLISBLACK

CONTENTS

Contents

UNFOLLOW ME

IDENTIFICATION

I am a black queer woman, and in case you haven't heard, I am having a moment. In this moment, it is more important that you know what I am than who I am. So I'll start there. I am an influencer. I am #BlackGirlMagic. I am a girlboss. I am diverse and I am included. I am an antiracist, radically honest, culturally relevant, intersectional womanist dyke. I am grant proposals and safe spaces and important new initiatives. I am self-care and self-love and self-empowering selfies. I am a national bestseller, a true triumph, an important story that will keep you glued to your seat and leave you in tears. I am the perceived expert of an experience, a fresh idea, a yardstick for liberal progression and conservative regression. I am a tiebreaker, a vote. I am just like you, but also, I am here to block you, drink your tears, cancel you from my cultures, and remind you that everything you have to say is irrelevant. I am in the room, seated at the table, holding a megaphone. And

I am so loud that all I can hear is my own feedback, an echo.

This is how I win now. Or at least that's what I'm told.

This book begins in 2016, when I was working in diversity and inclusion at a large nonprofit organization in Tacoma, Washington. Twenty-nine years old, with a frustrating lack of ambition, I mostly sat all day in my swivel chair, reciting rhetoric on conference calls and adding to the diversity of the place. Yes, I was selling my identities to the nonprofit machine, and no, it wasn't the first time. There were jobs where I led with my blackness, jobs where I led with my queerness, and jobs where I tried to lead with both at once. Before that, I'd spent five years working with my mother as a cultural competency trainer, scripting people and labeling their structural flaws as "misunderstandings." Often we just recommended team building. We were almost always invited back.

But I was growing tired of paycheck progressives, so like many people with a gripe, I uploaded a minute's worth of my feelings to my Instagram account. I called white people out for their intentional gradualism, their masking of a desire to maintain their racial status with varying displays of eternal naivete. I left myself out of it. The next morning a road had opened for me, and a choice about whether to take it.

Obviously, I made another video. And another and another and another. Soon there were offers to speak and write and I found myself with an inbox full of ego-pleasing options. My follower count grew by the tens of thousands and my face was all over specific corners of the internet. People called me by my social media handle instead of my real name when they met me in person. They asked for pictures and book recommendations and advice. One follower left the same comment underneath every video, encapsulating the appeal: "Jill is always black. And she's always on point, never off."

She was also, it struck me, the expression of a flattened identity, on repeat. I wanted to enjoy it, revel in the benefits like other identity influencers. I wanted to chase the headlines and react to them for easy content and more likes. But I couldn't. And after a year or so, I was just parroting the expectation. Following the rules I made. If you are interested in a book where I follow the trend and sell you an articulate account of my oppression, this book might disappoint you. If in order to see me, you must turn me inside out and be confronted with enough difference to make you feel privileged, then this book might disappoint you. If you are in search of an education that will ultimately allow you to know me better than I know myself, this book might disappoint you. And if you want to use this book as a reference to sound current and concerned at a diverse dinner party, it will disappoint. This book is not a comforting script or a way to win in a debate with a troll. I'm seeking something else.

I seek to go beyond cultural narratives and focus on what is universal about living in a world that quickly reduces you to either an exception or the rule. I seek to change the way we write about who we are so that we can stop mimicking each other for acceptance and personal gain. I seek the parts of us that can never be labeled. I seek to be on the other side of this moment. Yes, I seek truths about what it means to be black and queer and a woman in a dominant society that re-creates everything in its own image and calls it a success. But instead of avoiding my own compliance and accountability, I seek to aim the questions directly at myself, challenging the current narrative about race, gender, and sexuality and examining all the ways that I benefit from it.

I use stories from my own life to remind us that change is constant and growth is necessary, inside and out. (My mother has reminded me to tell you: The names of individuals who figure in these stories have been fictionalized. Any resemblance between the fictional names and those of real people is coincidental.) Ultimately, this collection is a look behind the curtain of identity, a search for the answer of why we fight so hard to stay so disconnected. It is an exploration of honesty, self, and ego and what exists beyond rage and being right.

Hi, liberal white people that like to name your kids after deciduous trees and maybe go to the local Unitarian church and also live in an unassuming and intentionally disheveled Craftsman-style house in a neighborhood that black people can't afford anymore. Hey. While you're here, I . . . I just thought I'd ask you a question. Um. I've always wanted to know. Like, but. How come everything's about you? Yeah, I just . . . I just noticed. 'Cause, like, even down in the comments, like, you're down there being like, "Oh, hey. Like, I . . . I don't mean to make this about me, it's just that . . ." And then you keep going and then, like, I mean, you make it about you. Like, everybody sees you doing it. And so I was just curious, like, how come, you know? And an example would be like, what is an "ethnic potluck," right? 'Cause that's an example of how you're at the center of everything and everyone else is just an "other." We're just accessories to your enriching cultural experience that you call life, where you just dabble in things and we're here to let you do that, right? *Yeah?* Well, if I'm here to just season your life, I'm going to make sure you're extra salty when I'm done.

—*Jillisblack*, October 6, 2016

STILL, UNTIL

How did all of this start for you? It's been four years since the beginning they mean, and since then, I have been asked this question more than any other. Wherever I happen to end up, it is always there waiting, always anticipating my arrival before I arrive.

The "all of this" they mean is my single gram of sub-demographic micro-fame on social media, and the "you" they mean is Jillisblack, which is the "you" that *I* perform on social media. The one who made the "Dear White People" videos and then later the "Dear Black People" videos and then later the "Dear Jillisblack" videos and then, soon, no videos at all. Because *I* can't do it anymore. Because *I'm* changing and *she* can't. Because I am an entire person, a much longer story, a more complicated answer. And because she's nothing more than a minute-long recorded performance of a truth that's always changing, a script that I've sloppily handwritten on copy paper or discarded receipts, an embodiment of the most comfortable parts of *my* ego, uploaded by *me* and fed until *she* is absolutely full of it by *their* likes.

When Jillisblack starts, there aren't as many versions of the same thing yet. Not as many bold characters using their boldest language to describe whiteness and what it does or doesn't do well enough for the kind of people who call it "whiteness." I go viral in the summer of 2016, and by the following spring I am one of a million versions of the same thing, "selflessly" building a platform off the artful articulation of collective anger and grief.

If I want to get shared, I have to go further and further, say more and more. I have to push the envelopes with the letters until I seem like the one who cares the very least about hurting anyone's feelings. If I post a video on social media and people's feelings get hurt, what I'm saying must be true. Because the truth hurts, doesn't it?

Social media can also turn on you, call you out for everything it had initially chosen to ignore or forgive you for. It archives what it has noticed about you for when you betray it. And I know that because I've done that. So I know I have to be careful.

The elephants in my room—my "obvious" proximity to whiteness, the fact that I haven't mentioned being queer since I became more known for being black (*who are you afraid to lose and why?*), my refusal (so far) to acknowledge the ways I benefit from colorism, my off-centered mouth and imperfect teeth, my unchallenged masculinity and who/what it could cause me to ignore, my lack of solutions, my need for internet attention, the fact that I can never be as "woke" as *she* claims because she's so desperate to claim it in the first place (*and why is that, exactly?*), how I don't even have *that* many followers, for real (*so don't act like you're* somebod*y, okay?*)—can begin to trumpet all at once.

When we feel betrayed by someone—even a stranger—suddenly we notice everything about them that was always there. Every elephant.

So, in the beginning, it was all about what I was willing to say as Jillisblack. Then it became about what I know better than to say as Jillisblack.

Jillisblack *can* call out white people (specifically and in general) and America as much as she wants. Jillisblack *can* question symbols of the black elite, celebrity and (social) media, respectability politics, capitalism, hope, and progress.

Jillisblack *can't* call out things people grew up loving or still love or feel represent them and their experience in the world—historical figures, fictional characters, singers, movies, cultural icons, influencers. Even if those things are actually using their money and support to bet against them, to make themselves rich or powerful, to buy their own safety. Even if those things are just extracting the biotic natural resource of their unwavering allegiance and depleting it in the process.

I know because I still love all the historical figures, fictional characters, singers, movies, cultural icons, and influencers that I feel represent me, too. And because no matter how good I've gotten at dealing with the trolls, I'm still not ready for a mass unfollowing.

I don't come close to one until much later, when I announce that I'm married. (Jillisblack can't announce that I'm married.) Some people unfollow because they think that my marriage makes me complicit in an agenda to destroy the black family. Some people unfollow because they think that my marriage makes me complicit in a heteronormative construct that reinforces tradition and capitalism. Other people unfollow for reasons they don't bother to tell me.

Jillisblack is a watchful negotiation of these rules.

*

SHE STARTS ON a Friday afternoon, in the parking lot of a TwinStar Credit Union. I'm there to pick up my five free checks for the month and record a video for social media. So far, my posts have been about being high or broke or one because of the other. Or they're about the slightly alternative dating rituals of the slightly alternative and highly ritualistic. Or the common social media practices of exclusive friend groups, bougie and brunching in Brooklyn with grad school tote bags full of travel-size natural hair care products, gently motivational weekly planners, and deteriorating music-festival ticket stubs. Or the unspoken rules of the hip black queer community, inescapably connected by years and years of inner-circle dating and early internet reliance. All the things I know or am, say and do, want or act on. All the mirrors that allow me to see myself in public. And the critique that's accurate only because it's really just a confession.

I'm not fashionable, but I make an honest attempt—mostly when I know I'll see some of you, and/or I know I'll be photographed somewhere that is social-media-worthy, or when I have a photoshoot with a photographer who posted asking if anyone was around today to be shot in profile in front of a brick wall or a bridge.

But if I could figure out how to get away with wearing Eddie Bauer graphic tees and flare-legged khakis for the rest of my life, I would, y'all. Or rather, I would dress exactly like I did in the sixth grade, but forever. The only reason I don't is because I know that these days I'm actively attempting an image. And I know that my chosen image comes with a uniform. An aesthetic of sorts. It's how we identify each other in public/at a Drake concert. I know that I must fully engage with my hair. I know that my bold prints and patterns must be layered and plentiful. I know that my jewelry must be wooden and African and from Etsy. I know that my A Tribe Called Quest T-shirt must be showcased. I know that I must wear outfits that allow for full-body mobility in case I need to quickly share an article or request a Lyft to meet a friend for tea or do some yoga. I know that I must look like I just got back from a life-changing trip to Iceland or like I'm about to go to a music festival where Erykah Badu will be closing or like I just finished watching *Love Jones* in a college sweatshirt while eating an acai bowl at all times.

I get it.

But this video is different. This day at work has been particularly frustrating, and I'm sick to death of all the good intentions and best practices and identity expertise. I'm tired of programmatic care and fixing something from a distance and the soft whine of gradualism as it stretches to make itself more comfortable in my body.

This time, I'm sitting in my car, in the rain, clutching a few notes about white liberalism and the performance of trying and an eternal promise of *soon*, almost. And the notes are scrawled on the back of a return envelope for a bill I can't yet afford to pay, and the rain is almost too loud for what I have to do, so I wait.

But I don't know how to wait anymore without checking my phone. So I move through a series of evolutionary ticks: text messages, WhatsApp notes, Facebook notifications. Then there's Instagram, Instagram again, Google Chrome. My last search was "how tall is Brandy?" I already don't remember the answer. But, wait. It's right there—5' 7".

Also, she's an Aquarius. Which makes sense, even though I don't really know Brandy like that.

But don't I, though?

When I'm done, I check my work email. There's nothing from the large nonprofit where I am employed as a diversity and inclusion educator, no missed call from either of my bosses. They don't look for me when I arrive late or leave early, because that's what they do, too. Being mostly unaccounted for is part of the organizational culture.

And when one of my bosses happens to be in the office long enough to see my miserable corner cubicle, dark and unoccupied, my chair tucked, and it seems like maybe I should be there, *doing* something, my answer is always the same—I'm working remotely.

Even if I had been sitting in that corner cubicle, watching the rain through the one-way window, there would still be only the performance of work, my seemingly transfixed eyes staring at an old email until it was time to go home.

I was hired to ensure that the regional offices were following up on their elusive diversity and inclusion efforts through a variety of in-house training and quarterly committee meetings. I quickly learned that my actual job was to enthusiastically agree with everyone in upper management (via email, Zoom call, or in-staff training) that everything that could be done to make the organization more diverse and inclusive was already well underway. All remaining issues were budgetary, not behavioral.

It's a job that could be completed in an hour or two a week, but I manage to perform the remaining thirty-six or so hours into a full paycheck.

White people, you're always educating yourselves. When do you finally just ... get it? Because black people have had to learn you so quickly in order to survive, so I know it's possible. Tell me, why is it taking you so long? Why is it so hard? Why is it costing you so much money?

> Why do you need so many workshops and train-
> ings and seminars and talks and panels and
> so . . . much . . . *time?*

When the rain finally lets up, I record my video and get it right in exactly three tries. Then I filter it, caption it, hashtag it, upload it, refresh it.

Okay, two likes. I sit in my car until the first comment comes in. Refresh again. Okay, it's good. They like it. They've noticed my haircut. They've tagged a friend.

Good, okay.

I spend five more minutes watching, waiting, refreshing, reading. Then I get out of my car, walk through the rain, and kindly demand my checks.

*

THAT NIGHT, EVERYTHING is the same. I cook dinner in my family's low-income apartment, turn on the music, call everyone in, and we all grab our food and gather. It's me, my mother, my brother. There are also two matching vapes filled with legal Washington weed for me and Chris, a glass of red wine for my mother. We sit around the long table that we inherited from a stranger and eat our vegetables, talk about nothing, speculate about the government or lack thereof, talk about money or a lack thereof, laugh. Listen to the screaming children who live next door with their screaming parents, and look out at the view of Mount Rainier from the tiny deck.

If only this could be enough for me, for what I want and what I think I'm supposed to be at twenty-nine years old. If only I didn't need so much attention all the fucking time. If only I could stop romanticizing my own displeasure, disinterest, distance.

But I was going to do something bigger than this one day. Beyond it. Something that wasn't diversity and inclusion work for an oversize nonprofit. I was going to finally reach my full potential and stop relying on tall tales of its existence.

I can't die selling my identities to an oversize nonprofit. I just can't.

So I disappear into my bedroom, with the stark white walls and the thin carpet, collapse onto the futon, and check Instagram. The video is doing well and I'm almost offended because why this one? Why now?

It isn't even funny.

But also, fine. This is okay, too. As long as someone knows what I mean and tells me so. Because that's what this social media is about for me—being heard, understood as some curated version of who I kind of am. So maybe this one is the right one after all.

*

SATURDAY, I WAKE up to twenty thousand more followers on Instagram and a text message from a friend who lives in Oakland, California. She links me to the video I shared yesterday, but now it's on Facebook, too. It sends me into a small panic, the reality of my face and my words escaping from the pen. A reminder of how uncontainable the internet is.

My friend is excited, warns me to probably stay out of the comment section. But like, *whoa*, dude! That's *you*, she says. Congratulations. *You're everywhere.*

I tap the link and go straight to the comment section. I learn that I'm a fucking liberal, a victim, the problem with everything. I learn that I don't know what the fuck I'm talking about, that I'm an ungrateful nigger who should leave America since I hate it so much, a racist dyke who needs a dick in her mouth, a dumb bitch who needs to be taught a lesson. I learn that I'm overcompensating for not being black enough, the type we've all heard from enough already, thanks. I learn that I think I'm better/smarter than everybody even though I'm not.

Oh, and I should go fuck myself.

I also learn that I'm worthy of marriage, that I'm not bad even though I probably could've said it without the profanity, that I'm a queen even though I'm a little bit too masculine, a mix of Daria and Angela Davis (who knew?). I learn that I'm brave (on the internet) and important (on the internet) and that everyone should be required to hear me speak my truth (on the internet).

Over coffee, I tell my mother about it.

"So, you know I posted a video yesterday, right? On Instagram."

"Oh, okay. Uh-huh."

"Well, this morning I woke up and I have like thirty thousand likes on it and, like, all these new followers, and I—"

"Shit."

"Yeah, and a friend sent me a link to where it's been shared on Facebook—well, a couple of people have—and that link alone had over a million views already."

"Well, Jill, that's kind of a big deal."

"Yeah, right?"

I show her the video. I tell her how it started.

Just tell the truth, white people. Say that you'll never give any of it up. That you're flattered by the attention. By watching people spend their entire lives fighting for so much of what you already have. Waiting on a world you were—oh, shucks!—born into. Given. The one where the only downside—the only real bummer—is that other people must suffer in order for you to have what you want. The one where all of the numbers show you winning at a game where you're both a player and the referee. Tell me, do you think you got lucky to be born as you instead of me, or do you think it was God? And tell me, do you love being able to call yourself privileged when the only other way out is accountability? I have to tell you, what you see as privilege wouldn't be good enough for what we deserve.

She asks me how I feel and what I'm going to do.

But I don't know how I feel, so I ignore that part.

"I mean, I guess I make another video soon. I guess I keep doing it. I don't know."

But I *do* know. It's not the video I thought would do it, but the reaction to it is exactly what I've been waiting for. A chance to be more publicly appraised. A way out of anonymity and into visibility for saying stuff that I really mean. Actually believe.

I want to use Jillisblack. I want her to be honest without consequence. I want her to say everything about race and racism, power and privilege, hierarchy and hypocrisy that I can't say at work without getting fired. I want her to take risks I can't afford to take. I want her to speak without interruption, any way that she wants, for every time that I couldn't.

Maybe other people want to use Jillisblack, too.

So I spend a quiet weekend thinking about how to do it well. I study the comment section of the video. I make myself read every single one.

I strategize about how to avoid rhetoric traps and how to win against a troll without seeming like I care. I consider how to avoid the question of "But if what you're saying is true, what are you going to do? And if you're not going to do anything, then why are you saying anything?" I have no practical solutions yet, so I'll need good excuses. I think of what I should wear and how I should cut my hair and I come up with a rhythm for the recitation of the words.

I hide all the elephants I can and attempt to quiet the ones I can't.

And on Sunday, I sit in the parking lot of our apartment complex and record another video. Sit in the car and notice how quickly the likes come in now, the comments.

This is how all this starts.

Nothing and nobody warned me.

I think I'm using something against itself, but it's using me against myself.

*

A YEAR LATER, the Lyft driver asks you, "Why Harlem?" And it could mean a million things, really.

You tell him that you're going to a party, and that you always enjoy the ride to the party more than the party itself.

He laughs, says something about the pain of having to go places you don't want to go. Something about his son and his son's education. Something about moving here young, learning quickly, having to or else. Something about no regrets that sounds full of nothing but.

Eventually he remembers the radio, starts nodding along to the music, says, "It's a good night for a party."

It must be sarcasm or small talk, because the wind is whipping and the sky is full of deep, dark drama. People on the street—weary and accustomed—clutch their umbrellas like it's always fucking something. You watch closely like the visitor that you are, say to yourself for the millionth time something you already think you know.

Jill, you can never, ever live here.

Say out loud, "It's not that kind of party."

And you could mean a million things, really. But none of them quite matter. You want the beginning of the small talk that you've grown to adore, require. Circumstantial conversation with someone you're supposed to think you have nothing in common with. Happy to talk without talking *at* or in spite or in spite of. It's made you want something confidential and off record, and everything—absolutely everything—is on record now.

The people you sit next to on planes or share rides with become a break from the noise, an opportunity to drop the script and improvise. The more of these conversations you have, the more out of practice you realize you are with saying exactly who you are.

"Well, not a *party* party. An event, really . . . at Langston Hughes's house."

You know why you say it so specifically when less detail would do. You know that you don't need to, so you can't quite sell the words as casual. You immediately begin to worry yourself with all the possible implications of an unnecessary detail uttered aloud. What does it mean about you if you have to brag and pretend it's necessary for the story? I mean, it's Langston fucking Hughes, but who even cares, right?

You.

You care.

And you want him to care, too. You want him to care so much that it's worth the cost of a Lyft from Brooklyn to Harlem at rush hour. You want him to care so much that you get to convince yourself you told him for his sake instead of yours. You want him to care enough to be impressed.

He nods, merges, cares very little or not at all and goes, "Oh, okay. What's the event for?"

You quickly consider your options. Find that you both want to wave this line of questioning away like an accident you didn't seek out, *and* you want to be heard, to talk. To find out more about yourself from someone who is curious enough to ask you.

Not Jillisblack.

But Jill.

You.

Maybe you want to say, "I don't understand my life right now, okay? There were places and opportunities and circumstances that I wanted, sure. But I never actually believed that I'd have them. And now I'm in New York, in this car, on my way to someone else's idea of a party, and I have no idea what to do with myself. So, please. Just *like* me. I want to know that I still deserve it even when I'm not her."

Maybe you want him to think of you as different. Different from the other black girls who rely on the armored vehicle of social media to yell into the partially open windows of all the white people they used to worship who now just follow them. Those black girls who pretend their anger is wildly different from that of a scorned ex on a hot night, drunk-texting all their friends about how ready they are to move on while stalking the ex's comment section for reasons to stay mad. The ones who talk more about the ex than they do about themselves. The ones who can't stop talking about how much they don't care anymore. The ones who hope the ex is watching them not care.

Those black girls.

You.

So you say, "Um . . . it's for, like, people who other people think are going to change the world in some way. It's being sponsored by some publishing house, and you know what? I didn't even get my invitation directly. Someone got me on the list. So I'm not actually one of these people who's going to change the world, but I'm allowed to be around them for a night."

He smiles at you in the rearview mirror, proud like a father you don't have.

"Oh, I get to drive someone around who's going to change the world, huh? You should've said something earlier!"

You shake your head. "No, I'm not. In fact, I don't even do well at events like this. I feel out of place. I don't know what to talk about. I think if I were one of them—these people—then I'd probably know what to say to them, right?"

"Oh, don't even worry about that. They're going to love you."

You already know that they won't, but you don't want to disappoint him. Instead, you look out the window at New York—children dressed up as adults. Adults dressed up as adults. Custom assumed to be universal. Everything moving quickly, choreographed by predictable restlessness. A giving in to motion above everything else. As if things that are still or quiet can't change.

"It's not even that I want them to love me. I think I'd rather love *them* for once."

You say it quietly because it's a loud lie.

You do want them to love you. If they did, you'd convince yourself that you like them.

You want them to think you're brilliant. If they did, you'd convince yourself that they must really see you.

You want them to laugh at all your jokes. If they did, you'd convince yourself that they have a pretty good sense of humor.

But in case they don't, you were already skeptical before you ever arrived, right? You even have a witness.

"Fuck. I hear that. I hate *everybody* in this city!"

Your witness laughs, swerves. There's a lot of honking, but he doesn't seem to care.

You laugh, too, because you're scared.

"Well, these kinds of events are hard. Everyone just wants to talk about themselves and they look at your outfit while you answer their questions and you just stand around performing self-importance. We don't ever talk about who isn't in the room, you know? We just keep saying we need to get them in there. One day. Somehow. But do we invite them? No."

And if this is how you feel, then why do you go? Why do you choose the outfits so carefully? Why are you excited to finally be one of the invited? And why don't you ever stand in the center of the room and scream? Interrupt? Why don't you ever betray your own interests?

Since he doesn't know how you're meant to win the game you've chosen to play, he doesn't need you to be grateful for the party, the platform, the ounce of fame. The *micro*-fame. People who don't know your game sometimes give you too much credit for the way you play it. Sometimes they give you less because they don't understand how to win at their own. And sometimes they know the rules to your game better than you do. This is when they can sell you back to yourself for a price. Make you a trend you think you started.

Because he doesn't know, he says, "Are you happy doing what you're doing? Do you feel like it's important?"

"I guess. I mean . . . sure? Maybe not. I want to write a book, really," you tell him.

Sure, a book. If that's what's next, then yes.

That.

"Oh yeah? A writer?" he asks excitedly.

"Yeah, sure. That's why it's a good idea for me to be at this party."

"Hey, look. You got this. It doesn't really matter if you hate these people. You just go in there and get what you need from them. They want what you got and they got what you need, so fuck 'em, you know? Fuck 'em."

"I don't know if I need them yet, because I don't know what I want yet."

He can't listen because now he's talking to himself, too.

"People are out here for themselves. Period. You have to be thinking about you if you want to make it. You don't have to love the party. You just have to be at the party. Shit, sometimes you gotta *be* the party. But no, you don't have to like it. Just go in there and get yours. Fuck that."

"Is that how it works?"

"Hey, why not? And they invited you for a reason, so."
He shrugs.

It's easy.

You don't have to like the party.

"Yeah," you say quietly. But you're not sure. And you weren't even invited, really. You're a favor for a friend.

"Fuck 'em," he says again.

"Fuck 'em," you say for the first time.

But you win differently, so you mean it differently.

*

THIRTY MINUTES LATER, you find yourself standing in a room full of diversity efforts—two of everything that exists so far, like Noah's Ark. The preservation of identities. Intentional about it, though. Highly stylized, well traveled, and expensively educated, well on their way, their fantasies worth everyone's reality. Sometimes they're more honest one-on-one than in the art. But the art is the reason for the suffering and the suffering is the reason for the party and the party is the reason for the diversity, so it's good everyone could make it out in the almost rain.

You look around, trying to get a lay of the land, but then there are hands on your shoulders and you're being told by two grinning, staring white women—presumably from the publishing house—that they're so glad you could make it out.

Grinning, staring.

You find your name tag.

Still grinning, staring.

You grab a gift bag. There's a card, a book, a notebook. *Staring.*

Wait, now *grinning*, too.

They tell you to please help yourself to the table of food. Vegan fried something, vegan macaroni and something, vegan red velvet cupcakes.

And yeah, you're vegan, but not like this.

They tell you there's a bar. Yeah, if you head to the back where all the other people who need some help getting into character are standing. Straight back and to the left. Can't miss it.

Slightly nostalgic R&B music plays, and the representation nods its collective head on beat as it discusses its latest projects. And right in the middle of it all, watching from where it hangs above our heads, a painting of Langston.

After at least two awkward introductions, you start to get worried, frustrated. It has been a full ten minutes since your arrival and Jillisblack is nowhere to be found. You need her to shake hands, exchange the pleasantries that mean she'll do almost anything to get to the next level, exchange email addresses, smile like she needs this (because she does). You need her to pretend that everything is fine, simply because it's always the same.

You have a conversation with someone else instead. It's the most challenging of all the challenging conversations, and you're not sure whose fault it is. But also, it's yours.

For starters, you kind of look alike. She's the most obvious other you in the Ark. Moves her hands a lot when she talks, her wrists loose and concerned. She adjusts her glasses when she's not talking. Her hair when she is. She sips her champagne, watches you from behind her thick black frames. She makes her entire living emphasizing her points, and so far, all you have managed is some extra grocery money. She has a blog. Went to Columbia. She asks you if you've ever met Solange. That's when you know that she doesn't know that you weren't actually invited to this party. Not the way she was.

She asks what you do and then listens to you by saying "uh-huh" a lot. That's fine, because you're not doing a good job explaining what it is that you do. Mostly because you don't know what it is that you do. You know only what the thing you do does to you.

You have to explain it that way in order to explain it at all, and *that* way sometimes makes people scared for you.

"Um . . . I basically just. Well, I had a video go viral about a year ago . . ."

She perks up, "Oh, okay."

"Right, and I kind of grew my social media from there. I write these one-minute-long letters to white people, sometimes black people, or whatever, and I record them on video, upload them."

"Oh, okay. That sounds cool. But like, what are the letters about, exactly?"

"Well, I could lie to you and—"

"Uh-huh."

"Yeah, I could lie to you and say they're about white people or black people, but honestly, I think they're starting to just be about me. They're about parties like this and what I've learned by being at parties like this and what questions I have after parties like this. They're about all the things I haven't been allowed to say at work but now get to say online. So, I—"

"Uh-huh."

"I guess I'm also trying to get to the bottom of who we all mean when we say we're fighting for 'us.' Or at least when I say it."

"Uh-huh. Totally."

"Yeah."

"Do you deal with a lot of people being mad at you or a lot of trolls or whatever?"

"I have trolls from all sides. And they're all super angry and super scared, but for different reasons."

"Uh-huh, yeah. But I bet it's mostly got to be, like, racist-ass white people, right?"

"Um . . . sometimes, sure. But, I mean, there's also—"

She nods, turns to face the room, starts looking around for a person who isn't trying to figure themselves out in every conversation they have. It's not that kind of party. And anyway, she wanted you to say the right answer, to play the shared game.

You were supposed to call yourself an influencer, but roll your eyes at it just enough to suggest that it doesn't mean anything. You were supposed to say that you create content around race, power, and hierarchy, and when you're not filming content for a creative project, you're working on your book proposal.

Your book is supposed to be about your identities and what other people think about your identities and how you learned to love to write about them. Your book is supposed to be about being the token other and how you achieved personal success "in spite of" that token otherness. Your book is fourteen of your worst encounters with white people and a workbook they can use to help themselves not be the worst.

It could've evolved from there. She would've known what kind of business you're there to do, which rooms you're both in, and how you could either help each other, pretend to help each other, or avoid each other altogether. You could have made assumptions about who you are behind your interpretation of the same character. But your actual answer let her know that you don't yet know what you're going to do with yourself, and that makes you a dangerous person to network with or steal from.

Luckily, you're saved from her disappointment in you by a greater horror—as you almost always are. The person who got you on the list has arrived. She walks up to both of you after walking up to someone else first—of course. She smiles at the other you, hugs her. First. Then she slowly turns to you and says, "Oh, Jillisblack. Hello."

You used to follow each other online, ran into each other on another app. Sent each other text messages for a week. Then you got busy and stopped texting.

So, okay. There's a bit of tension.

It's your fault.

"Hello," you reply. "Nice to finally meet you in person."

She looks at your entire outfit from toe to head, tilts her head.

"I like your hat," she says with a smirk.

It means *fuck you* in every language.

"I like it, too. Thank you."

She smiles, but it's more like a dare.

Then she turns back to the blogger who knows what she wants and asks her questions about some news she's heard about her through the grapevine of doers. An opportunity, a deal. Something about Apple. Something about money—but they laugh about the money.

"We deserve to be compensated. These white folks have been cashing in on us forever. How much are they paying you? Oh, nice."

You still don't know the going rate of your identities in rooms like this. You don't know if you're selling yourself short. So you don't belong in the conversation. You walk away when you can no longer trust what you might say and before you completely ruin your chances of a future fireside chat with the popular blogger or a good word from the person who brought you there to both punish and promote you.

You never know.

You text your friend to let him know that you'll be ready to meet up much earlier than you originally thought. In fact, if he's ready now, that works, too. Yeah, he can just text you when he's outside. And in the meantime, you go get another drink from the bar and assess the room, try to find the best place to wait and hide.

Suddenly, you are jarred into immediate cultural confusion when Omarion's "Touch" begins to play over the speakers.

Why?

For *whom*?

Up until that moment, it had been all Sam Cooke and Boyz II Men, and this is something else.

You scan the room defensively, protectively. There is no DJ, so there is no one to blame, no irony to be found. Your eyes meet the photographer's—a middle-aged black man in designer glasses, wide-leg stonewashed jeans, and a fedora. He's standing next to his assistant, someone who looks like the girl from everyone's high school that was universally beloved for being both popular *and* nice.

The three of you look at each other, point in the air as if the song is playing in the atmosphere, laugh. And then eventually you give in, take the chorus together, insert the right choreography at the right time.

> *We cannot lose, just let it touch*
> *(Touch)*

For the first time that evening, you find overlap that isn't forced. A sameness that isn't just for show.

But there's another person in your periphery. One of the white women from the publishing house watches you with her hands folded neatly behind her back. She's the Noah who saved you from the life-threatening storm of your oppression. The only one with a boat big enough to fit a couple of everything.

She looks happy to see you having so much culturally authentic fun together, and you imagine her congratulating herself in a horrifying internal dialogue. She's gotten all of you here, hasn't she? You're dancing to Omarion under a painting of Langston Hughes, aren't you? This is a win, proof of her progressiveness. She can walk around a room of sparkling clean "BIPOC" and all the other letters that she uses to spell the same word. And you're eating the vegan fried something and telling each other about your very important work that's going to help everyone get free by winning an award and making (us) a lot of money.

You almost want to tell her with a careful knowing and wry grin, "Oh, hey. I'm queer, too."

This is alternative assimilation—a quiet compromise and a wide stance. Both feet in. And you've shown up in Harlem to mingle with the people who know Solange so that you might one day know her, too. To figure out how they earned their connections, their book deals, and their invitations so that you might one day have them, too.

So that you can say, "Wait, wait, wait. No, I think maybe we can fix it with representation and exceptionalism after all. I think social media micro-fame is totally a form of rebellion against the capitalist regime. As long as it's mine, it's justified. If it's someone else's, it's selling out."

And, you *do* want to write the book. You just worry that it comes with too many compromises, too many fake smiles, too many white hands neatly folded behind too many backs, too many personal brands. You worry that you'd have to spend too much time explaining your presence in the room.

And now you're worried that you'll have to write it as her.

But for the same reason you get your hair cut before filming a new video. For the same reason you "accidentally" say Langston's name aloud. For the same reason you don't stand in the middle of the room and interrupt, you'll write it.

You want to belong in a room of people who are going to change the world, who know what they want and how to get it. Isn't this the dream? Where you told your younger self you'd end up someday?

You find the bathroom and lock yourself in, stare at yourself in the mirror, ready for some straight answers. Ask yourself:

Like, is this it?

No, *stop*.

You.

Look at me.

Is this it?

Do you need to be applauded? Do you need to feel special? Do you want them to make you an offer you can't refuse? Is that what you're waiting for?

Is this really fucking it?

You say *progress*, but maybe you mean money. You say *unity*, but maybe you mean money. You say *revolution*, but maybe you mean money. Maybe you always mean money.

Will the money eventually get you to write the book that you wanted to write anyway?

What does the book even mean to you? What will you do to get it in people's hands? What will the gimmick be? What will you edit away that was too much, too soon, not palatable enough? How much money does the book have to earn in order to make you worth the risk? Will it be easier for them to just go with the book that the blogger who kind of looks like you is writing?

How will that make you feel?

Is she a more willing you with fewer run-on sentences and less trepidation?

What if it's not the money that scares you and it's not the money's fault? What if it's not the book that scares you either? What if it's you?

What if you're not ready to admit that you're already selling the identities, but for $45,000 a year and an annual conference in Denver instead of a million-dollar deal and two weeks' worth of vacation selfies in Bali?

You're already doing it.

Not having enough money isn't working. Can't you learn to love the rooms just until the revolution comes?

You're already doing it.

For an ounce more of fame and security, can't you be grinned at and keep dancing through it? Grin back?

Jill, look. You don't stop showing up to the party. That's silly and it's not the point of any of it. Your discomfort, your not knowing what you want, is more about you than anyone else. You don't stop ending up here. Here is where your work is. So you have to learn to trust yourself at the party. You have to know yourself in the room. Then, one day you confess about the parties. You write a book about the rooms that will make the rooms worth it.

You promise yourself in the mirror, and when you're done, you wash your hands. Dry them on your carefully chosen outfit. Return to the party like it's yours.

Fuck 'em.

Dear white hippiecrites,

You're here because you want me to remember that we're all human beings, living under the rule of a few evil men who love money, and when I focus on race, I'm losing sight of the real enemy. And really, we should unite against the capitalist regime and take our power back as a human race and stop being consumer-driven sheeple.

And, I mean, like, sure.
But here's the problem—like, you're so fucking racist.
You're so fucking racist.
And you always want race to be the first exception made in that list of priorities, you know?
So, here's the thing, hippiecrites. Like, I get it.
They're poisoning us and you're racist.
Excess is destroying our ethics and our planet.
And you're so racist.
Yup, me too. I'm a vegan as well.
And. You. Are. Racist.
So I think the question then becomes, like, when do you stop seeing me as a part of a culture that you can steal from to enhance your own supposed enlightenment? And when do you

stop just *backpacking* right through my actual existence?

Let's not play games with each other, hippie-crites. Like, you know, when you come here and you ask me, like, when am I going to see us as a human race?
I mean, like, after you.

[*softly*] As always.

—*Jillisblack*, February 8, 2017

A CONSEQUENCE OF US

I live in my grandparents' house for a year as an adult, in the add-on bedroom with the thick burgundy carpet and the king-size bed. In that room there's a walk-in closet filled with extra decorative pillows, holiday gift bags, broken things too expensive to discard, and dead insects. Holy and hanging on every soft-pink wall is a cross or a Bible verse, written in impressive calligraphy and hung with multicolored pushpins. This is my grandmother's way of reminding you that Jesus is hers.

Sitting below the crosses and calligraphy and sinking deep into the carpet is a collection of multigenerational furniture. It's so heavy and so settled that it will be hard to move when my grandparents die. I think about this often and feel dutifully guilty, as if it's wrong to remember that one day they won't be around. As if death is more untrue for them than it is for me or anyone else. As if the things we refuse to say aloud don't exist.

My grandfather is a deep rich brown. He loves Cadillacs and most gender roles. My grandmother is inexplicably pale. She loves indulgence and being sick. Together they love "get rich quick" business offers and Blue Bell buttered pecan ice cream. I know very early on in my life that they aren't like the grandparents from television or the books my mother reads to me at night. I know that they're mean. Their house doesn't smell like fresh-baked cookies *or* a pot of greens and their hugs aren't warm. But they do love Jesus. Jesus seems right for grandparents—even if my grandparents' Jesus is a bully who hates tomboys and loves new outfits.

That year, my grandparents call me instead of Him whenever they need something. They drag the *J* and the *i* of my name out across re-laminated floors and down hallways until it reaches my room from wherever they are in the house. By that time, the last half of it is always drowned out by the echo of the first half, over time making me miss the harmony of the double *l*'s at the end.

That year, I am called to fix uncooperative remote controls for uncooperative new televisions. I temporarily repair the printer that my grandmother uses for the weekly Bible study class she teaches at the nursing home. I spend hours on the phone with various customer service departments and order her the anti-aging face creams and the jewelry sets from the Home Shopping Network that she claims to need. I send new cell phones back to Consumer Cellular because the new ones never work right and the old ones didn't either.

It's the television's fault. The printer's fault. The phone's fault.

Strange.

Sometimes my grandmother calls me into her bedroom to try on clothes that she doesn't want anymore. I sit on her bed and listen to her tell me how much every item cost—again—as she covers me in a pile of Chico's women's petite size 2 blouses and pleated trousers. "I don't have anywhere to wear this now. Because you know at the new church, people can wear jeans and everything. You know those white folks don't care about clothes. Oh, and here! Take these, too. I got this set in all the colors they had because I liked it so much."

"You needed all the colors, huh? Just like . . . all of 'em?" I say from underneath the pile.

"Yes, Jill," she says. "I did."

"But you don't need them now?"

"No, now you need them."

My grandmother was once a teacher in the Oakland public school system. "I only taught in the flatland schools, you know, because that's where they needed the most help." Now, she thinks she's rich, watches Fox News, *Judge Judy*, and the Trinity Broadcasting Network all day from a couch where her small body is permanently imprinted into the cushions. She makes crude jokes when she thinks Jesus isn't listening, forgets to hide sometimes, forgets to be scared. She can't hear anything you're saying, refuses to wear the special hearing aid that cost more than the others. She says it makes everything too loud.

My grandmother remembers everything she wants to remember and discards the rest in prayer. She tells stories of the students from her classes in Oakland. She laughs at their reading levels and their sleep deprivation and the premature wisdom of forgotten children, forced to age right up out of their own bodies for survival. "Honey, those mothers could've done better. There's no excuse. And the children?" She slaps the table, shakes her head. "Some of them didn't want to learn. You couldn't do anything with them. They wanted to be on the streets like the parents, you see. And I would grab one of them by the coat—and honey, it would be so dirty I'd hate to do it—and I'd say, 'If you don't get your little criminal butt in that chair!' Sometimes, honey, I'd have to threaten them, because that's what they knew." She shakes her head again, then bursts into terrifying laughter.

I listen to her stories and I think to myself, "Jill, is this you, too? Are you more like her than you can see?"

I don't think so. But I can't figure out how I could've escaped it all.

Often some reminder of separation is necessary to sustain the black middle class, which is flimsy and circumstantial and unstable. The black middle class comes with lots of different identifiers and status symbols; there are many different ways to perform it. The most important thing is to know exactly which performance you can achieve from where you are and what you know. You try to spare yourself the embarrassment of thinking you're pulling off one performance only to have the people you believe are *your* people tell you that you're not one of them at all.

They think it's sad that you believed this lie about yourself.

Strange.

Or maybe hilarious, sweet. And sure, they'll point you in the right direction if you ask. They'll say, "I think that's actually your group right there. Just take the stairs down a little bit and make a left." You've just become their reminder of the separation they've achieved, and because you have your own reminders, you know exactly how little they think of you.

My grandmother uses the Oakland public school system as her reminder of the separation she achieved. She uses the mothers who worked all night at factories and the mothers who were neglectful because they were so busy self-defending and the mothers who did sex work to provide for their children as her reminders. She always mentions the one who would "do that kind of work" all night and drop her child off every morning. At first, my grandmother tells the story like she's championing the plight of the black woman, a life of always having to reach for what you need. But eventually, she just laughs. This mother will always be the butt of an untold joke. My grandmother thinks she's performed her way out of a type of blackness that is a punishment. A type of blackness that is sad.

Hilarious.

She could get away with being herself by buying herself out of accountability. For the black middle class, good parenting can be replaced by class ascension. So my grandparents paid for private schools and Cadillacs from the white dealership and lived as far in the hills of Oakland as they could afford. They bought an RV. My grandfather worked at General Motors and had a janitorial business on the side. My grandmother shopped at I. Magnin, enjoyed her evening screwdriver before bed.

Isn't this how the white people do it? Don't white people buy things, take things, and hide from their children? Don't white people act first, apologize never? Anything white people do first, the rest of us get to do next . . . right? A middle-class motto of "If it can't be good, at least it can be white."

But you don't shed blackness by shedding black culture. You simply end up like a black Russian doll, undressing out of yourself into infinity, always further within yourself to go. Either lost or found in self.

I live in my grandparents' house for a year, walking back and forth between my add-on suite and the office with the leaning filing cabinet, the old encyclopedias, the laminating machine, a closet of my grandfather's rarely worn clothes and photo albums with fading frills overflowing from the sides, and the drawer of blank cards and stickers. A room that smells of the 1970s, of overcompensation, of parenting better in photos than in practice, the glorification of the past. When I walk through the mostly carpeted house—a long walk, a long house—all the furniture makes noise, exhales in response to my steps. Nothing is balanced. Everything is made vulnerable by my presence.

In the office, my grandmother sits at the desk, recording all the paid bills on a sheet of paper, no wig, glasses low on her nose, draped in washed-soft cotton pajamas. When she speaks, it's in the dialect of the snobbish, judgmental black matriarch that we've romanticized. Maybe out of our own desire to escape the responsibility of kindness. Maybe because trauma made romantic allows us to still be in love with our community perpetrators. We shape them into types and defend the types instead of the people.

In the beginning there are more of us. There is a great-great-grandmother. There is a great-grandfather and great-grandmother. There is a great-uncle who is a professor, head of a black studies department, lives on a farm. My grandmother's brother. The one person besides herself that she can't ever stop talking about. He wears a cowboy hat and talks loudly, confidently. He calls my grandmother a *schoolteacher* on purpose. Tells her with a smug smile that it's okay that my grandfather didn't graduate from college, because he's so industrious. Good with his hands. A hard worker. His sister is his reminder of his achieved separation. But over time, people begin to die and take their side of the story with them. Lies get stronger in the one-sidedness of history recounted.

I live in my grandparents' house for a year and my grandfather and I don't talk much. He knows me more than she does. Not better, just more. People tell him things that they won't tell her. He knows bigger secrets. Sometimes we look at her and laugh. Neither of us feels guilty about it.

He likes to talk to me about the money I make when I get booked for a speaking engagement. It's not often, but it's usually enough to last me for a couple of months when it happens.

"They pay you that just to go up there and run off at the mouth, Jill?"

He means it in earnest, so I respond, "Yeah, they do."

He's kind of proud. I know because he says, "Well, alright then. That's not too bad."

"Nah, it's not too bad."

"How long you reckon you can do that job for?"

"I guess I can do it for a little while, Papa. But eventually, I'll have to do something else. I can't stay on the internet. I want to write a show or a book or something. Plus, it's not really a job, so . . ."

"Well, that's alright. That's alright."

"Grandmommy thinks I'm saying racist stuff for money."

He laughs. "Well, that's alright. As long as it's for money."

My grandfather is different from my grandmother. He loves money but not elitism. He likes when people are good at things without thinking they're too smart. He wants you to know that you aren't better than him and that he can tell when you think you are.

Sometimes he likes me.

I live in my grandparents' house for a year, with no job and no plan. But I could feel something coming. I was so sure of it that I wasn't even embarrassed to tell people that I was living in a room in my grandparents' house in Alabama, in a town I know better than any town in the world—buying my groceries at the Kroger twenty minutes away with twenty-dollar bills from my grandmother's thick billfold and the remaining money from my annual Black History Month gigs.

"Your event sounds great. When is it?" I'd respond to emails, already knowing. Already quite certain.

"Oh, it's in February!"

But because I'd almost exclusively offered up my blackness but not my gender or my queerness to popular media for money, I had a long off-season.

Black History Month was everything.

I live in my grandparents' house for a year, happy for months. I was reading every book about ego and consciousness that I could safely charge to my Discover card with the five-hundred-dollar limit and upload to my Kindle. Books about ego and consciousness written by people who had ended up exactly where they wanted to be, but then found themselves somewhere else. Spiritual teachers and former millionaires who had given up everything they knew for the pursuit of something more infinite. A God that isn't given. One you have to seek within yourself.

Because I had grown so used to a comment section, it was a relief to be called out on all my bullshit in such an intimate way. In my grandparents' extra room with the soft-pink walls and the sinking furniture that will be hard to move.

I still make Jillisblack videos in my grandfather's workshop because I'm not ready to let go of the ways social media has changed my life. Because I don't know how to live without the granule of micro-fame, the validation of likes, the heart emoji.

It's frustrating to feel happier without it and still think I need it.

My grandfather finds out that I'm filming in his work-shop. One day he says to me, "Go out there and see if what I did works for that stuff you do on your phone."

In the shop, he's cleared out a space in the corner, hung a piece of drywall to use as a backdrop, moved a lamp and a chair in front of it.

I go back inside and thank him and tell him that it's perfect.

"Alright then. No big deal. Just took me about a half an hour," he says.

I live in my grandparents' house for a year, sad for days at a time. It would catch me right away, in the morning. I would know. It would take me over, talk to me in a condescending voice. "This whole place is doomed and there is nothing to look forward to. There is no impact big enough, and let's be honest, you'll never try anyway. You're scared and lazy. And look at you now. You can't even get out of bed. So weak that you can't even not be sad. Your ancestors didn't die for you to be *sad*. You must be one of those new blacks with the curated Instagram pages and the time for long captions. The new blacks stuck between generational goals, nestled in the reality of what they were supposed to want, in on a secret about what happens behind the closed door of capitalist progress but keeping quiet about it. You're weak. You're complaining about other people's problems. You're everything you critique. A moron. A traitor. Just as judgmental as your grandmother. Just as much talk as your father."

It would talk to me for two or three days at a time. And then one day I would wake up and forgive myself, remember myself, know myself again. I didn't know what to do with that other Jill, so I'd pretend not to know that she'd be back. Or sometimes I'd pretend that I knew the door she entered from and that I could close it whenever I wanted to, with enough green juice and exercise. But then I'd wake up on a Wednesday or a Saturday and know I'd awoken repossessed. "Good morning, you fucking hypocrite. What will you not be able to do for yourself today?"

I live in my grandparents' house for a year, in the moment. When I wasn't temporarily absent from my body, I was remarkably present in it. Rigorous in my seeking. If the books told me to breathe, I breathed. If the books told me to go sit in the forest, I would drag a lawn chair over the short bridge as my grandparents watched, confused, amused. I would sit in the middle of the trail that connects my grandparents' house to my aunt and uncle's house, across from a clearing in the woods where the birds would congregate for gossip and berries, and I wouldn't move. The trail that had not been made when me and my cousins were kids. We had walked along the street, enticing the cars with dancing and noise, unconcerned with consequences, in the moment.

One of the books suggests that I turn off most of the lights and stare at myself in the mirror until I start to feel disconnected from my body, from this reality. This feels important, since I had started being banished from it without warning. So I try it—once. After a few seconds in the near dark, I scare the shit out of myself with my own eye contact. Never try it again, decide it's less important than everything else because it isn't as easy as everything else.

It is from my grandmother and her fear of my queerness that I ever began to see it in myself. The way that I know it's real is that I can't hide it from her no matter what I do. Growing up, I watch myself carefully, try to adjust accordingly. But she knows anyway. She says I should be carrying a purse. I should always swing my arm in rhythm with my steps when I walk. It's more ladylike. I shouldn't be wearing jeans. But my girl cousins wear jeans, so I know it's just me who shouldn't and I know why. There's something suspicious about just *me*. And I shouldn't bite my nails either—it's masculine. Everything about me that's masculine is my mother's fault.

When I'm eight or nine years old, I figure out that people think that a lot of things are my mother's fault. This doesn't make sense to me, because my mother's smiles are real and she doesn't ask me to do anything ladylike or be anything I'm not, other than a little more quiet on Saturday mornings. She's funny and I can tell that she doesn't take any shit, so I don't either. She listens to me when I talk. She gets her hair cut into her signature short style at the barbershop, but sings Dianne Reeves songs while she sits on the couch and combs out my hair in our tiny living room. She buys me stonewashed jeans and on Fridays I get to rent a movie at Movie Gallery and sometimes—if it's payday—we get Little Caesars pizza. I love payday. I know that it's just the two of us and even though it doesn't feel like anyone's missing, everyone else can only see my father's shadow. I know that because she is a single parent, nothing counts. We don't count. Everything good about us is the result of something that should've never happened.

I live in my grandparents' house for a year and, once, I invite my future wife to spend the night with me in that room with the thick burgundy carpet and the king-size bed. I tell my grandmother that I have a friend coming by to see me and she'll leave late, out the back door. My friend and I are just working on a writing project together. No big deal. When she arrives, my grandmother spends an hour showing off her shelves.

In the living room that was once the carport, my grandmother has four rows of shelves where she displays family accomplishments—graduations, cars, vacations, old and new houses, certificates of recognition, photos of all of us when we're looking our most traditional or our most attractive. The only way you're described is by what you've achieved in capitalism or in class performance.

My uncle has the most real estate on the shelves because he's the most desperate for family approval and because he buys the most stuff. He has two sons but supports only the one who's desperate for *everyone's* approval. My uncle is always lonely, so he requires a lot of cheerleaders, flashy titles, and large suits. He talks a lot, makes a lot of promises, gives a lot of speeches, goes to a lot of events. Then he heads back home to sit alone in his big, empty house where the roof leaks and nothing is *quite right* up close. He sends my grandparents articles about himself filled with lies that they know are lies. They frame them and rest them on a shelf with the others.

One time he asks my grandmother to put me on the phone so he can get the number of a rapper he's heard I now know. It's the first time he's asked to speak to me in my entire life.

I manually drop the call.

I live in my grandparents' house for a year and one time my grandmother says to me, "What do they call you? Jill is black? Now why would they call you that? Since when are you black, honey?" She laughs and laughs and laughs. She smirks, loves and hates me in equal measure in moments like this. It's her way of reminding me that she's been here longer than I have, has seen more and less than I could ever imagine. We sit at the kitchen table, the seasonal plastic table cover noisy and sticky beneath our arms, and she laughs as I talk about us now. *Us.* Black people now. I update her on the trends, the news, the way we talk.

She says, "That's what y'all are doing, huh? They were doing all of that when I was a girl. Guess y'all think everything y'all do is brand new, don't you? Y'all trying to figure out how to be what you already are, huh? Well." She throws her hands up. "I guess you can't figure out anything else to do but be black. Honey, don't you already know you're black? The only people confused about it is y'all."

I can't deny it.

I live in my grandparents' house for a year and one day I find a Consciousness and Transformative Studies online graduate program. A school in California, of course. A school where I had done a semester and two days of law school years ago. Seems like a sign. The website uses all the words from all the books I'm reading day and night—the luxury of time, few needs, and my grandparents' house. I tell my grandmother I'm going to grad school so that she'll stop worrying that I'm a loser and so that I'll get a break from worrying that she's worried that I'm a loser. When she asks what kind of program it is, I lie to her and myself and stay intentionally vague. "Like, spirituality," I say. "Religion?" she asks. I nod, shrug. Sure, why not? What difference does it make? What harm does it do?

She starts to cry, calls my aunt on the phone at her office, tells the receptionist it's important. "Honey, you won't believe it! Jill is going to seminary school!" A blessing. Thank you, Jesus. She knew all along that one day it would happen. She knew that if she kept praying, I'd accept Him into my life as my one and only savior. Jesus knew, too. He always knows, and that's why they're friends.

In January, my grandmother gives me $100 and tells me to go buy a dress for my cousin's wedding. Well, first she gives me a $50 bill and I shake my head, remind her that I'll need shoes, too, of course. Or else I can't go. She says, "Yes, that's right. Because I've seen your shoes." She laughs and hands me another $50. The next day, I go to the thrift store and spend $15 on a mid-length black dress with long sleeves. When I try it on—which I do at home and not at the store because I don't quite care if it fits—I look like I'm in the "Addicted to Love" music video and everything about that is just right. Next, I go to the Dollar Store and I buy a pair of shoes that feel like they're made out of black construction paper, a two-pack of stockings, a brush. I proudly pocket the remaining $68, feeling like a winner.

The wedding is better with an edible.

There is a white minister from a campus church who reads everything from a book that might be the Bible. There are no vows, no stories told about how they figured out they were meant to be. There are no secret smiles, no tears, no nothing. He just reads from that book that honestly is probably the Bible, asks them to repeat a few lines back to him, and it's over. And when it's over, I feel victorious. Filled with righteous indignation.

There I am in that living room with all these people who believe that marriage is sacred and the kind of love I've found can never be sacred.

But I'm not done yet. I want more.

When it's time for the bouquet to be tossed, I already know it's mine. I fight for it because I know they don't want me to have it. And when I get it, I laugh and bow dramatically. "Thank you, thank you!" I proclaim to the people there who aren't my family. The ones who don't know that I've ruined it. I wanted to ruin it, show how silly all of it was. The pretense and the promises, all the things that it meant to be married. The way *marriage* was just a word for a kind of adulthood that so many people choose.

I catch the bouquet and it's a bit of a disaster. The whole family knows I'm queer, yes, but they ignore it. I ignore it, too, for all the things it isn't worth having to finally say. Yet we all know that there's something about me—more things than one—that make this ridiculous. My family is traditional, respectable, following along behind the others, careful not to get too lost, and I am too lost. What I am is too far.

In the middle of someone's speech, my grandmother walks over to the piano and begins to play—loudly. My cousin panics, widens her eyes at my aunt.

"Mama, get her," she says desperately.

When my aunt is finished sitting my grandmother back down, they all have a laugh at her expense, and

I hate it. And I hate that I hate it. I spend the rest of the evening by her side like she's mine more than theirs.

I live in my grandparent's house for a year and in February I get married at a courthouse in Atlanta. The next morning, I drive back to my grandparents' house and respond, "Not much," to my grandfather when he asks what I did in the city. He knows whatever I say is a lie, but he doesn't say that. He just smiles, "Alright. Well, grab me the trash can out of your bathroom. Man comes tomorrow to get the trash."

He looks tired. My grandmother is worrying him, staying up all night looking for ways to sleep. I don't think I owe him anything, but I'm not quite sure.

I say, "Papa, do you have time to play a game of dominoes later?"

He smiles, shrugs, "Well, let me see. I've got to finish my yard, but after that I can probably beat you once or twice, ol' Jill."

I nod and go back in my room to get the trash can. By the time I return he's already forgotten that he's asked for it.

In that house, scriptures hang from the wall, the calligraphy menacing, a reminder of the black people they had fought to be. The black people with enough money to blow. Enough money to go to the white campus church thirty minutes away, enough money to talk about how black people need to do better, know better. But not enough money to desire freedom. Not enough money to not spend a significant slice of their time reminding everyone that they have enough money. Not enough money because there's never enough money and they don't have enough money to know there's never enough money.

I live in my grandparents' house for a year. It is a reminder of all that is sad and strange, hilarious and sweet. Separate.

A consequence of us.

DEAR YOU
(My Favorite Cousin),

There is a long house on a narrow street that winds tight around the trees that make for quiet neighbors, whose shadows stretch across the pavement like needy children begging to be held, and shade the threshold of a freshly mowed lawn, the crumbling concrete of a wide driveway, the edge of an increasingly false reality.

This is the house I know better than any other house in the world. The only house I will never be able to leave behind. Even when I leave it behind for the last time, finally meaning it for the first time. My picture still hangs on the wall, my image nailed through the fading wallpaper right next to a heavy interpretation of Jesus.

More trustworthy as a memory than as a reminder.

At least for now.

In this house, there is a room that I make mine for a year. But for a number of Junes, Julys, and Saturdays, many years ago, it was a room made for trying out discouraged things and trying not to get caught, the ears of the grandparents proving to be much less sensitive than the ears of your jealous sister and the mother she'd run to go tell.

You, cousin. We were the last two girls born before the boys started marching their way into existence, one after the next after the next in a single-file line, bringing with them significantly louder summers and the kind of cruel competition that is meant to mimic masculinity, prove it to someone.

We were born just months apart (you first) and made natural best friends by both choice and convenience. Our names were always paired, joined together in others' speech as naturally as the people they named.

In this room that was once ours, there are permanent stains on the carpet from the times it had no choice but to absorb the mishaps of our insatiable childhood clumsiness, all the spilling over and falling down. The lamp on the heavy dresser that sits underneath the window has a broken knob and we will always be the only witnesses to its final turn.

We spent our childhoods together making up stories for ourselves and for our dolls (you only had Barbies, and I only had Kens), making plans for who we wanted to be when we finally got old enough to decide for ourselves, making fun of the grandmother who was always making fun of us first—for our weight, our skin, our interests, our sins. We weren't old enough to make excuses for her, so instead we made jokes at her expense. The laughing made us feel powerful, the protagonists in our own fictional world. A world like the ones we saw on television, where brave kids win against everyone who wishes them harm. All the returning villains.

On television, there's always a villain, so having a villain is normal. The grandmother is the villain who wants to drag us back to Earth and spoil all the fun. That's normal.

We stay up until morning watching all the shows we're not allowed to watch and take turns standing guard at the door for when the grandmother decides to catch us in the act of being sinfully interested, lectures us for over an hour about the danger of seeking outside information, reminds us that Satan loves curiosity.

It's the door through which he enters the soul.

But we get older and Satan starts knocking because there is suddenly nothing more necessary than outside information. He's in the unmentionable details and shocking revelations of the aging that happens in private. He's in the tension that has started to underlie our conversations about boys, friends, proms, popularity. He's in the way the grandmother likes to pull one of us aside to tell us what the other has said. Asks if we know for sure that we can trust each other, after all.

The competition that we've always found ourselves in, fueled by dueling adults and the bets they placed on us to win, fueled by symbolic success and the price of its many secrets, fueled by gender and its role models, becomes all that there is between us.

Your parents are doctors and they never had to be anything but doctors. There are no requirements, no standards, no expectations from our grandparents because the doctors have done their part to make the family different, better. You and your siblings were sheltered to show that you could afford to be, so no one was allowed to mention it. How you didn't know how to answer the phone or go in the store to grab a loaf of bread or socialize without arranged activities. Your whining, crying, begging, failing—it was failure. Which is okay. Though we called it being spoiled, which isn't. And when you failed, you were reminded that you were the children of doctors, better than other black people whose parents had other jobs. Better than your cousin who didn't have a father. Better than the black kids at your church who went to the local public school with other black kids. Better than anyone who didn't have a pool. And when we fought in the summers, tired of all the free time and tired of each other, you would quickly make me your reminder of the separation. My mother may like me and we may have fun with each other and we may go to the museum on a Saturday with a packed lunch and a half tank of gas, but your parents are doctors. And the doctors don't have to like you.

And besides, everyone knows I like girls.

We don't have time to stand guard for each other because we're too busy learning how to do it for ourselves, against villains we never saw coming.

The year I live at my grandparents' house, I barely see you. When I do, you romanticize my life now. You need me to be the one who's okay. Need to make living unrealistic, something that only a few of us will ever get to do. I shake my head at this familiar game. I'm too old for it now. Not a teenager anymore. Too much has happened. Too much hasn't happened yet. Instead, I try to tell you that sometimes I'm sad and that the social media popularity isn't what it seems. The followers? Single gram of micro-fame. I don't know how I'm going to pay my bills and I don't know what I'm going to do with my life, and social media moves quickly, won't last forever. I have to *do* something. Look at me. I'm right next door to you. We're kids again and adults now and we're both right here together. It's not so funny anymore, the chaos that adults make. It looks different from inside. And some days I can't even open the blinds, stare at myself in the mirror thinking, "This is it? This is all you have for me?" But your reality is reinforced by your fantasy of mine, so you say, "Yeah, but . . ."

I am tired of *yeah, but*s and I am tired of fantasy.

We used to laugh about coming from a family of liars. A family whose social status is more supposed than actual, the illusion of it sustained by new furniture and old shams. But it's an illusion we think protects us from something. If we are believed to have enough money or education, a respectable-enough job or family, maybe we stay safe from the realities our grandmother says we can't handle. The ones she says aren't ours.

You get to believe in it more than I do, because it's pretending to believe in you. You weren't saved from the narrative by being the child of its underdog, an outlier. Yours was supposed to be good, right, better. So you never got to question it or see it as unfair, and you never had to fix anything that was broken.

Even through it all, even though you've stopped returning my calls or wanting to know what I think, even though the grandmother says the two of you have started to get very close, actually, even though I have become more circumstance than choice for you, there are still moments in that room—maybe on Thanksgiving our junior year of high school after we've been ejected from the formal dining room for laughing through the group prayer—that we are the protagonists, the brave kids.

There's the time you fall asleep with the news on and wake up to the sound of our phony uncle's voice on CNN, claiming that black people should be more concerned with silver rights than civil rights. We're in that room in the long house when you tell me, and I say, "No way!" and you say, "How could I even make that up?" and we both laugh until we cry, because of course. Of course he said it.

But then we get even older, and there is nothing under us to absorb our outcomes anymore, no one to laugh at except ourselves, nothing to blame on Satan.

For the year I am there, you are right next door. In the room that has almost always been yours. In the house that *you* know better than any other house in the world.

I can't make you text me back. I can't make us friends again. I can't make you want to visit me in that room.

I mostly see you if I need tampons and can't afford them. I cross the bridge and walk through the forest that sits between the grandparents' house and the house that you know best and ring a doorbell I've been ringing ever since I grew tall enough to reach it.

I'm always excited to see you, hopeful that this time you will surprise me, invite me in.

But every time, you meet me at the door, and there we stay while you cycle through your comedy routine about being a terrible cousin and an awful friend, before quickly sending me back through the forest and over the bridge with twenty or so assorted tampons wrapped in loud pastel-colored plastic. Loud familial silence.

In the house, there is still a grandmother and a grandfather. The grandmother still has her mind, and the grandfather still has his body. The grandmother still has her long-term memory, and the grandfather still has his part-time job. The grandmother still holds grudges, and the grandfather still holds his tongue. With age, their survival has become a joint effort, a group project with a major deadline. But maybe that's all it ever was.

We used to know who they were. We used to laugh at how far everything had gone, how unhappy they all seemed, how ridiculous we looked in our caps and gowns, sitting side by side on a shelf of grand spectacles.

We weren't supposed to take this on, continue it. We were supposed to know it well enough to disbelieve it, run from it.

The essay about living in that house for a year is how I'm saying goodbye to the narrative I know best. The room, the grandparents, the aunt and uncles, the cousins. All of it.

I don't want to lie and I don't want to compete. I don't want to repent for sinning in public. I don't want my picture mounted on a wall of unearned sacrifice.

The grandmother keeps asking me what the book is about. What I possibly have to say that's worth people's money, interest, time.

You and I used to be bound by all the things we couldn't ignore about that house, that narrow street, that false reality. So I'll tell *you* instead. Write to you out of everyone, because you are the only one I'll miss when the truth that we used to know, together, becomes mine alone. And you can be the witness to that cycle—the one

where we name a family problem and inherit it out of
fear—as it takes its final turn.

Love,
Jill

FLY HOME

I'm in Philadelphia to moderate "A Conversation on Race & _____." I touch down, take a Lyft to the hotel, talk to Marcus in a Black Infiniti QX60 about our '90s R&B favorites, know that I'll make him laugh if I mention "Last Night" by Az Yet, mention "Last Night" by Az Yet, laugh with him, arrive, tell him that I had a good time talking to him, too, check into the hotel and find my room on the fourth floor, choose to sleep in the bed closest to the bathroom, grab my phone, learn the hard way that it's *just a little* too late to still order Uber Eats, berate myself for eight to eleven minutes for not thinking to do it when I was still in the Lyft talking about Brian McKnight, console myself with thoughts of all the food I'm going to order the second I wake up, text my mother, unpack the basics from my backpack, lay them out on the extra full-size bed, remember that I have an apple in the front pocket, eat the apple while watching two episodes of *Catfish* on the hotel television, scroll through social media and get very mad at a person I follow but don't really know for disagreeing with me about something people disagree about, throw my phone on the other full-size bed, turn off the TV, try to remember why I'm so mad, remember and get mad about it all over again, brush my teeth in the stark white bathroom, stare at myself in the mirror, pull the shower curtain closed so I can see my hair better, have a fight with myself as if I'm both me and the person I don't really know who made me mad, win big against the weak arguments of my own reflection, get back into the bed I chose and turn the extra pillow sideways, turn off the lamp and reach for my phone in the dark, realize that it's still on the other bed, say "Fuck" to an empty room of myself, tell myself that I don't even fucking need it, accidentally think about social media and get mad again, say, "Fucking shut up about it already. We get it," to an empty room of myself, twist, turn, consider grabbing the phone, decide against it, try to fall asleep for two hours, twist, turn, try to wake up for three hours, notice that it's suddenly one hundred billion degrees in the room, walk over to the wall unit and turn on the air, grab my phone, check social media, feel anxious, remember that I can order Uber Eats, order Uber Eats and start to feel a little better, consider posting online that I'm in Philadelphia, decide against it, watch a marathon of *Cutthroat Kitchen* until Uber Eats arrives, walk down to the lobby in sweatpants and a coat I wouldn't have packed had I anticipated the heat, avoid as much eye contact as possible, retrieve two bags of food from Yvette, thank her, make my way back to my room with the two bags of food, open the bags and spread everything out on the desk so I can see it all at once, put half of it in the fridge and tell myself not to forget it when it's time to leave, sing three words of "I'm So Excited" for an audience of only myself, eat the other half of the food while watching *House* on mute, drink the carrot juice I ordered to feel like a lifestyle coach, text my mother, scroll through the notifications on my phone, scroll through the notifications on my social media, watch a video with a million views of a child hitting an adult in the face, scroll through the ten thousand comments, ignore the ones about how the child deserves what she has coming to her, ignore the ones about how she's a grown-ass woman trapped in a little girl's body, ignore the ones about how it would be kind of sad if it wasn't so funny, feel unsettled, throw my phone on the extra full-size bed, watch an episode of *Law & Order: SVU*, feel unsettled, mute the TV, call my mother, talk to her about how much I hate social media, listen to her tell me I don't have to do it, hear what I want to hear because I called to complain, hang up and look at the clock, take a quick shower under a weak stream of lukewarm water, get dressed, pack the basics back into my backpack, tidy the room, take a selfie, request a Lyft and make my way down to the lobby, spot Luis in a silver Dodge Durango and wave, listen to Luis sing Ariana Grande as I watch Philadelphia through the window, arrive very early, thank Luis and tell him that he has a beautiful voice, sit in a park for an hour watching people push strollers, walk over to the museum, meet the contact person and follow them to the room where the panel will take place, meet the panelists and listen to them talk about what they have in common, moderate the panel, finish and wonder if I was the best choice for the job, feel guilty about never being as "Jillisblack" as people are expecting, feel angry that I feel guilty for not being a 2D image of myself that lives on the internet (but only after four or five takes and a filter), thank everyone involved and request a Lyft, get out of there as quickly as possible, look outside for Meredith in a burgundy Ford Flex, spot her parked across the street and run to catch her before she leaves, throw my suitcase in the trunk and say a winded "Hello," spend the ride in silence, arrive, thank Meredith, grab my suitcase from the trunk and head inside, remember too late that I forgot my food in the hotel fridge, pull up my boarding pass on my phone, wait in line, show my license, take off my shoes, closed-mouth smile at anyone I make eye contact with, get patted down, find the one available electrical outlet at my mostly empty gate, plug in my phone, remember that I have work in the morning and set my alarm for 6 A.M., check Instagram, sigh.

Fly home.

Dear black revolutionary internet intellectuals,

Yo. Like, eventually there are only two answers. It's racism or it's self-hatred. It's *racism* or it's *self-hatred*. It's not really that complicated. And you can keep writing all of the things and saying all of the things, and when someone critiques you, you can do that thing where you bring up all the white schools that you went to and all the white publications that published you and validated your super complex feelings about racism and solidified your intellectual wokeness—which, *yeah*, totally a thing. White validation will always point us in the direction of revolution. I agree with you. *And* I think that you should continue to rely on the very systems that you're critiquing to explain why you're qualified to speak. *And* I think you should continue pretending that you can both separate yourself from black people and defend blackness. *And* I think that you should continue making money off of it, too, because what's a bigger motivator to fix a problem than to make money off of the problem existing? Like, what can go wrong there?

I'm even trying to think of an example of when exploiting black people for money went wrong for black people . . . Let me think of it.

Hold on.

. . .

I'll think of something.

—*Jillisblack, January 15, 2017*

THIS IS HOW IT STARTS

When they ask you how it starts, you know they don't mean the part that happened at Highland Hospital in December 1986, when your best friend birthed you into the world—or at least into a town called Oakland—and gave you your first and middle and last names.

Your father wasn't there, so neither his first nor last name appear on your birth certificate. You know now that your mother used to jokingly refer to him as "Mr. Withheld," among her friends. But never in front of you.

In front of you, he was named only by the position he still refuses to fill.

She was careful about him then. Not for his sake, but for yours. The first years of your life, you have no idea that fathers are supposed to be any different from the one you have, so yours is perfect.

Fathers are supposed to come around once in a blue moon with two other kids you don't really know but who are suddenly supposed to be your older brother and sister, because that's what your father does. Fathers are supposed to run your bathwater too hot and leave you (alone) in the tub to go talk on the phone, because that's what your father does.

Fathers are supposed to be a special occasion, because that's what your father is.

When you're four years old, your mother moves you both to Alabama because she needs to raise you somewhere else. Somewhere slower but with longer days. Somewhere more affordable than Oakland already isn't in 1990. You try to miss your father but you don't know how to do it. Missing him is what reminds you that he exists at all. How do you miss him differently from that? From farther away than never close?

When cable television and public school have forced you to trade in the comfort of your own fallacies for the pressure of the collective ones, you have no choice but to start asking questions. You gather up the courage (or the necessary disappointment) to want to know him beyond the character both you and your mother have created in his place, the cardboard cutout of him that by now is so bent out of shape that it can't even stand on its own two feet. And you don't want to spend your entire life propping it up just to see its face.

So you broach the subject while sitting in the passenger's seat of your 1987 Chevy Nova, the beige fabric hanging from the ceiling and framing the back seat like stage curtains. You practically have to beg her for this part of the story. You have to tell her that hearing the excuses is finally getting harder than knowing the truth, but you say it with the less practiced language of a second grader whose face is always partially hidden between two signature braids, and behind a giant pair of gold Nickelodeon-brand glasses.

She tells you the stories about him that could be more helpful than harmful. She tells you the ones where he's smart or funny. The one about how they met. She tells you that you have his nose. That you can draw because of him. She gives you a version of him that you can see yourself in. She saves the rest for later. Maybe some parts are saved still, either forgotten or for what.

Alabama comes with humidity and hurricanes, Confederate flags and college football, chicken-finger chain restaurants and packs of chitterlings on sale two for one at the big Winn-Dixie in Opelika, an aunt and her husband and their kids who live forty minutes away.

The water bugs scare your mother more than the flags, the food, or the family.

In the beginning, you move from one apartment to the next to escape them. At least, that's what you gather from what you know about her and from what little you know about the world. Because you don't really know about money the same way you don't really know about fathers, you don't know how much you don't have. But you know that not having a lot is something you should probably learn to lie about if you don't want to get made fun of at school or at your aunt's house.

You know that you don't have a tape player in the Nova, so you can't choose your music. You think that maybe having money means the same as getting to choose. But until you have it—until you're rich from being a famous actor or a local doctor—you can only scan the FM stations in an endless search for something that isn't country or gospel or static, especially when there's nothing around you but tall trees and trailing kudzu. And because the options are limited, you have to know how your mother feels about every song—new or old. She keeps saying to you, "I like *talent*, Jill. Skill. That's why we mostly keep it on 104.1" (Jazz Flavors), whenever you forget and make the mistake of asking her why you can't listen to what everyone else is listening to.

You end up knowing more smooth jazz than any other kind of music, but you learn to lie about that, too.

She tries for you sometimes. Especially on Fridays after work, when she's sighing a little less from all that must be done to make do and due dates. She turns the station to 105.7 and waits for them to play the first song after a long commercial break.

And you wait, scared to even sing along to the first round of the chorus, because you know she won't last long. Even while basking in the warmth of an upcoming weekend, she can take only so much noise.

"Oh no. Uh-uh," she always ends up saying. "We can't do it, Jill. That music is made to destroy us. Seriously, Jill. They want you to think life is about money and partying and disrespecting women. Is that what you want life to be about?" Thankfully, she doesn't expect an answer. She just turns it back over to Jon Lucien or Gato Barbieri, and the sounds of Catalina Island roll in like waves from the speakers.

It's also why when your mother gets the black Saturn and the black Saturn has a tape player, you can listen to your Tevin Campbell or Brandy tapes. Everything else is for your room.

Anything by Immature is for your room.

The Shaggy "Boombastic" single cassette tape is for your room.

"That's why we got you the headphones, Jill," she says.

Even though it stops you from being as cool as some of the kids in your school who know all the words to all the popular songs, it also makes you want to know your own taste in everything. You want to know what you don't like and why, and how to explain why as well as she can, as passionately as she does. Developing language around liking things seems a lot less interesting, and you want to be interesting because you like being noticed— especially by adults.

Even by your grandparents, who by then have moved from California and into the house next door to your aunt and her husband and your cousins, and already started stirring the pot that promises to one day boil over, start a fire.

When your grandmother moves to Alabama and sees how close you are to your mother, she becomes particularly fixated on wedging her way in between. Intent on exposing your mother to you as someone you may not know as well as you think you do. She tells you that mothers and daughters shouldn't be best friends. She asks if your mother has been taking you to church. She asks you if you've spoken to your father. She calls him a mistake and you feel an unfamiliar urge to defend him, but only as a way of defending your mother.

They ask you how it starts, but they don't mean the creative writing lessons or the acting camps or the art classes your mother saved or shifted priorities to pay for, drove from work to pick you up from.

She would make dinner in your small apartment kitchen, still wearing her shoes and purse, singing the memory of the last song she had heard as she poured the required green vegetable from a can and into a one-quart pot with a missing lid.

Your mother has books everywhere. There are the thick green-and-black law books that she says are filled with things you better learn something about fast if you're black and broke in this country, like us.

You're glad she knows what's in them so she can know for both of you.

There are books displayed on the coffee table, crowded onto the rows of the bookcase you helped her put together—the one that arrived in a box at the door of the new house she buys in rural Alabama when you're seven and she's twenty-eight.

There are books on her pressed-wood bedside table with the beige tablecloth from Kmart, and yours with the navy blue one, too.

Every night before bed, she makes you scoot over and she reads to you. When you're younger, you choose *Berenstain Bears* or something from the *Just a Little Critter Collection*. You like the illustrations of the animals, the anthropomorphism, the idea of learning enough lessons to be considered good.

Sometimes you choose your favorite book about a black girl your age who *also* just has a mother. Or another about a black girl who doesn't appreciate the dress her mother sews her for a party because she wants the one her mother can't afford instead.

These lessons are harder, closer to home.

Later come the fiction books about enslaved children and girls who *also* don't hear from their fathers. There are illustrated versions of simplified Shakespearean plays that she got from Alabama Shakespeare Festival in Montgomery. You take day trips there on the weekends and random federal holidays, bring lunch from home and sit in the grass with the ducks. You walk around the museum and look at the pictures of the actors performing plays in the theater down the hall. The one that's so grand and dark and exciting that you almost can't stand it.

You tell your mother that you want to be an actress or a writer or work in a school cafeteria because you like pretend and books and food.

She starts letting you make your own lunch and she takes you to see *Malcolm X* at Carmike Cinema. When you get home, she shows you his autobiography in the bookcase, opens the cover and points, says, "Your name is right here. All the important books are already dedicated to you. They're yours."

She pulls *Invisible Man* from another row of books, "Especially this one," she says. "This one is going to be important to you one day."

She takes you to see *Panther*, buys the coffee-table book about the making of the movie, buys the soundtrack and plays it for months on end. You love it because it's the only time you can get away with listening to so much rap at once.

She takes you to see *Philadelphia*, too. Even though your head barely reaches the top of the reclining seat, you eat your gummy bears quietly and pay close attention.

When your teacher frowns, asks why your mother would take you to see "those kinds of movies," you understand what she means, so you tell your mother, and she writes your teacher a letter, volunteers to come talk to the class about black history and anything else your teacher is uncomfortable addressing.

"We're in Alabama, sweetie. We have to make sure they know who they're dealing with, don't we? She'll be fine. And if she's not nice to you on Monday, you tell me, and I'll have a talk with your principal. But she'll be nice. Trust me," she says, resolute.

You learn that whenever your mother is resolute, she's also psychic. When she's braiding your hair before school and she's telling you how she envisions your life as you grow older, you trust it. You head straight toward it like it's been predetermined by the stars.

One morning, after hundreds of slightly revised versions of your future predicted, she sees you going to college in California, writing books, changing the world, and you suddenly have a favorite.

When you're seven years old, you come out to her for the first time. You say it simply, because to you, it seems simple.

"I like girls."

Your mother says, "So, you think girls are pretty?"

And you say yes.

She tells you that it's okay to think that girls are pretty and asks if there's anything else you want to tell her. But there isn't, because first you need to figure out if you think girls are pretty or if it's something that might not be as okay.

So you wait.

She dates very little in front of you but tells you funny stories about men she has dates with sometimes, the ones who will never make it to meeting you. But then there is one who seems the readiest and the least threatening. The one who knows well enough to tell you that he's going to propose before he does it. Knows that you need to be there when it's in the idea stage.

You never actually grow to like him, but in the beginning he's okay enough, you guess. You're more curious about the new lifestyle that the marriage promises. With him around, there's suddenly more indulgence and excess. More eating out and more outfits, bigger vacations and a bigger house. Eventually, another room for another kid.

When you're nine years old, your mother picks you up from school and hands you an envelope. You open it quickly, excited to see a card, hoping to find money inside. But nothing falls out when you shake it, so you move on to reading it. This is how you find out that your mother is pregnant. A card congratulating you on getting to be a big sister.

But who the *fuck* ever asked you? Where was your warning, the request for your input when this was in the idea stage?

You rip up the card and scream at her about how much you hate it—all of it—and it feels good to try out rebellion. It's a new kind of release.

Your mother allows it for a while, tries to tell you how she understands, and you carry on, ranting and raving, just to see how far she'll let you go. Just so you know for the future when you need to rebel again.

When she finally says, "Okay, Jill. Now wait," in that way meant to remind you that's she's different, but not that kind of different, you find her limit.

You mark that spot.

Your mother lets you choose his middle name. "Christian Slater" is one of the coolest names you've heard by the time you're nine years old, so Christian it is. Your brother arrives in July 1996, just like he was always meant to.

Becoming his sister is one of the most important things you ever become.

In a way it all starts when you begin to perform being funny in public and in public school, because it's important to you that you be impressive, do your part, hold up your end of the bargain you were always making with your mother.

It was as if the two of you were always silently promising "You do your best by me and I do my best by you, got it?"

But then doing your best gets complicated because all your crushes are (still) on girls. And doing your best by her begins to mean lying, but you never want to be the one who doesn't make good on your promise.

It's not that you think your mother will have a big reaction or take badly to the news. It's more that you don't want to alter her expectations for what your life will be. You don't want to surprise her.

In school, you can't quite figure out how to be both yourself and everyone else, too. Get what you want and get what adults want for you, too. So you stop trying.

You can't explain why your mother seems relieved when you start caring less about grades and more about figuring out what you believe in, how those beliefs will shape your life. She shows up to parent-teacher conferences, obviously excited to tell them how much she doesn't give a fuck what they think of her child, but in the language of a woman with a lot of debt from law school and a low-paying nonprofit job. Her sentences are short and to the point. She returns all questions with questions. She rushes them through their answers.

She's on her lunch break. What else?

"Maybe you're the problem," she says, straightening her blazer, "Maybe it's not Jill at all. Maybe it's your class."

She seems way more excited to defend you than she ever did to see your outstanding report card. You change schools—and teachers—a lot. She is almost never satisfied with what the school system or the after-school program or the world has to offer you. She wants everything to be better than it is, as good as she thinks both you and your brother are.

In high school, you do nothing but start drama and join the club, because by now you care only about world peace and the girls you have crushes on, the ones you write about in your diary. Three or more times a week, you update a nonexistent reader on how many words each crush has said to you that week, desperate to tell someone who gets it.

You wear your giant political buttons—the ones you pick up at protests and political potlucks organized by the mostly white and performatively multicultural Unitarian church—pinned through the rough, multicolored fabric of one of your many Baja jackets. It's probably the jackets and the tie-dye T-shirts (the ones your mom's friend from Oakland taught you to make when she visited for a week over the summer) and all the hemp jewelry that earn you the title of "Most Wanted by the Fashion Police" in your unofficial senior poll. But you don't mind. In fact, the title is the point.

You spend most of the day hanging out in the nooks and crannies of your school, talking shit with your friends and avoiding class. But you never miss your curfew at home once. You still help with your brother and you still clean your room after only two asks from your mother. You would still rather be at home, talking about the world, than in the world, talking about home.

Even if it turns out that your stepfather is more threatening than he originally advertised.

He's brought with him a world of screaming and threats and cops and sudden change.

You want to believe in good and bad because you believe you're good. But your stepfather makes it impossible. You have to learn how to live with a character you wish you could understand more. You want to know what he thinks he's defending himself against. You want him to make sense. But he doesn't want to.

So you do the work of forcing yourself to see him as complicated. You come up with hundreds of different explanations for him. Make him into a hundred different people. Learn to believe that you like some of them as a way of making life easier.

Becoming someone who would eventually gain a moment of micro-fame on social media might have started when your mother learns of a mismatched caravan of old southern activists who are heading up to D.C. to protest the war on Iraq. She says to you, "I know you have school, but let's be honest, you're not doing anything there. And this is school, too. So you should go. I think it'll be good for you." And you know that she must be worried more about your restlessness than about her paranoia to even suggest it.

You go and going changes your whole fucking life.

The first leg of the trip is from the church to Huntsville, where you will join the people who have the van big enough for everybody. You drive there after school with a British woman who teaches English at Auburn, and that night you both stay at Steve and Mary's house. It's a predictable old bungalow with rainbow afghans draped across every piece of aged furniture and a record collection so massive that its stacks have spilled into the unlit fireplace and stayed long enough to gather dust.

You sleep in their thirteen-year-old daughter's extra bed, and all night long she tries to talk to you about bands you've heard of but don't want to talk about, and her mean friends from school, and what you like to do for fun.

In the morning, you are more ready for the road than ever.

The caravan of eight picks up the last person in Knoxville. Someone your age. He has a lime-green mohawk and tells you before you can ask that he's an anarchist. You have to pretend you know what that is, because asking questions is still something that embarrasses you, and because you have a feeling that he likes to give a long answer to a short question.

You have Indian food for the first time in Virginia and stay awake to keep Steve company as you finish the drive into D.C. You sleep in a hotel room with eight other people who, like you, think they have all their own ideas. In that moment, your ideas agree and it's a massive relief—the first moment of relief from shared ideas that you ever have.

You agree that you want peace on earth, equal rights for all, an end to corporate corruption. You want people to invest in love and freedom and hope instead of domination and greed. You don't know if you disagree on how to get there, because you don't talk very much about how to get there. Only where you need to go.

You look around the room and feel alone with yourself in a way that you've never felt before. It's not lonely. Just new.

The next morning, you lose yourself in a crowd of protest signs and alternative aesthetics, and it feels so good you want to cry. You walk the streets of D.C. and try out being this version of yourself that you think just might be your entire self forever, in person.

When you get back home, you tell your mother all about it even though you've had to call her at every stop you've made, there and back. You know it must cost a fortune because you aren't calling after 9 P.M. or on a weekend, and no one you know is really texting yet because it's way too expensive.

Your mother tells you that you seem older, and it's still your favorite compliment to have received.

When you get back to school, your science teacher, who doesn't like you—who knows you're not taking anything seriously—asks where you were and why she should let you do the makeup assignments. You don't really care to do them, so you tell her the truth. That you went to D.C. to protest the war because your mom says it's just as important as school.

She smiles at you like she's seeing you for the very first time, grabs you by your shoulders like a coach, cheers.

"That's *it*! That's the real stuff, Jill!"

And this time you smile, because you're seeing something about her for the very first time, too.

She allows you to do the assignments you missed and never unsees you again. So you finish out the rest of her class by taking it seriously. This is the kind of bargain that you know and respect, so it's easy to honor it.

One weekend, your mother shows you the undergraduate catalog from the weird school in San Francisco where she went for law school and you walked across the stage with her at graduation. She says that it's for people like you and you don't know which "like you" she means, but you know she's telling you to *run*.

To go be yourself somewhere farther away, for longer.

New College asks for transcripts but the admissions office informs you that good grades are the very least of what they want from you—which is good, because you don't have any good grades to give them. Instead, they require a five-page answer to the question "How do you plan to change the world?"

Happy to finally be asked, you finish it in an afternoon, write about how you will use your acting and your writing as tools. People need to be *convinced*. The people trying to change the world for the better need to make what we believe in seem like the only option, the only solution. A real no-brainer.

Don't you have to sell it if you want other people to buy it? Don't you have to make them need it?

And when they send you your acceptance letter and you know that you're leaving Auburn, Alabama, for San Francisco, California, in the fall of 2004, you're too overwhelmed to be excited.

Also, there's a girl that you found on the internet. You talk to her every night on the phone for hours, and lying to your mother makes your body feel less hospitable, your stomach less accepting of its contents. So when she finds you crying on your bed with the door closed, your first instinct is to eject something vital.

"What's going on?" she asks in that voice that means you better tell her before she gets too worried.

This time it's hard. You recognize the tone and what she expects, but this time you can't. You don't know how to make it come out of your mouth.

"Jill."

It's a warning.

"1 can't tell you," you say with your head between your knees.

"Did someone hurt you? Are you pregnant? Wait, Jill, are you on drugs?"

"No, none of those things."

"Is it about a boy?" she asks.

Instead of the vomit you were anticipating, the truth makes its way from your gut and up through your lips and you say, "It'll never be about a boy."

And even in the moment you think to yourself, "What kind of fucking Lifetime movie, *The Truth About Jane* shit is this?" and you wish that there was someone to watch this happen, to laugh at the parts that aren't funny to you just yet but will be later.

"You like girls?" she asks, looking at you through narrowed eyes.

"Yes! Yes, I like girls."

She nods for a moment, then promptly slams your door, manages to shock you even more than you've shocked yourself. Because no, you never planned on telling her, for reasons you can no longer remember, but still, you thought that maybe . . .

But then you hear her footsteps making their way back to your room. She swings the door open and walks over to you and it happens too quickly for you to even consider the options for what might happen.

"Jill, I thought something was actually wrong. I thought it was something *bad*."

She's mad that you would scare her, and you tell her that you were scared, too. She gets yet another reason to demand more from the world on behalf of her kids, and reasons were the last things she needed.

When she drops you off at the airport in the fall, waves as you make your way toward the security line, she's the saddest she's ever let herself be in front of you.

It's an affirmation you never knew you needed.

*

NEW COLLEGE SCARES the shit out of you because something feels eerily the same.

You thought you'd finally be an insider. For once, a part of a welcoming majority, united by an overwhelming desire to right the wrongs of greedy white men in suits, fight the good fight.

But in a school full mostly of white people with radical philosophies and acid-birthed solutions for someone else's problems, you feel more outside of a culture than you've ever felt, the only one of everything, always raising your hand to point out what's missing from the conversation, but also being enough of it for them to feel like it's there.

Eventually, you start taking pleasure in interrupting their theories with personal experiences and points of reference that they couldn't know or disprove. Being outside becomes useful. Being the only one with a first-hand account makes you an indisputable source. An expert.

You get used to that feeling.

You take a class called Writing Well I and have a writing teacher (New College doesn't call them professors) who gives you a B on your first essay. And as someone who has barely graduated from high school out of an utter lack of interest, you can't explain why you care. Why it's suddenly not good enough.

But also, you can. Because you want to be the winner this time. Now that it's *your* stuff, you want to be good at it.

For the next essay, you write about your roommate at Ansonia Abby—the student housing facility you are living in since New College doesn't have dorms. All the students from the fashion and language schools live there, too, making for the kind of diversity that no one means.

Your roommate is from Japan and she is in San Francisco to learn English. She shows you pictures of her boyfriend, brings you bananas from the cafeteria when you decide to sleep in. She is neat and considerate, and so are you. You say "Good morning!" to each other every morning and "Good night!" to each other every evening after she kindly asks you if you're also ready to turn the lights off. Even if you aren't, you say yes and go to bed, too.

One time she asks if you will help her review for a test, and it's the most you ever talk. The next day, she leaves a piece of chocolate cake she bought from the bakery down the street on your dresser, along with a thank-you note.

In the essay you describe the bathroom you share, the hair products, the clippers you use to shave your head,

her Herbal Essences rose-scented shampoo with direc-
tions that you can't understand. She's in San Francisco to
learn English and you're in San Francisco to learn
double-talk.

You get an A on the essay, and your teacher (whom
you call by her first name) pulls you aside to tell you how
much she's looking forward to reading your weekly
assignments.

You're taking an experimental performance-art class,
a class on Freud in the media. You're also taking a class
on revolutionary African literature, but you lose interest
after your teacher tells you how much he paid for his
Italian leather shoes. How he wouldn't be caught dead
wearing anything else.

But that's not the only reason.

There's a tension between the two of you that you
can't name. A tension that you've never felt before with
another black person—especially a black person at New
College. In fact, you are all overly friendly with each
other, winking and shrugging at each other across the
room of white actors and activists.

When you ask questions, he smirks.

When you answer questions, he laughs before he
responds.

When you tell him that your final project will be on
Indigenous Australian culture, he says, "Of course it
will be."

Like you're obvious to him. Predictable.

You never completely diagnose it, but it doesn't even matter. Because suddenly, you care about nothing but Writing Well I and the weekly essays you're assigned. You write each one to the very fullest of your ability. You can't think of another time you've cared like this or when it's meant so much. But she can tell that it does, so she writes you detailed notes all throughout the paragraphs, full-page notes on the back of the last page. She notices almost everything you do on purpose and tells you when it works.

You fall in love with what you can do with an essay. The contradictions you can name without implicating yourself in any of them, the way you get to control the narrative. You learn a new way to sell something.

The final exam—a timed personal essay on anything you want—was exactly how you desired to end the semester. You write and write and you do it joyfully. For fun.

That's why at the end of the year, when everyone who showed up to even half of the once-a-week classes—sometimes literally with a pet macaw on their shoulder or a banjo instead of a book—gets an A, you want to burn the entire building to the ground.

No one would think that it starts when you confront your teacher in the café because you don't know how to stop being angry without an answer.

"Jill, you wrote great essays in this class. But everyone was trying their best. It wouldn't be fair to give you the highest grade if everyone was trying their best. Don't you want them to feel encouraged?"

It'll be a full decade before you write another personal essay, and you never write to the best of your ability at New College again. You don't have to. You get As with minimal effort so that no one feels like they're re-creating the patriarchy.

You are taught by alternative capitalists, egalitarian egomaniacs, and old-school hippiecrites with time to spare now that some time has passed. Many of them are desperate for the good old days when their gripes were the most progressive, frustrated to hear the language change without them. Angry that they could get something wrong now and quickly become the enemy of the later generations of themselves.

And even though your teachers were educated at Ivy Leagues and are the children of famous writers and actresses, agents and politicians, they have chosen to come teach you the lessons of their heroic half-rebellion. Pass on their politics for the sake of their own personal preservation. They believe that your belief in them and what they believe is what makes you smart. So the trying doesn't quite matter.

They needed Harvard, but somehow you only need them.

And everyone who needs them should feel encouraged.

After you leave the school and return, and even after you leave again and it closes its doors for good—without immediately repaying money owed to staff and students or honoring the agreements of its own ethical framework and without a real apology for its incongruous actions—the obsession with spotting anyone and everything that isn't who or what it claims to be, that doesn't live in complete agreement with who and what it says it is, intensifies. It started within your own family, for your own protection.

You don't want to get burned again. Not even by yourself.

So you begin to see your own contradictions as weakness, develop a fear of finding out that you're not who you think you are and an additional fear of being called out for it by other people.

Maybe it starts with fear.

*

YOU'RE IN YOUR midtwenties when you begin facilitating "cultural competency" trainings with your mother for nonprofit organizations all over the California Bay Area. She's the one with the real experience. You've spent most of your twenties working odd jobs and signing on to message boards to earn participation credit for online classes, trying to avoid being a contradiction by not being much of anything at all.

But you have a queer identity and a generational perspective that lengthen the list of training topics and widen your potential reach in a room. So she mentors you, teaches you everything she knows about nonprofits. She teaches you about mission and vision statements. She teaches you about grants and how they fund programming. She teaches you about all the different levels of staff and what they do. She also gives you tips on public speaking, teaches you social service lingo, shorthand.

Your mother is always finding new clients to train and new trainings to give (Culture & Media, Boundaries, Family Advocacy Parts I & II, Queer Advocacy Parts I & II, Conflict Resolution, Home-Visiting Basics, Strategic Planning, Organizational Storytelling & Timelining, Outreach & Engagement Parts I & II, Restorative Justice, Team Building) because she's friendly and relentless, and so you're always throwing on your Banana Republic sweater and your "serious pants" and getting in the passenger's side of your Hyundai Tucson, inching down the congested freeways of progress, surrounded by Blizzard Pearl, Blue Ribbon or Barcelona Red Metallic Priuses (diversity) with Hillary '08 and Obama '12 bumper stickers (inclusion), headed to some training, somewhere.

In the beginning, you're just along for the ride, unconvinced that a training can actually change anything. But all the nonprofit organizations that enlist your services are receiving grant money for working with adopted and fostered children and the stakes are too high.

If you don't take every question from the foster parent who wants to know if she can let a queer child sleep in the same room as the other kids she's fostering, and if you don't answer them in a way that doesn't shame her into shutting down, there's a child who suffers for your apathy, your waste of an opportunity with a person who's asking a hard but seemingly genuine question—the system they're in will impact them whether you believe in its intentions or not.

Yeah, it's all fucked. But you're in the front of a room with twenty pairs of eyes on you and the clock moves slowly. So you might as well try.

You better try.

Together, as the disarmingly weird, multigenerational comedic duo, you and your mother become a team like no other. And it works.

Instead of implicating themselves in the experiences of their token diversity employees, nonprofits hire the two of you as the insider outsiders (or the outsider insiders?) who can affirm and suggest from an impossible distance, take no one's side but the children's. You're there to reinforce the organizational vision, hold management accountable, and strengthen everyone's comfort in working through new or "culturally challenging" interactions with coworkers and clients.

But everyone wants something different from you. The social workers want you to put their supervisor on the spot at least once, make them have to admit to something they've done wrong. Like made an assumption about a client's racial background in a weekly meeting or crossed a boundary with a supervisee during an all-staff training. You know we've done our job when a social worker smirks, raises an eyebrow, hides a laugh, turns to a coworker, and shares a secret smile.

The clinical supervisors want to hear that change starts at the very top. That they're trying to get the job done with limited time and resources and they don't feel heard or supported by the regional director. You know what would also be helpful? A script for how to handle a variety of cross-cultural incidents and staff complaints. They want to know what they can say and what they can't. They want one size to fit all as long as it makes the workday shorter.

The regional director wants the training to check off a few boxes for the old grants and even more for the new ones. They want to hear that they are more proactive and culturally aware than other regional directors. They think it might be helpful to review the mission and vision of the organization, make sure they are culturally current so that they can update them on the website.

You both do it until you can't anymore. Until you don't know what you're saying or why you're saying it. Until your favorite organization—the one that seems most sincere in its efforts, most connected to the work and the clients—closes its doors for lack of funding while organizations that exist only to chase grants thrive.

Until people you train begin to get sick and, without health coverage, die.

Until one of the organizations wins all the grants and expands into communities it knows nothing about. Suddenly it can afford to hire you for every type of training you've got, one at every location, and you can't say no.

Until you think of your mother saying, "But what is the social services incentive to ever solve the problem? They'd put themselves right out of a job," and you can't stop thinking about it.

Until you ask the group with all the money a question, "What do white people offer in a cultural exchange?" and the white queer woman who is a director gets defensive, doesn't understand that it's a trick question designed to make white people admit that they have culture.

"You're saying white people have nothing to offer?" she asks incredulously.

"No," you respond, meaning it. "I'm asking what white people offer—culturally—in an exchange with someone of another culture. When we discussed diversity, people talked about all the language and yummy food and rich traditions people bring into the office and how that benefits the overall culture of the office. Alma asked if tradition is always beneficial, and as a room, we agreed that it's not. Just now, Sam was sharing some of the things he had learned from his travels through Asia and how they had impacted his life. I asked if he felt like he had offered something in exchange for what he learned—which we agreed doesn't always happen. Then

Natalie asked if that kind of exchange should always happen."

"Right. And then you asked what white people offer in return for what they get. And I'd have to say *a lot*," she says, laughs, leaning back in her chair, crossing her arms.

"Great, perfect. Did you want to share some of what came up for you or should we turn it back ov—"

"I'll share. Infrastructure, resources, educational opportunities . . . *um* . . . in some cases, actual money, aid. I know a lot of smart white people who have dedicated their lives to scientific research, public health, helping people. Generous people. Um, teachers."

"And you feel like those things are all cultural? And part of white culture, specifically?"

"What is *white culture*? Why is that so broad?"

"Well, that's what I'm asking. That's what we're trying to figure out."

"I think they're part of American culture, and white culture gave you America. A place where we're allowed to have this training."

You're in shock because she's supposed to think it, sure, but never say it in public. At work. That's not how the script goes. And because she's already gone too far, she keeps going still and ends up saying how proud she is to live somewhere where people care about each other, and other people should be proud, too—even if it's fucked up sometimes for people like her or "you." You don't know which part of you she's talking about. The parts you share or the parts you don't.

Most people disengage, look down at their phones or their laps or a handout. The one black employee starts mumbling under her breath, "Fuck this shit," and the people she works with start to stare at her, and your mother tries to save it by suggesting everyone take a break, come back and move on to a small-group activity. But the room has changed. And you realize that when the training is over, you and your mother will leave and the time some director told you she gave you America will be nothing more than an anecdote, a memory from your training days. Something you remind each other of when you want to get mad for fun.

You don't work there. The stakes aren't as high.

You never return to that office. When you run into the director at the other offices in Oakland or in trainings for upper management, you exchange smiles and leave it at that.

After a few years, the trainings are more for the organizations that like you and want to see you back again, doing something. *Anything.* So there are always new trainings. New topics. Part fours and fives of old trainings.

But Barack is still president. Federally recognized gay marriage is right around the corner. Police shootings are still mostly local news. People need only so much cultural competence when everything is going so well.

Jillisblack and the sub-demographic micro-fame start when you and your mother visit your brother at school in Olympia, Washington, and fall in love with it. The trees, the coffee, the air. The parks and all the available parking. Mount Rainier. You feel like you can breathe. Like there's space for your breath.

The last day of your trip, you sit together at a coffee shop downtown, right in front of the window. You tell her that you're dreading going home. That it feels like you're leaving a new one.

"I agree," she says, casually sipping her coffee like she hasn't already made up her mind. "Maybe we should try it."

A few months later, you do.

In Olympia, your mother is overqualified for every position she goes out for and you get hired only because you're black but also queer.

Olympia does queer. Black is out of its wheelhouse.

So you work as a program coordinator at a small nonprofit for queer youth. Then you leave to go work for a large nonprofit, where you're paid to "do" diversity and inclusion. When they hire you, they tell you that it was a plus that you are black, but also your queerness allows you to do more trainings in the community—which gave you an advantage over the other person they were considering for the position.

You don't actually know how to do anything they're asking you to do besides train, but you know how to interview for it. And you'll do whatever you need to do, sell whatever part of yourself the job requires, because there's rent and groceries and cell phone plans.

You need your cell phone plan.

You're surrounded by trees and coffee and air, but also an impenetrable level of whiteness. And yes, it speaks to you in the grocery store, makes room for you on the trails. Asks you how long you've been vegan and gives you a high five. Sends its "kiddos and doggos" over to say hello to you at the park. It's mostly friendly and so are you.

But at the time, it's also lonely. You feel like a permanent exception, a guest. Forever being asked what event you're in town for or what your major is at Evergreen. You run into people you've met before who either seem scared to say they remember meeting you or genuinely don't.

Because you're lonely, you're on Instagram more than ever. You get high every night and follow everyone that you wish you could hang out with in real life. Sometimes they follow you back. The more followers you gain, the more likely they are to follow back. And the people you follow, follow each other.

For once, you're not the only version of anything that you are.

These strangers you share identities and interests and musical taste and exes and politics and hairstyles with become your community.

A chosen community of people like you from all over the globe. People who finally make you feel like the majority. People who are either in agreement with you or quickly unfollowed, replaced, forgotten about. People you've never met but feel like you already know.

You begin to post a few times a week.

This is how it starts.

[Dear Dad]

Because I found you nowhere
I choose to find you elsewhere
In men whose layers
Have kept me warm in the absence of your
apology.
I will sew a father-shaped quilt
Out of the fabric of these better men
And when it's time
I will pass it down.

Love,
Your Daughter

—*Jillisblack*, June 2017

A FRIEND OF MEN

As always, I am assigned the middle seat on a flight to New York. By the time I find my row, there is already a woman fast asleep in the window seat. Her face is tucked into her antecubital space, and her body is folded into its very smallest shape so as not to disturb anyone. I sit down in the middle seat—24B—between her and the empty seat, and wait. I want to see who else is coming before making a decision about how I will best fit.

When I see him walk up the aisle—early forties, white enough, maybe divorced or divorcing, maybe someone's father—I know it will be him. He's wearing a blue-checkered button-down shirt, relaxed-fit weekend khakis, silver-rimmed glasses on a squarish face. I can't help but notice that he's just a little bit shorter than me, a little bit bald on the top.

I know I'm not supposed to notice all the little bits, because that means I'm looking too closely.

At first, we barely make eye contact, choosing to keep our smiles tight, polite, and fleeting. He slides his smart black carry-on into the overhead bin, points at his seat. My right elbow leaves the armrest, my right thigh slides farther center. My entire body shifts left, closer to the folded woman. I make more room for him than I leave for myself, and when he sits, he stretches out into every corner of it because it's there.

"Hi," I say, dropping my voice, using my countertenor.

He, unsuspecting to the point of insult, stares at me blankly, then says, "Oh, hello."

There is silence for a while, and the occasional apology for any unexpected touching of shoulders, elbows, knees. Then the apologizing grows too tedious and the unexpected touching too expected, so what remains is the silence. As we reach a cruising altitude and the "fasten seat belt" light fades, I turn to him and say, "Do you want to do your own thing, or should we have a conversation?"

He laughs, surprised. Then he shrugs a *Why not?*, turns his body toward me.

"How do we start?" he asks.

*

*

MY MOTHER STILL tells the story, asks if I remember Michael and the preschool teacher who would tell her every day that I was the only one who could calm him, bring him back down to earth.

He is one of my earliest memories. Not of another person, but of myself.

He had all the attention, always kicking and screaming, upset and inconsolable. On the rare occasion that he was allowed to be in a room with the rest of us, it was only a matter of time before he'd have to be picked up and taken out, a bright red emergency. I remember being relieved when the tantrum would finally happen and I could stop waiting for it.

I couldn't figure out why there were boys in the class who could sit still, color, take naps, play games, and make friends, and then there was Michael, who couldn't do any of those things. What was *he*?

Because the other boys were the majority, they weren't all that interesting. Why learn more about them if they already made sense? If their alikeness was already forming a pattern?

Why not solve the difference of Michael and actually get somewhere? Figure out if I was more like the boys who could sit still or if I was more like him?

I already knew I didn't seem like the other girls. But I didn't know why that difference didn't make me an emergency like Michael.

I know there are a number of reasons why Michael was prone to make a scene. But back then, with few points of reference or ways to name what I saw, I found him to be absolutely fascinating. I wanted to understand what I sensed: that he was a small part of a much larger story about carrying out contrary impulses.

I knew I couldn't scream or make a scene like Michael could. But I wanted to know *how* I knew. More than that, I wanted to know why I didn't *want* to scream or make a scene like he did. Why, to me, it felt out of the realm of possibility, and how he knew he *could* do those things in the first place. How he let himself do them.

How I didn't.

I wanted to understand that gap between.

I remember approaching him, sitting with him in the corner, saying nothing. I remember doing it day after day, until one day I started asking him questions—at least the questions I had learned so far to ask (maybe thirty or so, but it was enough)—and handing him toys to try. I remember him trying to answer through the lingering tremors of his last bout, his skin tight from the layers of dried tears.

I also remember the praise I got for my ability to subdue him with my focused attention and how it felt—how powerful I felt even though I didn't yet know the word or my own desire for it. Michael got attention for his outbursts, and I got attention for soothing Michael. Eventually, he sought me out whenever he was upset, exploded even bigger when I wasn't around to ground him with questions about himself.

Michael was the first boy I ever felt responsible for, ever took on as a way of trying to be more myself.

> **Mutualism:** A form of symbiosis that is characterized by both species benefiting from the association.
> **Parasitism:** One organism benefits while causing the other harm.
> **Commensalism:** One organism benefits while the other is unaffected.

After Michael, there was Samuel. I was visiting with my grandparents in Oakland for a couple of months, going to their church down the hill. Samuel was in my Sunday school class. I would go over to his house and marvel at his toys, take the opportunity to play with them without my grandmother watching carefully for signs of what I might be or want.

His toys were hard metal and thick plastic, ramp and pulley, construction and demolition, law and order, fast and flame. On his bedroom floor was a giant activity rug that looked like a town. There were winding roads and stoplights, municipal buildings and trees.

I loved it. I loved anything that imitated real (adult) life.

I liked dolls, too. One time I brought them to Samuel's house, spread them out on that rug and told him he could choose the ones he wanted. He laughed like I was stupid, told me that dolls were for girls, and so I put them away.

We spent the next three hours racing Matchbox cars in circles.

I could do what he did *with him* when it was just the two of us, but he could never do what I did, with or without me, *ever*. No one could see him do it. Not even himself.

Later there would be more and more of these friendships, all made out of the same threads.

There was John the Freshman, whom I am assigned to sit next to when I have to retake physical science my sophomore year of high school. He's the quarterback of the JV football team. Wears camo, jeans with cowboy boots, and—on game day—his blue-and-white jersey. The class sits in three lines of paired desks. I sit next to him and his camo in my tie-dye shirts and antiwar buttons. We don't talk until one day we do, and then we don't stop talking for the rest of the semester, nearly obsessed with our own novelty.

I'm writing a story about a girl who falls in love with a boy she meets in rehab, and every day John the Freshman reads my new pages and gives me feedback. The one time I come to class without anything new, he shakes his head at me, lays the guilt on thick, "This is no good, Busby. I need to know what happens."

When the teaching assistant tries to move us to quiet the constant talking, we're both so genuinely distraught and loud about it that by the end of the week, he's moved us back and warns us that we'll have to be more quiet, less disruptive.

But then John starts dating Jenna, the junior varsity cheerleader from my debate class. They're a hometown tradition, and I'm disappointed that he's finally stopped contradicting himself in such an obvious way.

It's so fucking boring.

After the end of the semester, we never speak again, and years later I find out that he joined the navy, proposed to Jenna in New York, married her back home in front of all their classmates, who also know how to sit still, color, take naps, play games, and make friends.

Even when the boys were called my "boyfriends," they were really just friends. I would choose a favorite, flatter him with my sudden interest, ask him to be my boyfriend. Having a boyfriend meant freedom from being asked why I didn't have a boyfriend, so I was hardly ever without one if I could help it.

Aggressive mimicry: A form of similarity in which a predator or parasite gains an advantage by its resemblance to a third party.

By junior year, there were other things that influenced the way I made my friends. So there was Kahlil. He was secretly gay like me. It was almost all we talked about because it was the one thing we couldn't talk about with anyone else. We would leave debate class to go do "research" and instead escape to the deepest, darkest corner of the library to update each other on everything new that had happened with the people we had crushes on. We would analyze the interactions or lack thereof and decide what we were going to do about it—which, by the way, was absolutely nothing.

We had in common this circumspection, this hesitation.

I was scared of not being liked and possibly being killed for *who* I liked. He was scared of God's wrath and even more scared of his mother's.

*

*

THE WOMAN IN seat 24A has yet to move a muscle.

The man next to me is opening a package of cookies.

I ask him if he lives in New York.

He asks me if I live in New York.

I ask him if he likes living in New York.

He asks me if I live alone.

I tell him that I'm married.

He asks me how long I've been with my husband.

He nods, recovers quickly enough, says, "Oh, I see."

He asks me how long I've been with my wife.

He asks me if I've only ever been with women, stumbles over it.

I ask him if he's only ever been with women.

He laughs nervously. "Yes, yes, yes!"

I don't laugh.

"It's a real question," I say.

He stops laughing. "Yes. Yes, I understand."

A flight attendant announces that they will now be starting their complimentary food and beverage service.

He takes out his wallet.

Tells me he's going to get a beer.

Asks if he can buy me a drink.

I shake my head.

Say thank you.

"But thank you," I say.

I ask where he's from.

I ask if he misses Vienna.

He asks where I'm from.

He asks which one feels more like home.

He tells me he's never been to Alabama.

I tell him it's not for everyone.

He says nothing ever is and I agree.

I ask how long he can stay in New York.

He tells me his job is moving him to Geneva next week, and as he says it, he breathes a sigh of relief. "There are trees everywhere in Geneva. And I will have time to see them. I am excited, yes."

I ask him what he does for work.

I ask him if he likes it.

I ask him what else he does.

"I want to retire in five years and study baking, pastries. Then I want to open a dessert shop."

He asks me what else I do.

I tell him that I'm working on a book proposal.

He asks me what the book will be about.

"No matter what I say it's about, it's actually about me being scared. Of other people, of the internet, of trying too hard. Or it's about power. How we make ourselves feel powerful when we don't feel empowered."

> **Batesian mimicry:** A form of biological resemblance in which a noxious, or dangerous, organism (the model), equipped with a warning system such as conspicuous coloration, is mimicked by a harmless organism (the mimic).

He nods, doesn't say anything, stretches his legs, sips his beer.

"I took an edible," I tell him for no reason.

"Ah, good for you. I just do alcohol."

He reaches for the *Sky* mag, flips through the pages back to front, stretches his legs, sips his beer.

Then he asks, "Do you feel like you have power?"

"Over myself—so yes. Over anyone else, no. But I try anyway."

He looks at me like, *Say more.*

"It's hard. I feel most powerful when I feel like I'm being myself. But I don't even try to be myself in public. Like, the idea of going out into the world as just Jill scares the shit out of me. So I'm always a little bit in character. And that character feels more powerful than I do."

He nods, smiles.

"I'm not sure that other people often feel like themselves either—even these people that we're supposed to think are so powerful," he says.

"Do you feel like you have power?" I ask.

He thinks.

"Well, I don't know. In this country and where I come from, too, I am certainly given a lot of power."

"Do you have power that you didn't get from someone else?"

"Yes, sure. But I'm talking about power in the . . ."

"In the society?"

"Yes, in society."

"In society I have power that I get from other people, too."

He looks at me like he can't tell if I'm serious.

He asks, "What is your character like?"

I laugh. "Funny. Dry, you know. Unimpressed. Kind of . . . removed. Unemotional. Hard to know. She likes to dominate conversations because she likes to convince people of how smart she is. How she can't be tricked."

"Are you sure she's not just you?"

"Of course not."

We laugh.

The flight attendant interrupts us with the offer of coffee or water.

"Coffee," I say.

"Coffee," he says.

"Black," I say.

"Black," he says.

The steam dances—coffee too hot to drink—and we sit in a preferred discomfort, a learned compromise.

When the plane lands and the flight is over, we exchange email addresses, hug at the arrivals gate.

"I hope you do well with your book," he says.

"I'm going to write about you."

"I don't believe you."

"You'll believe it when it's true."

"Maybe not even then."

"Oh, *there's* your real power!" I say, and we both laugh.

Leave it.

*
*
*

THREE HOURS AFTER I land in New York, I find myself at a trendy restaurant with a rooftop bar with a group of a certain kind of friend.

Jillisblack makes different kinds of friends than I can. So I am now friends with the kind of men I couldn't have met without her. The kind who knew me as her, first, and think they are getting to know her better whenever I show up as myself, instead.

They wanted the outdoor seating, and the table is too small for all of us. It's also the only one available, so we try to make it work. I sit wedged between Shawn and Louis, their after-work biceps wide and imposing inside summer-tight short sleeves. There's also Jared and the two Kyles and Marcus. We are all black, a few of us queer, but I am the only woman at the table. And I notice because I have learned to notice something I am when I am the only one of it.

Shawn was the first friend, and still my favorite. Successful, late thirties, charismatic, and flirtatious, an underdog done good, a black man in a suit on Monday and a jersey on Saturday, good-looking to enough people that it had become a relevant identity, all dressed up as himself with somewhere else to be.

He knows it. He does himself as an act. On purpose.

I like the on-purpose of him and he likes that I've noticed what's on-purpose about him, so we're friends.

"Jill, you still vegan?"

"Always."

"Alright, well, look. I'm sorry you can't eat any of this good-ass food. Kyle, are you getting wings, man?"

"Yeah, man. And probably, like, let me see . . . probably the plantains. I really don't need all that shit, though, man. I'm in Thailand next week, but I'm thinking of doing a juice cleanse as soon as I get back."

He caresses his torso, reassures himself.

"Oh yeah? My homie—you know Calvin?"

"Yeah, I know Calvin. That's the dude who's got the movie coming out, right?"

"Yeah, the documentary. He's a director."

"Yeah, Calvin. I know Calvin. He's a cool dude."

"Yeah, Calvin's a cool dude."

A table leaves, another is seated, the waitress is back with waters, drinks, ready to take our order. She answers all the questions, substitutes all the sides, says, "Yes, we can do that," smiles, nods, turns, smiles again.

"Jill, you saw *Homecoming*?" Kyle asks.

"The Beyoncé thing?" Marcus asks.

"No, it's not for me," I say, and brace myself for the . . .

"Is that even allowed?" the other Kyle asks, smiling, amused.

"Not at every table, no," I say.

"Why isn't it for you?"

"I'm just not a Beyoncé fan."

"I'm about to call every black woman I know and tell on you. That's what I'm about to do."

Laughter.

"Do it," I say, "so I can tell on you to every black woman you know, too."

Shawn looks at me, wants the real answer. "You don't think she's important?"

"Everyone's important," I say.

He waves his hands, rushing me to it. "No, for real."

"So you don't think she's a feminist, huh?" Louis asks.

"I'm more concerned that I can't say I'm not a fan without inviting that question. Years ago, when I could say that I wasn't a fan without inviting that question, *that's* when I was kind of a fan," I say, laughing.

"Are *you* a feminist?" Shawn asks.

"Are *you*?"

"I think men need to reevaluate our masculinity, for sure. And I think women are incredible. I think they're smart and capable and strong, and I think we, as men, need to be listening to y'all right now. I think rape culture is out of control, so . . . yeah. I'd say I'm a feminist. I'm not perfect, but I'm trying to learn how to be a better man."

"A better man or a better feminist?" I ask, sipping my water.

"I mean, shit. Both, I guess. Same thing, right?"

Later, after he declares himself a feminist who wants to be a better man, I watch Shawn walk by a woman at the bar, touch her, rest a hand on the small of her back, turn her around, lean in. I watch him tell her that she's beautiful. I watch the hand not move.

I wait.

I ask myself, "How does this work?"

I watch him begin a conversation with her. There is talking and smiling and I don't get it. What does this mean? Do I not understand something about straightness?

What if she and I don't agree about what a woman should want done to her body? Do I not get to say what a woman should want done to her body? Is attempting to do that inherently antifeminist?

Whose agenda wins here—mine or hers? What happens when we don't agree? Do I go with what she thinks or what I think? What if we don't want the same thing or we do, but we think there are different ways to get it?

What does feminism do in this moment?

In the meantime, how should I feel about him?

When I do it, when it's me at the bar—leaning in—how is it different?

Is it different?

And when it's me at the bar, with a strange hand resting on the small of my back—how is it different?

Is it different?

I've read articles about men and what we should do with them/about them/without them, where they belong, and what they deserve. I've taken classes and considered so many crowded intersections that it eventually led me to a crossroads.

I've been touched without an ask and I've been chased down a street by a man whose advances I refused. I've had my life threatened at home and on public transit. I've been the victim of circumstances I was warned about by matriarchs and media my entire life. I've been wrong about men and wronged by them, too.

Also, I've been believed in by men, helped by men, heard by men, seen by men, held accountable by men, loved by men.

There are men who are some of my favorite people in this world, the kind of human beings I'm so glad to have found on this planet, to know in this life. Not despite what they are, but because of who they are.

There have been moments recently when I've told other friends or people I've dated or strangers that, often, I find that my most intimate friendships have been with men, and they've looked at me like I am fighting against myself. Like I need to work through something—a trauma, or an unclaimed identity, or the absence of my father.

But because women casually share articles on how to stay safe while in a parking lot or at a party or while walking down the street or riding in an Uber or in a public bathroom or at school or while sleeping in your home or whenever you're around strangers or partners or family, and a number to call when he loses his job or when he drinks too much or when his team loses the big game, I know where the look is coming from, why the intimacy is a surprise.

Because I am a friend of men, I have also had to ask myself some questions. Questions about what I'm like now and what I would be like with different options, a bigger allowance.

I have to ask myself: What if I could build a world that protects me from my own insecurities? Makes everything I think and do the most important thing to think and do? What if I could believe myself more worthy of life and choice and time and understanding than anyone else?

Would I be him instead of me?

Is this why I've forgiven him instead of holding him accountable?

Am I me because I can't be him? Or am I me because I don't want to be? Because I never want to be doing the most I can get away with?

I have to ask myself the questions: Haven't I figured out a million ways to be forgiven? Haven't I tried to build a world that protects me from my own insecurities? Haven't I tried to make everything I think and do the most important thing to think and do? Haven't I believed myself more worthy of life and choice and time and understanding than other people? Not out of my identities, but out of my own fear. As a way to feel more powerful.

Sometimes we protect parasitic men by pretending there is a benefit, mutualism.

Sometimes we protect men who are obvious emergencies. The ones we allow ourselves to feel responsible for, take on as a way of knowing something about ourselves.

Sometimes we protect them out of closeness. Because we like or love them. Because we knew or know them.

Because the one we love—the one we thought we knew best—is the entitled one, who stopped doing what he *should* do to do what he's allowed to do instead.

Sometimes we protect ourselves from the inconvenience of hard decisions, conversations.

*

WE'LL BELIEVE IT when it's true.

Maybe not even then.

Dear black people,

Why do we care? What are we trying to prove to them? Why are we engaging in a 24/7 dialogue with white people and calling it self-love? Perhaps white people still know more about what we're capable of than we do.

Because here we are in a constant state of "Look, see, look! We can run, we can read, we can swim, we can think, we can go and do and see and be! Hey, white people! We told you, didn't we? Look! Please look at us so that it counts, because it doesn't count unless you're seeing it. We must prove everything to you because you are the standard. The call to our response. And we're a desperate, grinning version of whatever it is that you think you are."

And it's kind of weird, isn't it? They used to keep us in their game with threats and violence. Literally enslave us in it. Now we run back to it and call it success. Achievement. It's an accomplishment if they want us. We've worked side by side with white people to reshape our black reality into something sharp around the edges. This way, we can remain scared of stepping over what is immediately visible and into a version of ourselves that is more than race, rhetoric, rage, and reaction. Even better, when one of us is brave enough to endure the sharpness and attempt the unknown, we can call it a cultural betrayal and drag them. Back.

And yet.

We used to escape deep into the woods—the twisted darkness of southern expanse late at night—hoping not to get caught. Now we're even deeper in the woods in the middle of the day, praying that they discover us. That they notice. Waiting for an invitation to our own self-hatred, asking, "What took you so long? Why didn't you notice me sooner?"

—*Jillisblack*, September 20, 2017

FLOWERS FOR THE BLACK ARTISTS

in which the liberals, through their foundation, choose eight artists to retreat for a week on the coast in two four-bedroom houses.

in which the (nice, rich, white) liberals, through their (nice, white, liberal arts) foundation, choose eight (black) artists to retreat for a week on the coast in two four-bedroom houses.

in which the (nice, rich, white) liberals (colonizers with a heart of gold), through their (nice, white, liberal arts) foundation (tax shelter) choose (gift as a charitable deduction) eight (black) artists to (receive money/time/opportunity/access) retreat (passively network) for a week on the coast in two four-bedroom houses (off-season Airbnbs).

Of the eight (black) artists, two are writers.

I am the one who writes essays (about being black).

The other writes screenplays about (black) kids who are (also) robots.

The screenwriter, the painter, the muralist, the illustrator, the actress, the performance artist, the mixed-media artist, and the essayist.

> *The black artists are here doing the black arts, remember?*
> *Oh, that's right, that's right.*
> *They're artists.*
> *That's good, that's good. Okay, good. Good for them.*

When I arrive, I am assigned a room in the blue house—the one closer to the shops but farther from the ocean. In my room, there is minimal furniture. A twin bed with a nautical throw pillow, a blue-striped wingback armchair, a wooden bookshelf filled with white classics and a dutiful show copy of *Beloved*, the pages still crisp and tidy, unturned. In front of a large bay window, there is a writing desk, and on that desk there are blue and purple begonias arranged in a glass vase. Tucked underneath the vase is a small white envelope, a card inside that reads:

Jill,
Before the masterpiece, we must master peace! We hope you enjoy your time here, and that it inspires within you a willingness to be great!

I rest the card on the desk, sit on the bed, call my mother to let her know that I've arrived, wonder if all the artists got the same flowers or if mine were individually chosen. Like I was.

*

THAT NIGHT, WE are all welcomed to the coast by a man from the arts foundation. He smiles when he talks, apologizes for things that don't matter. We offer back to him things he gave us in the first place—a seat, a plate of the catered food, a bottle of water. He says he just wants to get out of there and leave us to it, whatever it is, but he'll see us on Saturday for the community Q&A.

"The people who live here are so happy to have you, and they're very excited to hear all about your art," he says.

> *Jill, we can't wait to hear all about how our racism influences your art.*
>
> *If you make us feel guilty enough, we'll call you brave for your efforts.*
>
> *You can't make us love blackness, but you can make us love the way you use it.*
>
> *How will you use it?*

On the walls are childhood photos of the homeowner's now-adult children. They spent their summers here, their growth spurts recorded on the door frame in permanent marker, meant to stay.

After he leaves, we convene in the yellow house for dinner. We sit around the dining room table with the curtains wide open on a window that belongs to them but is temporarily full of us instead: the screenwriter, the painter, the muralist, the illustrator, the actress, the performance artist, the mixed-media artist, and the essayist.

We squeeze in close, make just enough room for everyone to have a seat. We eat our catered food off their cobalt blue ceramic dishes, drink donated red wine out of their cups.

As it grows dark outside, the ocean view becomes implied, and we become less implied. We are reflected back to ourselves in the glass under the dim light of a low-hanging fixture, more easily seen by the neighbors walking their dogs or walking themselves around the neighborhood. We leave rings of donated red wine on their real-wood tabletop, talk and laugh so loudly that the porcelain teacups and family heirlooms rattle nervously in the cabinet, unused to so much vitality and bass.

We sit on display, swirl the wine, talk about what it means to be black artists (preservation).

They use us, steal our work, force us to compromise.

But how else can we get our art out into the world?

How else can our story be heard?

I mean, we have to do it, right?

Yeah, we have to do it.
It just sucks that we have to do it like this.
It does. It really does.
But it's worth it.
Oh, it's totally worth it.
All we have to do is take the cheese without disturbing the trap.
Easy.

We talk about what it's like to be nice white liberals (speculation). To live in this town without having a real big special talent, influence, or fame. To live here not as a somebody but as an anybody.

Oh, but what's it like?
To be you.
To be black.
Like you.
Write us a book.
Sing us a song.
Make us a movie.
About you.
That's really about us.
And the thrill.
And the bravery.
Of your soulful
Persistence.
We're paying you.

Sitting around that table, we don't talk about *the feeling*.

Instead, we go around the table and talk about the art that brought us to the coast. It seems like, in every case, blackness brought us to the art. I'm so curious about each of us. I'm so curious about us.

We are the chosen black artists.

We are "recently awarded," "semi-influential," "well educated," "sponsored by," "in conversation with," "newly important fresh takes and reverse spins." Here "on behalf of" everyone else. Everyone else who may or may no longer concern us.

We are the chosen black artists, taking up temporary residency in places where white people can afford to slow down, breathe, stay for good.

I listen to the painter, the illustrator, the actress, the performance artist. And when I speak, I sound like everyone else.

I talk in long monologues, answer questions about myself that no one asked. I like for my name to be known, and I like to mention other people's names, too.

I like to tell an intimate story about my personal relationship with a public figure. I like to be given credit for showing/knowing/being/spinning some-thing shiny and bright. I like to be stunning and prolific and devastating. I like to let everyone know that I'm here.

I am the overbearing parent of brainchildren and pet projects. I wax poetic about the black body. I will accept my reparations in the form of recognition. I crave the spotlight and I hope remaining seen can save me. I'll express myself into the great beyond.

If I lived in this town, I would have no special occasion or collective camouflage to save me. There would be no other black person to pay the price for my compromise. No black person who could've easily been me instead. I would be immediately identifiable, the only one mistaking myself for someone else.

And even though I'm not, I tell them that I'm working on a book. What's true is that I'm working my way up to a book, trying to stop pretending that I don't want the things I want. That's why I'm here.

As the next bottle of wine is passed and the mixed-media artist starts talking about making heads from headlines—I wonder what the point of a book would be.

If we could move enough units of something to live here, become a big-enough somebody to feel safe enough, we'd have to live in isolation, away from everything that is ours, the only one or two of something, their reminder of what's out there, what they're rich enough to get away from—with the exception of this one week, this one time.

This is their home.

We are the black artists.

Doing our black arts.

Resting our weary heads and tired minds for a week in someone else's summer hideaway, the black people with the permission slip.

There's an art to getting one, but that's not the art we say we're here to do, because that's the art that makes us feel the guiltiest.

And we're not here to feel guilty.

We're here to do the art.

We don't do it for the money. We don't need the applause. We don't need anyone to notice what we've made. We just want it, that's all. We deserve it, that's all. If we were white, we'd have it already. That's all.

I want it because if I were them, I'd have it.

*

THE NEXT MORNING, I sit in the backyard around the wrought-iron table with the chipping white paint and drink my coffee with the performance artist and the screenwriter. I ask them what kind of flowers were waiting in their rooms when they arrived.

The performance artist shrugs. "I don't remember."

The screenwriter shrugs. "Roses, I think."

They talk industry politics, gatekeepers, people they know who they think can get them in front of the right person.

I drink my coffee and watch them, always happy to observe and archive, until the screenwriter turns to me and smiles, says, "Jill, what are you working on here?"

"Essays."

"Yeah? Cool, cool. Smart."

"Yeah, thank you. You're working on the screenplay about kid robots, right?"

"Well, no. That one is being shopped right now. The one that I'm working on here is about these two friends—one is black and the other one is white. The black friend ends up at an Ivy League, becomes this super successful lawyer, and the white one drops out of high school and ends up on drugs."

"Oh, I see."

"Yeah, and then eventually the white guy ends up on trial for shooting a cop and the black guy takes his case."

"Dope," the performance artist says.

"The ol' switcheroo," I say, sipping my coffee.

The screenwriter looks at me, confused. "What do you mean?"

I excuse myself.

*

LATER THAT AFTERNOON, I take a long walk around town, note the architecture and the tension.

If I wanted this—the big house with the American flag and the tree swing in the small coastal town, I would be jealous of the seasoned air, the sound of continuous disturbance across the water, the nonsymmetrical facades and the steep gabled roofs, the little post office and the novelty shops, the white wine glasses clinking and the loud laughter. I would feel slighted.

If this were it—if the laughter didn't require the wine and the waves on the water weren't a reminder of friction—I would bury myself under all the lives that will never be mine and contaminate the soil with the acid of my blame/envy.

Or maybe I would want to run back to that house that isn't mine either and figure out a way to make the nice white liberals listen to me, buy my book, read my words.

Maybe I would want to sit down at their desk, the sun streaming in through the window and illuminating the dust (dirt, bacteria, pollutants, hair, decomposing insects, dead skin), and figure out a new way to say the same thing about the latest version of an ongoing problem, *speak on behalf of.*

Maybe I would insert myself in their collection, twist and turn the tired themes like keys in the door of a house near the sea where the bones have settled south and been forgotten about and the stench is hidden underneath the pretense, dead fish, and salt water and no one has to admit to anything—with the exception of a small plaque on a side street that sums it all up in a regrettable but ultimately necessary history. I would want to do that, too. I would summarize my regrets with the same words that satisfy my needs.

I would.

But also, I will.

Because I'm here, too.

The old switcheroo.

*

THAT NIGHT, I go out to dinner with the screenwriter, the painter, and the muralist. The owner smiles, waves us in excitedly as we are seated by the host.

The restaurant is located in the renovated home of a sea captain and is a shared-plate dining, cocktails with rose syrup, modern rustic, updated Mediterranean gastropub with sea-and-sand globe glass pendants hanging over each small table from the factory-weathered plank-wood ceilings kind of place.

Twenty pairs of watchful eyes pan, zoom in on us like dome security cameras, capture us from every angle.

They seat us directly in the middle of the restaurant, and while the screenwriter, the painter, and the muralist consider appetizers, I can't help but surveil the surveillants. Notice them notice us out of both curiosity and concern, having vigilance in common.

We sit around that table center stage, faces bobbing in and out of view, in or out of the shadows being created by a precariously dancing flame, and declare ourselves the winners. We don't care if they don't want us here. We don't care because, *goddamnit*, we're here!

We're here.

Chosen.

Yeah, fuck that.

We don't have to be wanted.

We just have to be here.

Preserving our bodies through our bodies of work.

Feared or, worse, trusted.

We don't care.

Fuck them.

And when dinner is over, we walk back to the house and talk more shit, and eventually we go to their rooms and quickly fall asleep in their beds. I feel like a kid coming down from a tantrum.

*

ON THE FOURTH day, I learn that the actress had daffodils in her room—which she happens not to like. I also learn that she is writing a play about her life.

"Will you be playing yourself?" I ask, as we sit outside in the matching white Adirondack chairs, sipping our coffee in unison.

"Definitely," she says.

She tells me about the industry, how she's had to fight for every single part she's gotten, how all the interesting roles go to the white actresses, how she can only ever play a friend or a coworker, a maid or an enslaved woman.

"Or like, somebody's baby mama or the ratchet black chick. You know, the stereotypes. And I graduated from Tisch, okay? Tell me why the fuck I got formally trained to play a stereotype?"

The man who lives in the house across the street opens the front door for his dog, who quickly finds his scent, reclaims his territory, runs back inside behind his owner.

"What's your ideal role?" I ask.

"This one. The one that I'm writing now. The play itself is all about my experiences in predominantly white spaces. Because I was one of *those* black girls, you know. I grew up in an all-white neighborhood, I went to prep school. I was on the rowing team, for fuck's sake! You know what I'm saying? And when I'd meet other black girls out in the world, I would be all excited like, 'Yay! Finally, someone who will understand me!' But they didn't like me because they thought I was stuck-up, or maybe they thought I thought I was better than them or something because of how I talked or because I was doing stuff that white girls did. But I was just being myself."

She shrugs, smirks.

"Did you?" I ask.

"Did I what?"

"Did you think that you were better than them?"

"No, I just thought I was different than them."

"Because you're a role that requires formal training."

She nods at me, smiles.

"You get it," she says.

I find a way to excuse myself.

*

OF THE EIGHT black artists, I am the only one who started on social media.

It's like I've done something backward. Cheated somehow. Because I wasn't chosen by an industry.

I was chosen by an algorithm.

And everything important that happens now, happens after that.

The other artists resent social media, say it ruins everything.

People don't have to be good anymore, you know?

People don't have to make real art.

People can get ten thousand likes off of nothing.

Artists have to actually be good to get noticed.

Artists have to put in the work.

Artists have to perfect their craft.

Now they want to ask us how many followers we have?

Are you fucking serious?

But not you, Jill.

Your account is different.

I tell them that it's not and they laugh.

Of course it is. Or else you wouldn't be here.

*

ON THE FIFTH night, I sit on the back porch with the muralist and smoke a joint.

"What kind of flowers were in your room when you got here?" I ask him.

"White lilies from the lily-whites," he says, laughing and coughing, "if you can fucking believe it."

He passes it to me and I watch the smoke rise in the darkness, suspend, disappear. I inhale into an escape and exhale into an answer. "I can absolutely fucking believe it."

We laugh, and I pass it back to him.

"What's it like for you in this town?" I ask him.

He sits up, scratches at his beard, "It's a little bit weird, but it's cool out here, you know? It's peaceful."

"What's it like walking around as a tall black man?"

He shrugs. "I mean, I'm definitely getting some stares out here, right? But like, of course. That's everywhere. For the most part, though, everybody I've encountered around town has been really cool. Friendly."

"Do you think it's because they know what we're here for?"

"Maybe. I don't care why they're being friendly, to be honest. I just want them to keep doing it. I don't want any problems. Shit, I speak to them first! They're probably like, 'Damn, who is that friendly black guy waving at us from across the street?' But they wave back!" he says, laughing.

I laugh, too. But I start to feel paranoid as we rock in the owner's chairs, haloed by the porch light and obscured by the smoke we make.

"I've never heard quiet like this in my whole life," he says. "Where I live, it's always loud."

"Will you ever leave New York?" I ask, already certain of his answer.

He shakes his head. "Probably not. I like the energy of it, the pace, the culture. The food. *Us.* That's home, you know? I don't think I could ever really leave and be happy. I'd miss all the things that made me who I am. That remind me of who I am."

We sit in silence for a moment, passing the joint back and forth until it burns into an end.

I excuse myself.

*

ON THE DAY of the (Black) Artist Community Q&A, the two writers, the mixed-media artist, the performance artist, the screenwriter, the actress, the muralist, and the illustrator get all dressed up to go on display. It's time to show and tell what the permission slip, the quiet, and the ocean got us/them. What we came away with and what it's worth. How we earned our temporary keep.

The event is hosted by a (white) painter who lives in a contemporary Georgian-style house right on the edge of a retro downtown and a seemingly limitless sea. All the furniture in the living room has been moved to one side to accommodate resident artists and aesthete residents.

As promised, the man from the arts foundation is back for the pudding. This time, he's joined by several colleagues who walk around the spacious living room making small talk with each artist, asking questions about schools and travel, presumed poverty and amusing privileges.

I find myself watching the waves crash through a sashed window with no curtains and no blinds, waiting to be saved by the pure force of my own awkwardness, as a man from the foundation engages me in a conversation about trying to force the artistic process, whether or not it is truly possible.

He has a friendly mustache and wears a silly tie instead of a serious one to let us know that he's different from the rest of them. Maybe he participated in a sit-in once or had his own run-ins once or twice, but either way, he's only working this job to help people like me. To keep the rooms fair for when we can't be there. He has the kind of smile that I once believed but disbelieve now. Mostly because I disbelieve myself whenever I'm around one.

Away from. On behalf of.

Pretending not to know what I'm doing.

> *Jill, you can justify absolutely anything for the promise of enough money or enough recognition.*
>
> *Enough time to be alone and gather your thoughts.*
>
> *They're going to use you anyway. Jill, why not go for the thing that you always wanted—that thing that's so expensive? Health insurance, maybe. They're going to use you anyway.*

Jill, your mother deserves everything because she did it without anyone else. Your brother deserves everything because they tried to sit him in a hallway in an Alabama elementary school and forget about him. Let them use you because you could really use the money. Let them smile at you and feed you and fill your room with begonias. Let them give you a break. Let them feel good for seeing something in you. Yes, you already know how it'll go. But maybe you can figure out how to do both well.

Jill, it's not like you want much. How much does it take? You just want to be okay, right? You want to go to the dentist once a year, not worry so much about not having enough. Maybe you can be the one person who makes it out of a lie alive.

Artists have to eat.

Right?

I come with new and old injuries, recently burned fingertips and aging stab wounds that I like to forget about whenever I want something. Whenever I want to ascend to a new level of complicity but call it curiosity instead.

They flare up sometimes.

Jill, are you going to write a book about being complicit just so that you can feel better about being complicit?

But Silly Tie doesn't ask me that question.

He asks, "The only way to do it is a writing schedule, don't you think? A few pages every morning."

Maybe he doesn't ask because he already knows that my presence is my answer.

"Sure, I agree," I say.

I think Silly Tie wants me to articulate my thoughts on being a . . .

Black. *Queer.* <u>Woman</u>. Born in Oakland!!! Raised in ALABAMA. The child of a *single parent.* The sister of a **black man**. Living in a <u>*low-income*</u> apartment when she goes #VIRAL!! (The later generation of a black family who worships money and materialism. Degrees. Whose coldness will often remind her of why what she wants won't work. Can't preserve.)

Work on wanting less.

To pay off the debt, I will write of the time I spent by the sea, the long walks in the afternoon among the welcoming locals and tiny nautical gift shops, gathering the output of all my big thoughts and important musings, tapping the tree of suffering for sap. Then I will be worth my weight in flowers.

"Do you write in the morning?" he asks, smiling underneath the very hairy situation.

"Not yet, no. But I'd like to start."

"Well, when have you been writing here?"

Sometimes (most times) I need the pressure of waiting till it's almost too late to force me into a sentence of accidental honesty. But that's not what he wants to hear.

"I'm one of those people who writes all night. I like to do it in the dark," I say, rocking on my heels and sipping white wine.

The truth is, I'm in bed every night by 9:30, exhausted from small talk and sun rays, the ins and outs of pretending not to sweat.

Before he can respond, we're interrupted by an announcement that the Q&A session is about to begin, and the (chosen black) artists are asked if they could kindly approach the front of the room and take their assigned seats.

I politely nod an "excuse me" at Silly Tie and make my way over to where the dark row splits the room. I find my name at the very end of the line, the chair closest to the door.

We are asked a series of questions about what our art requires of us and what we require of ourselves. We are asked about recurring themes.

Do current events show up in our work?

Childhoods?

We don't want to be the thing that you are.
We just want to know what it's like.
Take this money.
You can be our entertainment.
You've always been so good.
At making us cry.
At making us laugh.

At fascinating us.
You make us feel.
Like we can do anything.
Tell us what we are.
Tell us what we're like from the outside.
Tell us what we're like from your insides.
Give us that good gospel.
That old-time religion.
That soul food.
Or subvert it.
Freak it.
Remember everything you do
That surprises us
Is actually just the us
In you.
Clever, different.
Ironic.
Look, you're living in the big house.
For a week.
Make your reality.
Art.
(Is that preservation
Too?)

Arts programs come up. Arts programs in schools with diverse student bodies. Diverse student bodies. The importance of a break. The importance of a foundation.

Then we are asked to show or talk about what we've worked on since arriving.

When it is my turn, I smile at the audience, make a joke about the small problem of having *too* much time on my hands and *too* much beauty at my fingertips to write at length about the woes of the world.

They laugh.

I tell them that I'm only kidding, that I've begun working on what will be the beginning of my first book. I open the Google Doc that last saved just three hours ago, and read to them from an essay about Langston Hughes's house and of a choice finally being made in real time.

Dear Jillisblack,

Where are you? Like, hasn't anyone ever told you how social media works? Hasn't anyone told you that trauma is trending and you can sell consciousness for capital these days? Like, do it!

And you're commercial, which is code for classism, so don't you want to further develop your brand? The awkward aesthetic, the self-righteousness? Colorism helps, of course. And the white liberals think you're a challenge, so you can work that angle, too. That's great!

But Jill, you have to post. You've got to know and then grow and then unknow and outgrow your audience into more online relevance and popularity. Jill, there's sooo much race stuff you could be reacting to right now, like, so many quality racial topics. So, like, react. Reactions are shareable, and that's good for your account. And your videos were better when they started with "Dear white people," because it made your market more obvious. And this hipster accountability thing is cute, but where's it going? Like, where is your book? Where is your podcast? Don't you want to be verified? Don't you want to sell contrived authenticity like a product? Where's your packaging and solutions for your version of media visibility?

This is real life, you know?

So where are you?

—*Jillisblack*, April 9, 2018

LET THE LITTLE PEOPLE THROUGH

It's just barely summer in the South Carolina suburbs, and even though your mother's mammoth sunflowers are starting to grow uncomfortably tall in the small backyard and the same three songs are drifting from the wide-open window of a standard-size SUV by noon and the air is reeking of sweat, smoke, and watermelon-scented chemicals by the time the sun sets behind haunted trees and chain restaurants, it's just barely a summer.

Everything that's selling out fast is antiviral or antiracist or—with a talented PR team—both, and people are wearing their masks in public, just in case they are found out to be a loud or silent carrier of one of the things that no one wants.

Breathing around each other has become dangerous, so I CAN'T BREATHE masks are all sold out online, and the popular race-forward books with the stern covers and marketable titles are on the shelves or in the tote bags of the guilty left in need of a cause or a conundrum and the trendy middle in need of a script or a scapegoat and the retired Unitarians in need of a title or a toolkit.

We're stuck inside with ourselves, trying to believe the things we're supposed to think and to mean the things we're supposed to say. We're performing interpersonal politics in public, more conscientious than conscious, systematic in our approach, same or shame, safe or sorry. What's the difference?

We've caught ourselves in the traps we set for other people's contradictions, and finding no logical way out, we almost always give in.

Your marriage has ended and you've left Atlanta. Traveled up north to a different type of South. You're living with your mother in a house that's like all the other houses around it for miles. There are rosebushes in front, a friendly doormat, a spring-themed flag.

Your stepfather lives there, too.

You're living in the kind of compromise that capitalism creates. The kind that feels like the latter years of your childhood, after your single mother of one got married and became a single mother of two, but with a husband.

You lived in a different neighborhood then, on a winding drive of character houses and holiday decorations, block parties and trampolines, in another small southern town where college football is an ethic, and anything different is deviant, divisive, dangerous. You were the new black family on an established white street—a husband, a wife, a brother, a sister. Allowable only because you appear safe, aligned, malleable.

*

AT THE BUS stop, the other sixth graders ask if that guy is your real dad. They ask you where your real dad is then. They ask if you like boys, because you don't really seem like you do. Which boy do you like then?

When your stepfather feels entitled to the spoils of his rage, and you must drive the half hour to your grand-mother's house to spend the night, your grandmother calls your stepfather a good choice. Former military and a college graduate—the kind of college graduate that refer-ences it often, thinks of it as a kind of earned worthiness, a bulletproof vest—he is perceived as a safe and, thus, good, choice. Because he played football, joined a black fraternity, got a job, kept a job, he was a good choice.

Respectability makes him a good choice.

Your grandmother says forgive him and stay, and the next time she says forgive him and stay, and the next time she says, "You all have a beautiful house. I really think it's best you stay."

You already have an idea, but this confirms that money is important, and you start to wish you had more money than your stepfather so that you could win instead. So that people would give you the benefit of the doubt instead. So that he could move again instead. So that he could start over with nothing again instead.

*

BUT NOW, YEARS later, it's different. Now your step-father quotes CNN, tucks his short-sleeved company polo shirt into wide-legged khakis, watches reruns of *Becker.* He still works in middle management, calls the people who work for him thugs and idiots. Most of his stories are about work or alcohol.

As long as you've known him, he's needed to live in hell to feel at home. He's performed masculinity as abuse. He's yelled whenever someone was unwilling to lie for him, see him as he needs to see himself. He's yelled whenever he thinks someone has forgotten that he *can*, that he still knows how.

For half a year, he stays mostly quiet.

But you know it's coming.

It's the early half of an already hot Sunday when he stands in the living room and recites with a smirk, "You know, these cops are out here killing up black men in the street like it's nothing. It's dangerous out here for us. A real shame, honestly." He keeps smirking and staring and waiting for a response, and you realize that the words aren't said as information but rather as some sort of explanation for who and what he is.

But you already know. He's shown you.

So there is nothing to say. All your personal thoughts about him are in conflict with all your political thoughts about men like him whom you'll never actually know, whose secrets you haven't been keeping, and men you love, whom you've chosen, who are unlearning their way out of normalized abuse, too.

A week later the man from next door, with the three young boys and the wife who loves being a substitute teacher, is working on one of his antique cars in his standard white subdivision garage, a tiny radio playing only your favorite country hits from yesterday and today, and he's wiping the sweat from his brow with a stack of Dunkin' Donuts napkins. The man from the other next door, with the oxygen tank and the hot tub, is chain-smoking cigarettes on his covered patio. You're standing in the living room. *Poetic Justice* is on BET again—all the profanity has been removed to protect the innocence of neglected children—and your stepfather is on the other end of the phone. He and the alcohol are calmly informing you that they're on their way home to kill you and your mother.

Suddenly you are wide awake again. Back from that lie you tell yourself when you need to pretend that what you forgive, you deserve again.

And at the very same time, all around you, there's George Floyd as headline. George Floyd as topic. George Floyd as symbol. George Floyd as Sunday sermon. George Floyd as political tactic. George Floyd as distant idea. George Floyd as COLE SPROUSE AND KAIA GERBER REUNITE FOR BLACK LIVES MATTER MARCH AFTER HE DENIES THEY'RE DATING. George Floyd as KATHERINE HEIGL ON DISCUSSING GEORGE FLOYD'S DEATH WITH HER DAUGHTER: "HOW WILL I EXPLAIN THE UNEXPLAINABLE?" George Floyd as martyr. George Floyd as catalyst for change. George Floyd as *too hard too sad too far too obvious too public.* George Floyd as behind our reusable masks we are all the same. George Floyd as sacrifice. George Floyd as necessary. George Floyd as matter, moment, history.

Matter: Anything that occupies space.

Your stepfather is black and your stepfather is a man. He is himself, too. Your stepfather harms and your stepfather's been harmed. He is a product and a consumer. In exchange for clean breaks, and out of our own discomfort with our own humanness, we desire a perfect victim, a silent hero. We play God to find godliness. We ignore the details, uncomfortable with two or more things being true at the same time—not *right*, but *true.*

Real.

And in that moment, in the living room, where you are standing with your mother, as Chicago slaps Iesha in front of a beautiful overlook and whatever she says in response has been replaced with a more appropriate word, your childhood seeks a conclusion to a lingering story.

You and your mother fill the car with as many important things as it can hold, throw some clothes and toiletries into overnight bags, and when you're done, you leave in the dark with your dog to go stay in a room at the Country Inn and Suites where the shower doesn't work and the pool is right outside your window, bright blue surrounded by yellow caution tape, closed until further notice.

As the pool lights glow behind a curtain that won't close all the way, you both decide that it's time to go back to Washington. You miss the weed and the weather, the mountains and the trees. You miss the health care and the coffee. You miss the kind of racism that smiles at you first, plays you a few chords of something by Bikini Kill on an acoustic guitar that it doesn't even bother tuning, lies after.

You leave the news on just for the noise and wake up to different versions of the same story. *Another corporation has taken to Twitter to agree that #BlackLivesMatter. Businesses are starting to reopen, but is it too much too soon? In response to the protests, there are curfews in place across the country. Did you hear what Trump said? Did you see what he did?*

That first day, you head immediately west, away from the Spanish moss that hangs limply from the trees and the plantations that are now tourist attractions. You've told almost no one that you are driving cross-country. You don't want to hear the requisite fear in their voices, sense the concern in their texts. You don't need to be reminded of the virus, the protests, the mandates, the masks. You can't stay home because home isn't safe. The immediate trouble is inside, just as terrifying as anything else that wants you dead.

The last two days in the hotel, there had hardly been any time to think about anything else other than getting to Washington. You ship three boxes to your brother in Marblemount, organize the car, plan your route on Google Maps, review your combined budget, buy a few travel-friendly groceries, fold a few feelings neatly away until there is more time to try them on, decide what still fits.

And yet, there is George Floyd standing six feet away from you in the grocery store as you are smiled at by a man in uniform. George Floyd is in the tension outside, the humidity. He is in the reminder you give yourself in a hotel bathtub after you try to cry about one of the many things that's happened in the past forty-eight hours and can't. You remind yourself to look around, take it all in, move it around until you make it make as much sense as it ever can.

Because there is no way to avoid being black in America. There is no right time to travel. There is nowhere safer to be instead. And there is no time to waste. There is no old or new normal. If it's all fucked, then let it find you.

Whatever catches you, let it catch you in motion.

You drive your way through a few of Tennessee's forgotten exits, past the old Ford trucks with the fading support ribbons on the bumper, the gas stations with the peeling red racer stripes, the little black firecracker stands covered in dripping neon announcements, the flags and the crosses, the crumbling identities of forgotten whiteness, always holding on to itself so tightly that it breaks. Privilege taps you on your shoulder and asks where the fuck you are.

You steer the silver Hyundai Elantra that now holds almost everything you and your mother own in the world over the mountains and out of the sweaty grip of an angry white America that thinks it still has a chance against data, diversity, and digital. Still sees itself as more of a race than a concept, system, trap. An angry white America that hopeful white America finds loud, embarrassing, that it fights with at holiday dinners after one too many glasses of wine, that it unfollows on social media. An angry white America that hopeful white America blames for everything it doesn't like about itself.

That first night, you're in between large towns and too far away from the cities when it almost gets too dark. You stop at an exit that's almost the kind of exit you were looking for and check into a Quality Inn that sits right next door to a truck stop and across the street from a Huddle House.

The woman at the front desk behind the makeshift Plexiglas wall and superstore-size hand sanitizer sees your driver's license and asks if you're from Washington.

"California originally," you say, and even though it's true, it sounds like you're lying.

"Me too. I'm from California," she says, and your eyebrows lift without permission.

Now you both sound like you're lying.

"Oh yeah? What part?"

"Southern California. Like, right outside of San Diego."

"Ah, I'm from up north," you tell her. But she's never been, says it was never a place she needed to see.

She hands you your room keys through a hole in the Plexiglas and shows you where the ice machines are on the hotel map, circles them with a black Sharpie, just in case.

"You're all set," she says, smiling. "And in case I don't see you again, have a good rest of your trip."

It takes you too long to reorganize your wallet, too long to fold the receipt, find the card keys in your pocket, so you ask her how she ended up in Clarksville.

"I couldn't take California anymore. I miss it. I have family there still and I miss my family. But I love it here. It's easy and it's quiet. There aren't a whole lot of choices to make and nobody bothers you. In San Diego there was always something to go do. I always had somewhere I had to be. I moved here and there's not much to do and

I don't have too many places to be. Nobody is paying attention to us out here. Nobody cares what we're doing."

The next morning you walk your dog in the small plot of grass with the restless flies and the discarded Styrofoam. You are carefully observed by a trucker who doesn't smile back and someone who is sitting on the sidewalk, lazily smoking a cigarette and swatting the bugs away with a plastic hotel cup. And because you've lived as you for a long time now, you know that the staring can be about all or some of the many things that you are and how those things work with all or some of the many things they are.

When you get back to the room, you tell your mother about the staring. The vibe in the parking lot is off, and it's probably fine but, well, you know. It is, until.

Joe Biden is on the television talking about how "he was the guy in the room who always said . . ."

And the black political correspondents are on the cable news stations telling white political correspondents that they don't know what it's like to be black in this country.

But how can they ever know what it's like to know what it's like?

It doesn't matter.

Matter: Be of importance; have significance.

It's more lucrative to educate hopeful white people forever, to tell them that they can never know but you can teach them how to be better learners for $19.99/month. And it's more lucrative to come up with the curriculum, sell it to the hopeful whites so they can eventually sell it to everyone else. Make them an expert in what they can never know. Let them decide which of you is more of an expert in articulating an experience they can never have. Let them share you on Instagram with the caption: "Fellow white people, watch this. It's important."

But how do they know what's important about it if they can't even know who's telling the truth? If black people don't all agree, then how do white people decide which black people to listen to? What do they base it on—their agreement?

Your mother drives you out of Tennessee and farther into the middle of the country, where you are surrounded by nothing but America. On the outskirts of the outskirts, you mostly encounter windmills and crosses. Little square houses dot the side of the highway, and you try to imagine what it's like to live in the blue one with the broken swing set and the KEEP AMERICA GREAT sign in the front yard. What it's like to live within the whiteness that whiteness doesn't want, in a house with a yard sign that reads as one thing but means "Fuck you," in a town that's aging with you, where things close more than they open, where there is no one left to meet and nothing left to do.

But you can't. And you don't really want to.

A child stands in the front yard of the blue house with the swing set and the sign, holding hands with a white-haired adult and waving at the cars. You wave because when you've started denying yourself the enjoyment of your own humanity, then you've lost something vital. Something that doesn't feel theoretical. The child and the adult wave back excitedly, smile from being noticed, and it makes you happy even if it's not supposed to—not right now while your truth is defined by your dedication to anger. And maybe it's because they aren't wearing masks that you notice their smiles anyway.

Because you're supposed to know that when you wave, they win. *Fuck that*, the voices that are meant to keep you safe/sane say. *They don't give a fuck about us. What the fuck do you look like waving at one of their kids? They don't give a fuck about our kids, Jill! You must hate yourself to do some smiling-ass, Uncle Tom–ass, coon-ass shit like that. Do you hate yourself? Do you know your history? You think these white people really give a fuck about you? Did that white cop give a fuck about George Floyd? That white kid's going to grow up right there in that town and become the kind of white adult that shoots you in broad daylight like it's nothing, and you have the audacity to wave, you fucking traitor. What you forgive, you deserve. Don't you remember?*

You're supposed to know, or else you don't get it. But also, there are some exceptions.

You can wave if the waving makes you the president. You can wave if the waving makes you a global superstar with a global superstar husband. You can wave if your other hand is full of money, if your compromise has made you a resource.

But don't wave at that child who can't pay you or put you on.

Save your hands for the exceptions, for the opportunities too big to miss.

In front of you there is nothing but flatland split in the middle by straight road. Behind you are the white people who live in a house on the highway, with a view of everything they can already see. They're still waving in the wind like a flag.

If no one wants it, do we still call it privilege?

You stop for the night outside Kansas City, Kansas, or Kansas City, Missouri. You never figure out which one. In the morning, you walk your dog around a park that's right outside the hotel. There's a walking trail, a lake in the middle, geese in the lake, a roundabout. Middle-class details. Your dog is pulling on the leash, but she's cute, harmless, so the other people with dogs smile when she lunges at them. You shrug dramatically, laugh, play the part of "Who owns who here?!"

"She always tries to embarrass me in public. I don't know why she's like this," you say cheerfully, playing hopeless. And they smile at you with an empathy reserved for certain roles you know to play.

They say, "Don't worry. We have small dogs at home. What's her name?"

They never ask you yours and you never ask them theirs, and when you stop making small talk and say goodbye, you all wave at the dogs. Say their names, instead.

Then everyone smiles, masks around their necks.

That day, you'll make it to Colorado and that's all you care about. It *sounds* like something different from the South, from Middle America—even if it's not. You expect the scenery to change as you grow closer, but there is still just wind blowing red dust and flat earth meeting wide sky up until you finally cross the line and Google Maps says, "Welcome." The hotel sits between a cornfield and a gas station, and when you open the window in your room, the smell of manure wafts in and stays.

You eat sandwiches and drink red wine out of plastic hotel cups, and neither of you can figure out a way to say "Can you believe that we're here? Can you believe what had to happen?" with enough enthusiasm, so instead you just keep saying, "*Wow.*" You both stare out at the corn and say it over and over until the sun finally sets and the window becomes a mirror.

You have to make it to Washington. Then—*then*— you'll be ready to talk about everything.

Outside a natural-foods store, a white woman with a mask approaches, says, "I just want to let you know that we're with you. We're all going to fight this together.

You're not alone. It's just this president, you know? He's created so much division. If we can just get him out of there, I think a lot of this could get better."

What you are capable of—on this long journey across a country in its current version of the same crisis—is a tight smile and a nod. She does most of the talking, and when her effort satisfies her need and she leaves you with a final goodbye, you're exhausted. You and your mother look at each other and roll your eyes like teenagers on vacation, shrug at a promise that "progressive" whiteness makes you every few years, every time the ghosts of their necessary evil show up to the party and make a scene too big to hide but just big enough to hide behind.

Before she ever thought to notice you, before she was ever interested, even without her, you existed.

When you're almost done for the day, almost at the pet-friendly Comfort Suites in Ogden, Utah, that you googled while you were still in Elk Mountain, Wyoming, the dust starts. Soon the air is full of sand and years of accumulating debris, and the body of the car sways suddenly, the steering wheel jolts in your mother's hands. Feeling out of control and up to your neck in unexpressed disappointment and bad news, you grip the door handle until it hurts.

Your phone vibrates in your lap, notifies you that someone has messaged you on Instagram. From the notification preview, you can see that it begins: hi. Just checking

in to make sure that you're ok. i was also wondering if I
could send you some of my new . . .

*After every death we've managed to escape, what if it's finally
the windstorm in Utah? Not the man who just can't make himself
happy or domestic terrorism or the police. Not the things that I
believe in or the people that I love or the way that I am. Not the
toxic food or the toxic environment or the 5G. Not my mother's
breast cancer diagnosis twelve years ago. Not a mechanical failure
on my way to accept an award for being articulate in public. Not
the money or the stress or the lack of a vacation. Not the virus.
Not the president. Not the people who are only here to be right
about everything. Not me. No, of course not. It's going to be the
fucking windstorm in Utah. And the only thing to blame will be
nature and timing. The rest we ran from in vain. It was never
even meant for us. Our destiny was always leading us here, just
when we were finally starting to get somewhere.*

Your mother sits up straight, slows the car down to a
quarter of the speed limit. You imagine that the cars that
speed by in the left lane are endemic to the area, so used
to sudden bouts of low visibility that their eyes have
adjusted over time.

You ride in silence. When the wind finally stops, you
realize that it won't kill you, and that means that everything else still can. You're relieved and something else,
too.

"That got scary for a second. Shit," your mother
says.

"I know. For me too," you say.

You both laugh, joke about the wind that almost blew you away for good.

You make it to Ogden and check into the Comfort Inn from behind the blue tape. They're using the decline in business to renovate. So, in the lobby and in the hallways, there are exposed wires hanging from missing ceiling tiles, carpet covered in plastic tarps. The smell of fresh white paint reminds you that you still have one more chapter left to finish of *Invisible Man*.

You'll do it when you get to Washington.

Once you are safely inside your nonsmoking double room, you take a tropical hard-candy edible and spend eighty-six dollars on two yellow curries and a side of brown rice on DoorDash and begin to unpack the essentials. Your mother calls your brother on speaker to let him know you're done driving for the day. On the second floor, it sounds like two hundred wildly enthusiastic and unattended children from the local marching band are practicing a routine for some big competition.

Your dog begins to bark at the talented children in their special steel-toe boots and you can feel your mother growing tense at the noise and you're starting to do that thing where you keep asking yourself if you're high, which means that you definitely are, and from somewhere across the room your phone dings, letting you know that Justin in a white Camry is out front with your order.

Before you can figure out how to make yourself move, there is a boom quickly followed by a *hum, zap!* The room goes dark, and suddenly everything is strangely quiet, off. Across the parking lot, no one left the lights on at the Motel 6 either.

There is nothing to do but wander down the unlit hallway with your cell phone flashlight and to pry open the automatic door in the lobby to retrieve your order from Justin and ask the person at the front desk if she knows what's going on and for her to say it's lights out for half the town and for you to go back to the room and tell your mother while you quickly open flimsy containers of heavy food. And there's nothing left to do but note that the curry looks and tastes almost exactly like Campbell's vegetable soup and to ask yourself what you expected and to laugh and laugh and laugh and complain and use the complaining as a way to say a few of the things you've wanted to say for days and for your mother to go talk to the manager in that voice she's used your whole life to indicate that something or someone is about to be free, and to have the manager say, "We have two people stuck in the elevator right now, so, see? Some people here have it worse than you after all," and to have your mother come back from the front desk and tell you that you're getting moved to a newly renovated room on the second floor, where you spend the rest of the evening inhaling a fresh coat of white paint and the sweet scent of a small but necessary victory on a long but necessary day.

When you finally cross the Washington state line, you want to cry but you still can't, so you cheer instead. You stay in your brother's vacant house in Bellingham, where he and his old roommates still have two more months left on their lease. They're almost all moved out with the exception of a couple of beds, a kitchen table and chairs, and a couch.

It's a yellow house that sits across the street from a popular Thai restaurant on a short block of brightly colored houses in the desirable "Lettered Streets" district. This is the area of town where you can find coffee shops, breweries, protests, holistic veterinary care, expensive little houses covered in solar panels and prayer flags, rows and rows of lacinato kale and a line of mammoth sunflowers. At the end of the block is the ocean.

That night, you toast with a red wine blend and food from a grocery store cold case and look out at the trees. It stays light outside until almost ten o'clock and you can't believe that you had forgotten to miss that part of Washington while you were away from it.

While you're in the yellow house, you take walks around the neighborhood and say hello back to all the people who stop to ask what brought you into town.

"Are you students? No? Well, welcome anyway!"

On Thursday, your brother comes up to visit. You order too much food from across the street, and after you finish eating, you all take a walk around the neighborhood.

There are chalk memorials on the sidewalk for George Floyd and BLACK LIVES MATTER signs perched in almost every window, right next to a sleeping cat or a plant.

On your way back, you notice two white women standing in line at the Thai restaurant. One of them is staring at you, a smile slowly widening across her face. She points at each of you individually, then grabs her friend and turns her around in your direction.

"See? *See?* I told you! They *are* here!"

It plays out quickly and you almost don't believe it as it's happening, but she raises her fist in the air, starts chanting, "Black Lives Matter! Black Lives Matter! Fuck racism!"

You acknowledge her and keep walking. People are stopping on the street to see what all the fuss is about, and she uses their attention as an opportunity to rally them. "Come on, everybody! Let them know that black lives matter here!"

Her friend looks at you, smiles an apology, asks her to please stop making a scene.

As you're walking up the driveway of the yellow house, your body rigid with rage, she continues to yell after you, "*You* fucking matter! Your life fucking matters! Black Lives Fucking Matter!"

Matter: An affair or situation under consideration; a topic.

You all step into the house, close the door behind you, and through the walls you can still hear her insisting that you matter, but you don't know who she's telling, and she doesn't either.

That night, you try not to picture her. Instead, you finish *Invisible Man* with the window wide open and the sun still out. You listen to a couple fight about a cigarette that he wasn't supposed to finish but did anyway.

It feels like summer.

Do you ever think about why people unfollow you? I do. But more than that, I think about what the final straw was. Because let's be real here—if you post the exact same thing wearing the exact same T-shirt for three years, people will eventually realize you ain't shit and hit that button. And you know what? I wish those people nothing but good, seasonally appropriate joy and happiness. I do. But sometimes I *wake up* to forty-seven fewer followers. And I need y'all to tell me what happened. There you are living your life . . . using lines from Nayyirah Waheed poetry to help you recover from your latest breakup and, like, drying herbs and maybe watching reruns of *Moesha*, when all of a sudden you're like, "Uh-uh. Fuck that bitch, Jill. I'm done."

What happened, yo?!?!?!

I ain't even posted in four days and it's 5 A.M., tho!

Like, don't do that. Unfollow me in the real actual morning or in the late afternoon like you've got some damn sense. Unfollow me because I only like your photos when your mom's in them. Unfollow me because I'm always high and only sometimes making sense.

But whatever you do, don't surprise me with it. Have some decency.

Shit.

Update: To all y'all unfollowing me this afternoon, well played.

—*Jillisblack*, December 9, 2015

UNFOLLOW ME

The 2020 election is a few weeks away, and my family and I have moved to Olympia for the second time. This time, to the heavily forested outskirts of a capital city that hasn't changed nearly as quickly as we have since we left it four years ago to head back to a Deep South that's still just a little too deep for me.

After so many moves in the last few years, I have grown increasingly more uncomfortable with naming anything outside myself as a "home," worried that it will always feel like a trap or a setup. An identity too susceptible to circumstance to be an identity that I desire.

Not all trees are deeply rooted by nature. Some grow their roots close to the surface. If they're buried too far down in the dirt, growth stops, and the stress eventually kills them.

And yet, I am also happy to return to Olympia, and to remember the right streets to turn left on, and the person who still works in the alcohol and spirits department at Grocery Outlet. I see her every Monday when I drive the twenty-four minutes there from our house to buy heavily discounted, quick-sale organic kale and red wine blends straight from the southern region of Central California. I like that I recognize her even with her mask on.

The new place—with the yard that's just big enough not to intimidate and the quiet that makes me use my inside voice even when I'm standing outside, the quiet that's interrupted only by the random vocalizations of Steller's jays and northern flickers, the free-roaming long-haired cats that torment the eager short-haired dogs in fenced yards, the footsteps of the deer as they nibble their way down the fence of Taylor junipers that separate us from our new neighbor on one side, the one who waves when we see him—feels more like home than anywhere I've ever lived.

I panic. Anxious for the distraction of a calamity or a big, sudden decision that isn't about the end of my marriage or a big, sudden fight that isn't with my stepfather, or a big, sudden forward motion that isn't yet another quick move back.

I'm anxious for the chaos that doesn't surprise. The consistent one.

Luckily, I have a smart phone. It allows me to access my chaos from an outside source, fast and cheap. And by the second week, I've managed to convince myself that the other next-door neighbor (the one who has never spoken) is in some kind of angry white-pride militia. He has emphasized this level of cultural commitment by having a shaved head and several tattoos on his arms that don't seem whimsical or ironic. He also wears a concerning number of black T-shirts, the graphics made indistinguishable by the distance between us.

When he fills his hummingbird feeders with fresh nectar and doesn't make eye contact with me, I can just tell that he's the enemy. When he loads his young kids into the back seat of the family's Sea Glass Pearl Prius and it's absent of the important telltale Prius bumper stickers that I rely on to know how accepted my identities are wherever I am, it's obvious that he's plotting against us. When he mows his grass and does it in large headphones, blasting music only he can hear, I can just tell that he's not trustworthy. *And*, he does it all as if he doesn't want to be bothered.

But what's he bothered *by*, exactly? The threat of small talk or the threat of blackness? That I can't really know until I know makes me nervous, so I have to try to know as much as I can. And I have to seek out the information that confirms what I suspect.

Homie is a Proud Boy.

Luckily, every three seconds there are new articles published about the pandemic and the election and the worst year that only a few people saw coming. After reading the headlines and last paragraphs of a few of those articles, I'm feeling pretty fucking confident that the neighbor is a Proud Boy. And on election night he will emerge from his house to defend his promised land against social distancing, socialized diversity, and whatever else threatens his grip on the biggest piece of the pie in the sky.

But even if he isn't, can any of us really be too careful? What would be enough to validate my fear? Isn't all the fear valid when everything feels like a threat? If everything I hold on to might be mistaken for a weapon? If the stakes are so high that if I'm right, I just might die of it?

And I'm always trying to decide which one I'd rather be more—wrong or alive.

But I'm not wrong, right? Because militias are happening. And I'm not wrong, right? Because every time my brother goes for a run, I have to pretend that I'm not hyperaware of every long minute until he returns. And I'm not wrong, right? Because we live in a big, scary world where we control nothing and no one unless . . . well, you really can't trust anybody, honestly.

Unless they agree with you. Not only about everyone else and who they really are. But about who you really are, too.

Social media is suggesting that if I have a remote job, I should escape the United States and move somewhere safe that has really good internet connection. This way I can keep my American job and live *very* well in a country that has a lower cost of living. Plus, I don't even have to miss out on entertaining myself with the bad news from back home. It will follow me on my smart phone and make me feel included.

Something to seriously consider.

I read an article at 2 A.M. that screams its headline from the belly of my popular searches and mined data, BLACK MAN SET ON FIRE BY WHITE NEIGHBOR IN RURAL AMERICA! And even though the article eventually reveals itself to be about a lovers' quarrel over an alleged infidelity and stolen drugs, the truth of it doesn't solve my problem.

It's not about what it is. It's about what it *could have been* but happened not to be. What it *could always be*, until it is.

In the mostly white neighborhood of diverse incomes where I now live, there is a quiet war being waged. On front lawns and in the windows of houses, there are mostly small BIDEN-HARRIS, anti-Trump, and TRUST SCIENCE signs and a few large KEEP AMERICA GREAT ones, too. There are Bernie bumper stickers and faded Ben Carson ones, too. There are Tibetan prayer flags hanging from the turquoise trims of tiny houses, and there are IN THIS HOUSE WE PRAY flags in front of the slightly bigger houses, too. There are also badge-shaped security company signs highly visible in almost everyone's front yards—in case any version of God ever requires a helping hand or a little bit of backup.

I make an appointment to have a security system installed. If they all have them, then we *definitely* need one.

Every morning and every night I check the news on my phone so that I can be reminded of why I should always be scared or mad. How it's my civic duty. A way to participate.

Even though assumptions save some people's lives and end others', I figure they're my right at this point. And it's a privilege to get to *check* the news instead of being the news.

Remember that.

Perhaps the neighbor is a Proud Boy, so I must decide what I want to do about him.

But first . . .

I must finish the essay. The essay that is meant to be the last essay of this book, about Jillisblack and me these days. How we get along.

I try a lot of different versions of it, but in each version I stop just short of what I really mean. Hide it behind a breastplate of sarcasm. I don't give myself up, because I'm worried that it's not what anyone wants from me. When the truth is, I don't think Jillisblack's way of seeing everything as black or white—her way of believing that everyone who is not in agreement with her is actually in denial of themselves—works. I no longer thrive on the kind of hopelessness that she requires to get out of bed in the morning. I don't think she knows any more about anyone else than anyone else knows about *me*.

Still, I'm worried that I'm always hiding my desire in the bodies of the people I critique, holding them accountable for everything about myself that I can't yet admit to or escape from.

I'm worried that I'm like a child, always believing a game is broken and pointless once I've finished playing it. Once it's beat me.

I'm worried that I'm like Sisyphus, eternally useless and endlessly frustrated by performing a task that is a consequence of itself.

I should be writing the final essay, but instead I'm watching on the live security camera as my presumably Proud neighbor checks his mail and hides his agenda from me. Watching him reminds me of the only Jillisblack story I don't like to tell. The one I will absolutely never allow to be in the final essay of this book.

I don't tell it because I only tell the stories where I remain likable throughout or, at the very least, redeemable by humor, culture, time passed, lessons learned. Like the time I learned it was time to give Jillisblack a break from social media.

I don't tell it because that would be like scoring a point on myself for the other team. Trapping myself for the hunter.

I don't tell it because I would be admitting to the privilege of being alive long enough, potentially packaged well enough, nice-white-liberal-adjacent enough for the book deal and the edgy race-themed stories I've promised to tell—instead of the ones that promise to tell on me.

So of course I can't ever, ever, *ever* allow myself to write, "One time I got so tired of being agreed with on the internet that I had an hour-long conversation with a Proud Boy and it didn't end badly." Or, "Contrary to the popular narrative, the conversations in my DMs that ended the worst were with proud white liberal women who accused me of being ungrateful anytime my line of questioning was too unpredictable. Who were fine with everything I had to say about white people until it was about one of them. Not their new ways to be antiracist or their progressive politics or their intersectional book club or their black-and-white selfies of support, but *them*, and what they *actually* wanted from me. Not as a group of proud white liberal women, but rather as individual white women who would come into the comment section to (first) identify as proud liberals, then ask why I was so comfortable disappointing them."

I never asked the individual proud white liberal women why it is that someone screaming at them in ALL CAPS about how evil they inherently are, reducing them down to the internet definition of a "Karen," demanding that they save their unanswered questions for Google, dragging them by their Twitter fingers all across the internet and daring them to cry is found to be *absolutely brilliant! Soooooo fucking raw and real! THE TRUTH.* Met with a chorus of YOU ARE HOLDING MY MIRROR AND SHOWING ME WHO I AM! *Please tell me all about myself! Read me for everything I've done!*

I neeeeeeeeeeeeeeeed it!!! I DESERVE IT!!! I'll be quiet so I can be seen.

I never asked what the individual proud white liberal women get from it or how they know they're learning.

If you feel like giving up, that's how you know it's working!

I never asked the individual proud white liberal women how a public flogging would lead them to greater empathy and understanding of themselves and the world around them.

I imagined the answer was that it made them feel like they were somehow doing their civic duty, participating. Or maybe because they don't find who they follow for a flogging to be capable enough, human enough, individual enough to ever be self-motivated or strategic, insecure or conflicted, needy or indulgent. Like them.

But I should've asked.

Anyway, I don't tell the one story about Jillisblack that I don't like to tell, because I'd lose and I can't lose in public. That's what gets you unfollowed.

But if I could do it without losing, I would write about the time in 2017 when I am sent a direct message that reads, "You're a fucking monkey dyke and I hope you die soon and put us all out of our misery. You dumb fucking cunt."

It's poetic enough, but I'm too tired to be moved by it. I've only been a cultural commentator on social media for a few months at this point, and already the message is too obvious to still be entertaining. I can't work up enough anger to fight him with my usual sarcasm and practiced one-liners. Especially with no one watching.

Besides, I've tried it.

I've attempted to one-up a sad person from a smart phone. I know that even when I screenshot it and repost it for the sake of the collective ego, and my following declares me the winner, it can't be true. Spending my time one-upping a sad person is a way of admitting that I'm a sad person myself.

Performing critique for public consumption and social capital has made me a person who is always a little bit sad and very, *very* anxious.

And again, I've tried it.

He's come to me as a fourteen-year-old soccer player from Berlin named Ben who enjoys the musical catalog of Wiz Khalifa and posing with his friends in front of large symbols of big masculinity and who sometimes sends me photos of dog shit that he's named after me.

<Insert five Face with Tears of Joy emoji here>

He's come to me as a lonely white dad with a trucking business who just wants to know how claiming to know everything about people I don't really know shit about is soooo fucking different when I do it, huh?

<nigger>

He's come to me as a twenty-one-year-old women's studies major named Emma who wants to know why I'm talking shit about the kind of white people who actually want to help end oppression. The patriarchy. Colonialism. Etc. Emma is an ally. Why don't I want her?

<then maybe I don't want to be your fucking ally after all bitch. good fucking luck>

The day I respond to the Proud Boy who calls me a fucking monkey dyke, I almost can't help myself. I want to know what's on the other end of the conversation that I'm never supposed to entertain. The one that neither of us supposedly deserves, but for very different reasons.

I want to talk to the primary source. I don't want everything I think I know to come from someone else. Or a documentary or a think piece or a news report or a meme or a caption or a campaign. I want it straight from the horse's shit.

Straight from the boy with all the pride.

But Jillisblack is in the room, because now she always is. And she's staring at me with that smirk, the raised eyebrow. The oversize glasses.

She says, *"Really?"* but she means, "Why do you always have to figure out how to win?"

She's right. At first, that's what it's mostly about.

I know I can't win if I do what he expects me to do. I can't win if I give him the reaction he wants. I can win only if I surprise him or if I make him surprise himself.

So instead of trying to be clever, instead of trying to convince him how well I know him and myself and everyone else, instead of blocking him, I say, "Hi. What's going on?" And he immediately asks me, "Why are you saying dumb shit?"

I sigh, because if he's going to play it like this, I'm not going to end up playing at all. We both have to be willing to defy the gravity of it.

Jillisblack reminds you, "You don't even know if he's who he says he is. All you can see is a profile photo and a bio. Your Proud Boy could be anyone—a black person who's testing your allegiance, a JV tennis star, an ex."

I ignore her because I need him to be who he says he is in order for me to win. I tell him that I'm saying what he thinks is dumb shit because I believe it. I believe that all white people are lying about how complicit they are.

But, like, yeah. Obviously.

As am I.

The thing that bothers me, inspires the necessary rage, is that they're lying about what they already know. That they actually know better than I ever could about exactly what it is they're fighting to keep. That they pretend I'm telling them something new when I'm actually only allowed to tell them the same thing over and over again, but next time with more emphasis on the personal suffering. If they keep me running around in circles, always telling them who *I* am, maybe I won't notice that they're still who they always were.

Some white people's narrative will always call for the casting of black people in the roles of villain, idiot, sucker, submissive; but also, exception, token, muse, submissive. Anything that implies actual humanity would upset the balance and crash the illusion.

That's what I tell him.

He tells me that I must be talking about some dumbass liberals, because he doesn't give a fuck about that kind of shit I'm mentioning. He just knows that he has pride in who and what he is and no one is going to tell him not to. He has to protect himself and his family from being wiped out, and black people are stupid if they don't see who the real enemy is.

He tells me that only a liberal could listen to the crap I say.

I obviously can't argue with that.

He tells me that he doesn't get it because I don't seem entirely stupid.

I tell him that it's a strange compliment.

Jillisblack says, "What the fuck are you doing? Look at how he thinks he can talk to you!" She paces circles around my room, shaking her head and mumbling under her breath about self-hatred and internalized oppression.

He tells me that he doesn't mean it as a compliment at all. If I wasn't entirely stupid, why would I believe that the government wants to help me?

I tell him that I don't.

"This is so fucking basic," Jillisblack says.

He asks why I would believe that white people would ever willingly give up power just to hand it over to someone else.

I tell him that I don't.

"Power is subjective," Jillisblack says.

He asks why I trust the media to tell people the truth about what's really happening.

I tell him that I don't.

"We're the media now," Jillisblack says.

For a moment, he types nothing.

Jillisblack sighs loudly, says, "You have a hundred unanswered messages from people who actually agree with you. People who actually like you. Well, *me*, anyway. But you're so obsessed with the trolls and the naysayers. *Why*? Why do you feel more seen when you're questioned than when you're believed?"

Maybe I'm like the proud liberal white women who crave the accusations. Maybe I think the punishment will absolve and exalt me faster than the appreciation ever could.

I tell the Proud Boy that now I want to ask him some questions about what he believes.

"You're going to fuck this up for me, aren't you?" Jillisblack asks in disbelief.

It takes him a moment to respond, but eventually he types, "Go ahead."

I ask him if he hates black people and he says that he doesn't. But he knows that white people are better and smarter than black people and that America is proof of that. He says, "That's why you won't actually leave America, right? Only America would let you say this kind of dumb shit and get away with it."

"You deserve to read that shit because you're, like, *literally* asking for it," she says.

I have all kinds of things I'd like to say back to him about what white people are actually capable of and what America is actually proof of, but I want him to keep saying more and more of what he means.

I want him to say everything I think he'll say. I don't want to be surprised.

I ask him if he thinks white liberals are better and smarter than black people, too, and he says that he does. Because liberals lie to black people and talk shit behind their backs, and black people still trust them.

Jillisblack laughs.

I ask him if he's happy believing what he believes and he says, "That's a weird question, but sure."

I ask because it's hard to spend every moment in reaction to someone or something else. I wonder if I'm happy. Calling out, telling off, staying ready for everyone so that I never get caught off guard.

I ask him what it is that he needs to say to black people so badly that he's come into my inbox to say it to someone who so obviously disagrees with him. He says that in some ways, he gets it. Because he believes in white pride, he understands why black people would have black pride, too. That makes sense. He just doesn't approve of the way we're going about showing it. And if we keep blaming white people for all our problems, we'll keep having problems we can't fix for ourselves.

Oh, and if we keep believing white liberals actually care about us.

"Aren't you just blaming black people and liberals for all of *your* problems?" I ask him aloud in my room.

"Tell him that. Type *that*!" Jillisblack says, sitting next to me on the futon, jabbing at the screen with her index finger.

Instead, I ask him if he believes in anything bigger than whiteness, and he says that he doesn't believe in God, if that's what I mean. He says that God is another lie that people believe in just so they can feel better about their fucked-up lives.

I tell him that people believe in all kinds of things to feel better about their fucked-up lives.

He agrees.

We go back and forth until there is finally a lag between messages and it's a conversation that seems to be over. But after I've exited the app and sat still on my floor staring at the wall to avoid the screen and her gaze, and after I've started the work of avoiding an answer to the question of why I've done something so unallowed to get some answers I could've predicted, he sends another message.

"Don't open that," she warns.

I open it and hope he calls me a name so that I can get what I deserve, pay for my mistake sooner rather than later. But he doesn't. Instead, he thanks me.

He didn't expect me to respond like I did.

He gets lonely knowing all the stuff he knows about how the world really is.

He's sorry he called me those names.

He was just mad about what I was saying.

And he still is, by the way.

But he hopes I have a good rest of my day.

I make it all much worse than it has to be by not using this as an opportunity to tell him that I didn't mean any of it. That it was all just a clever trick to get him to apologize to me. Then at least I could still screenshot it, post it on my Instagram, laugh with everyone about how I fooled him, bested him. I could both indulge the conversation *and* use it to win.

I'd win.

But I don't.

I don't know what part of all the things that I am and all the apologies I've learned to give makes me want to not be rude just because he said it first. It doesn't make any sense. But I tell him thank you like it's about having good manners.

"You're self-hating as fuck right now, you know that? Do you know that you're the problem? Who needs white people when we've got you?" Jillisblack says from behind her glasses, suddenly back on the other side of the room.

I tell him that I hope he reconsiders how he feels.

"YOU *HOPE* HE *RECONSIDERS*? Are you trying to convince a supposed Proud Boy—who is definitely a sophomore at somebody's high school—to save money by bundling his cable and internet? Is that what this is? Is that why you'd be using a weak-ass word like 'reconsider'?!"

And he says, "Same to you," with a heart emoji, and that's that.

It doesn't climax with a callout. There is no follow-up story or public consequence. I try to forget about it and go back to making my weekly one-minute rants like it never happened. Like I didn't make it happen.

But Jillisblack knows, and she finds a way to tell everyone. Soon the "Dear White People" videos that she's become known for turn to "Dear Black People" ones instead.

Every single one is about a black person who says one thing but justifies another.

A black person who is an accomplice in a crime against themselves.

A black person who says "Thank you" in private and "Fuck them" in public.

A liar.

I know she's trying to get under my skin.

One time I accidentally tell another person about it. I am a little bit too high to stop myself and it slips out, lands heavily in the middle of our conversation.

"Wait, I don't get it, though," they say, looking confused and perhaps suspicious, "Why did you even talk to this guy at all?"

I try to explain, but no matter what I say, I can't make their eyes less narrow. I can't fix their frown.

I had a conversation *with* a Proud Boy instead of about one.

On purpose.

And I should know better. Because I'm me.

But more importantly, I'm Jillisblack. And even when I, Jill Louise Busby, haven't been understood as someone you can trust to not get played/suckered/bamboozled/hoodwinked, she *has*.

Maybe that's why I'm slowly allowing her to run my entire life. Maybe I think she's better at it.

Until now.

Three days before the election and twenty-five days before the first deadline for what will soon be this book, I realize where all this is going. I realize that I'm looking out the window at a sign that it's time to reveal a truth that doesn't declare me the winner. It's time to tell the whole thing.

Or the book isn't really mine.

It's hers.

I have to write it knowing that Jillisblack would read this essay and raise her right (my left) eyebrow in judgmental contempt, smirk and shrug and say, "How much did they pay you for writing this? No, really. Come on. How did they get to you? What did it take?"

She would say that she wasn't surprised, actually. That she could see this coming a million miles away from someone like me.

She didn't have to know me to know my type.

She would ask, "Did you figure out that other people were getting more popular than you and decide to pull the old switcheroo? Is this the new lane since the other one has gotten so, so very crowded?"

Was this easier to package up and sell to the highest bidder?

Can you not get mad enough anymore now that you've stopped running and you're writing the last essay of the book and you've moved into a neighborhood where you're just as worried to feel safe as you are to feel scared?

And she deserves answers.

If she were really here, able to read the words as herself and not through me, I would give them to her. Call her out by name the way she likes. Say, "Hi, Jillisblack. I miss you, too. You came into my life and answered questions I didn't even know I had. You caught me in lies I didn't even know I was telling. And you exist only on an app, a new world given to us so that we give in to a new world. It makes sense that you think you know every-thing and everyone. But you mistake preaching to the choir with speaking gospel truth. You think that all that you see and all that you say is all that there is. But it's just one account, and it isn't even firsthand. And to answer your question, nothing has been as easy to package up and sell as you were."

But in the end, this isn't an essay about Jillisblack or the "Proud Boy" who introduces himself and his wife a week later, tells us they've been meaning to run over to say hello, says we should holler if we ever need anything.

I could've been right about him. But so far, I wasn't.

It's not about a white liberal either. Or an election or a neighborhood. Fear or fact. It isn't an essay about who's right or wrong or who agrees or doesn't.

It's also not an essay about how Proud Boys are harmless lonely lovers of heart emojis, waiting to be engaged by indulgent social media personalities before reconsidering their choices.

That would be silly.

It's just an essay about what happened a few weeks ago.

One that I will never allow to be the last essay of this book.

*

*

*

AFTER A LONG hiatus, she starts showing up again. Looking desperate and scared like she knows the end is near for her.

"You're really going to end with the essay about the Proud Boy, huh? So you don't want the opportunity to write a second book, I guess. That's probably smart."

I look up one Monday in February and she is sitting on the edge of my bed, her back straight, her smile knowing. But I notice right away that she is due for a haircut.

"The only other option was to lead with it," I say, typing these words, sipping from a mug of black coffee gone cold.

"*Oh!* Bold choice that would've been," she mocks, "starting with a defense mechanism."

"That's not what the essay is."

"Oh, sure. Of course."

She stares at me, my fingers as they move over the keyboard

"I don't think you have enough followers to get away with this. Like, you're not famous enough to pull off having a conversation with your online persona. Because this is already kind of a 'memoir-in-essays' thing, right? *Right?* And you're only micro-famous, right? *Right?*"

I nod.

"Right. Bold choices."

I resume typing, trying to refuse her the attention she requires.

"You should let me write the book. That's the book people want. Look, once I'm undone, you can't go back. I can always be you, but you can never be me again.

Think about it. You want to write a book in a few years once everything . . . Fine, okay. No problem. But this moment is mine. It's the perfect time for what I do.

"You can't do what you do without me. You don't have your own ideas. You can't speak for yourself. That's not even your real face. You're filtered with thirty-five percent intensity Ludwig, contrasted, highlighted. I dress you. I get your hair cut."

She narrows her eyes at me. Says, "You'll miss me, you know. During an interview that goes left. When they ask why you doubt the intentions of white liberals in silly ties or white women who grin and stare. When they compare you to someone else who looks like you but who doesn't agree with you. When they ask you to explain how that could even be possible. You'll want me to do it. You'll wish I were in the room."

She's not wrong. She's an instinct. A history. A reaction. A weapon. She's a fight that's still in me, because it's not yet my initial instinct to relax, lower my shoulders, my eyebrow, my guard.

"They'll disagree with you," she warns.

"That makes sense."

"They'll ask about me."

"I want them to."

"They'll wish the book were mine, instead."

"The ones who do always did."

"Can we at least take the conversation about Beyoncé out of 'A Friend of Men'?"

"No."
"But it's a bad idea."
"I know."
"Tell them that it wasn't mine."
"Done."

ACKNOWLEDGMENTS

Thank you to Alma, Chris, and Joseline. For coffee-time realizations, celebrity gossip, book club, improv dance parties, hot water for tea, flute duets to Tamia songs, letters, loyalty, humor, and accountability. You are my best friends and the home of my most honest self. I love you like whoa.

Thank you to the Rhode Island Writers Colony. For the phone call that made it happen. For Ms. Dianne. For John. For the care and the aftercare. For the question "What are you waiting for?" For the Del's lemonade and Donny Hathaway. For Brook Stephenson. For existing.

Thank you to Jason Reynolds, Darnell Moore, and Michael Render.

Thank you to Katie Kotchman. For that initial conversation. For getting it right away. For the emails about that one reality show. For signing off with that infamous "All best." For every single thing you did to make this book possible.

Thank you to Callie Garnett. For the excitement. For the real questions. For the thoughtful pauses. For the patience and the push. For the postcard. For the kombucha jokes. For being so, so good at what you do. For bringing so, so much to this book.

Thank you to the team at Bloomsbury. You've all been amazing and working with you has been an even better experience than I could've ever imagined.

Thank you to my friends.

Thank you to the people who listened to my long, rambling WhatsApp notes about this process and, for whatever reason, didn't immediately block me. Thank you to all the early readers who took their job seriously enough to offer true feedback and necessary perspective. Thank you to the first person who read this entire thing and gave me my first review. It made me cry on the low but you didn't need to know that until now. Getting to share this with you was one of the very best parts of the journey.

Thank you to the Bolsters. I could not have written this book without your support.

Thank you to Joe Henry and Christina Fisher.

Thank you to the people I don't name anymore but who were part of making this happen.

Thank you to everyone I found online and who found me online, who shared my words or left a comment or liked a video or drove or took the subway to some event. Thank you for reading and listening. Thank you for calling me out when it made sense. Most of the time, it did. Thank you for always surprising me with the seemingly infinite boundaries of your support.

Thank you for reading this book. I kind of can't believe that you did, whoever you are. I hope that you enjoyed it or hated it or recognized yourself in it or wanted to throw it into a deep body of water and forget about it forever. I'm honored by any and all of those. Not equally, but still. THANK YOU.

And an extra special thank you to Omarion. Obviously.

A NOTE ON THE AUTHOR

JILL LOUISE BUSBY (also known as Jillisblack) had spent nearly ten years in the nonprofit sector specializing in diversity and inclusion when she uploaded to Instagram a one-minute incisive attack on liberal gradualism and the so-called progressive nonprofit machine. The video went viral, receiving millions of views across social platforms and making her the "it" voice for all things race-based and indulgently honest. Over the next few years, she amassed a loyal following of over eighty thousand people. She continues to use social media, writing, and film to expose contradictions, challenge performative authenticity, and campaign for account-ability. She lives in Olympia, Washington.